In Search of a Home

In Search of a Home

Nineteenth-Century Wendish Immigration

George R. Nielsen

Texas A&M University Press
College Station

Copyright © 1989 by George R. Nielsen
Manufactured in the United States of America
All rights reserved
Second printing, 2007

An earlier version of this book was published as *In Search of a Home: The Wends (Sorbs) on the Australian and Texas Frontier* (Birmingham University, 1977), © George R. Nielsen

The paper used in this book meets the minimum requirements of the American National Standard for Permanence of Paper for Printed Library Materials, Z39.48-1984. Binding materials have been chosen for durability.

Library of Congress Cataloging-in-Publication Data

Nielsen, George R.
   In search of a home : nineteenth-century Wendish immigration / George R. Nielsen.—1st ed.
     p. cm.
   "An earlier version of this book was published as In search of a home : the Wends (Sorbs) on the Australian and Texas frontier (Birmingham University, 1977)"—T.p. verso.
   Includes bibliographical references and index.
   ISBN 0-89096-400-9 (alk. paper)
   1. Sorbs—Australia—History. 2. Sorbs—Texas—History. 3. Australia—Ethnic relations.
4. Texas—Ethnic relations. I. Title.
DU122.S67N53 1989
976.4′0049188—dc19   89-31217
                                   CIP

ISBN-13: 978-1-58544-638-4 (pbk.)
ISBN-10: 1-58544-638-6 (pbk.)

To the memory of my mother,
EMMA MOERBE NIELSEN,
and my grandparents,
PASTOR AND MRS. EMIL F. MOERBE

Contents

List of Illustrations *page* ix
List of Tables x
Preface xi

CHAPTER 1 The European Background 3
2 The Australian Wends 13
3 The Texas Wends 64
4 The Wends in Canada, Nebraska, and South Africa 113
5 Wendish Folkways 119
6 The Wends, Comparative Frontiers, and Turner 125

Appendix: Personal Details of Wendish Emigrants 132
Notes 190
Index 207

Illustrations

Bautzen	*page* 8
Biar homestead, St. Kitts, 1969	37
School children, Peter's Hill Church, ca. 1890	39
Johann Herman Gersch and Maria Magdalena Kleinig, St. Kitts, 1883	40
Fred Dreckow's team carting wheat, Cleve, 1912	43
Carting wool bales, 1928	46
St. Peter's Lutheran Church, St. Kitts, 1910	49
Andreas Kleinig home, South Australia, 1929	56
Gus Dreckow's home, Yadnarie, ca. 1914	61
Wendish wedding party, Texas, 1880s	*page* 90
Ernst Bernstein and Maria Kulke, Warda, 1891	95
Picking cotton, Weise farm, Lee County	97
Johann Kilian family, ca. 1865	98
Gerhard Kilian family at home, 1899	99
Butchering for beef club, Vernon	100
St. Peter's School, Serbin, ca. 1900	102
Frame home, Lee County	106
Kurio log cabin, Texas Wendish Heritage Museum	107
St. Paul Lutheran Church, Serbin	108
Texas Wendish Heritage Museum, Serbin	109

Maps

1	Administrative Divisions of Lusatia and Extent of the Sorbian Language in 1886	10
2	Lower Lusatian Birthplaces of Australian Wends	19

ILLUSTRATIONS

3	Upper Lusatian Birthplaces of Australian Wends	22
4	Australian Location of Wendish Settlers	33
5	Lusatian Birthplaces of Texas Wends	73
6	Texas Locations of Wendish Settlers	79
7	Canadian Location of Wendish Settlers	115

Figure

Migration from Lusatia to Australia by Date of Departure: 1848–77	18

Tables

1	Production of Corn and Cotton by Population Groups	85
2	Possession of Draft Animals by Population Groups	86
3	Possession of Cattle and Swine by Population Groups	87
4	Farm Acreages and Agricultural Values by Population Groups	89

Preface

Interest in ethnic history is not a new phenomenon, but the intense interest of recent years is. Not only have new studies appeared within the last decade, but the entire subject has been drawn together through the publication of the *Harvard Encyclopedia of American Ethnic Groups*. The cause or causes of this resurgence are difficult to isolate, and they may vary from a simple attempt to locate personal roots by looking into the past to a complex phenomenon associated with racism, immigration, and civil rights.

This study is first of all a chapter in the history of a small Slavic group that maintained feelings of nationality, but never succeeded in possessing its own state. This people, the Wends (or Sorbs), migrated mostly to the United States and Australia in the days when the melting pot concept held sway and they were expected to become average citizens of their host countries. Cultural assimilation did indeed occur with the Wends, but they did not as readily lose their ethnic identity. The current interest in the Wends, therefore, is more historical in nature, or for personal identification, than it is a search for civil rights and race. The pluralistic concept of society that has been fashionable in recent years encourages diversity instead of assimilation and does not apply to the Wends because they had already been absorbed into the mainstream of society.

A second aspect of the study concerns the effects of the frontier on the assimilation process. Because most Wends were engaged in agriculture in eastern Germany, they generally settled on the frontiers of Texas and Australia where land was inexpensive and there began their life of assimilation. The approach here, therefore, is to describe the original setting in Europe, the nature of the two migrations, the conditions on the Australian and Texas frontiers, and finally the responses the Wends made.

The Wendish experience in assimilation was different from that of most immigrants in that they left a homeland where they had constituted a minority and had experienced pressure from the state to adopt the dominant German culture. When they migrated to their new homes, they again constituted a minority and witnessed the continued loss of their culture. But instead of accepting the culture of their host countries, they first assimilated with the German settlers, and then, with the Germans, were absorbed into the dominant society.

One of the problems with research on the Wends is that they left few written sources. Although they were a literate people, few professionals migrated and writing a diary or an account was not widely practiced. They did write some letters, but with few exceptions the only ones to remain are those reprinted in newspapers.

Another problem is the identification of Wendish individuals. Because they were under constant pressure in Europe, many Wends crossed the ethnic line. Even names are not a certain means of identification because many changed their names; people such as Lehmann, Schmidt, Krause, and Deutscher could be either German or Wend. Although Wends had their own surnames (such as Wićaz [Lehmann] and Kowar [Schmidt]), the German forms were usually used in official records.

An advantage in the study of the Wends is that, compared with most ethnic groups, there were not as many who migrated and therefore an attempt has been made to identify each Wendish family and collect information on the first two generations of each family (see Appendix). The most reliable pieces of evidence for identification of a Wendish family were, first, the village of origin, and second, family tradition. The cities in Lusatia were predominantly German, while many of the villages were almost entirely Wendish (Sorbian). A person whose birthplace was Bautzen or Cottbus was likely to be German, while a person from Werben or Dauban was likely to be Wendish. Ernst Tschernik's book, *Die Entwicklung der sorbischen Bevölkerung von 1832–1945* (Berlin, 1954) was helpful because it listed the villages of Lusatia and their ethnic composition.

The second source for identification, family tradition, could be extremely precise so that members of a family would instantly identify their ancestors as being Wends, or it could be so vague that someone scarcely remembered that his ancestors from Germany spoke a language different from German.

Individuals who came from villages with a large Wendish population or with a Wendish family tradition were included in the study. The possibility nevertheless exists that a few Germans from predomi-

Preface

nantly Wendish villages were included and that many Wends were excluded or overlooked because of inadequate records or insufficient evidence. The research presented here identified approximately one thousand Wends who migrated to Australia and approximately fourteen hundred who went to Texas. The probability is great that many more Wends migrated than the Appendix or the maps show, but that limitation can never be completely corrected. The purpose of the book, therefore, is to present an immigration history of the Wends and to examine their assimilation into the new societies.

Research with such sparse and scattered material was much of a back-and-forth procedure, where information at one stage of the study made little sense, but later, in context, could lead to valuable insights. The initial step was to find a congregation with membership records that included the village of birth in Europe. Very often the location of a single Wend, whether in a congregational book or on a ship's passenger list, led to others, because Wends tended to travel and live with other Wends. Membership in a Wendish emigration group was an additional means of ethnic identification.

As the Wends were tentatively identified, a sheet was prepared for each family, and on that sheet was recorded information from sources such as church records, census rolls, state death records, tombstones, passenger lists, naturalization records, and obituaries. Attempts were then made to locate the descendants of each family. Often they were residing in the same community in which their ancestors had lived, but if none were found, a search of telephone directories was made and letters sent requesting interviews or further correspondence. These interviews and letters often led to valuable information about the Wendish communities, the immediate family, and folk customs. While the bulk of this study was based on the records containing vital statistics as well as congregational histories, local studies, church minutes, newspapers, and old letters, the individual interviews and correspondence provided a multitude of isolated facts that, when placed together, sharpened the perspective.

During the eleven years that followed the publication of the original study, I not only received correspondence from many persons providing me with additional details, but I continued to collect and organize new information from my own research. Even though this second edition contains no major substantive changes, I have incorporated new details, made corrections, and added a concluding chapter on the Wends and the frontier.

A note on terminology is in order. The Slavonic inhabitants of eastern Germany are known in English as *Wends* or *Sorbs,* and the corresponding adjectives are *Wendish* and *Sorbian.* In scholarly writings Sorb and Sorbian are usually preferred, with good reason, just as the German words *Sorbe* and *sorbisch* are nowadays officially preferred to *Wende* and *wendisch* in the German Democratic Republic.

The emigrants from Lusatia and their descendants, who form the subject matter of this book, however, consider themselves to be Wends or of Wendish descent. They are English-speaking, but the words Sorbs and Sorbian are virtually unknown to them. I have therefore mainly used the terms Wends and Wendish, reserving Sorb and Sorbian for reference to the G.D.R. It would seem pedantic to apply to the Wends of Texas, Australia, and elsewhere the word Sorb—a word which they themselves do not know.

In the preparation of this book I have received valuable assistance that I want to recognize. Generous financial aid was given by the Australian-American Educational Foundation (Fulbright-Hays Program), enabling me to conduct research in Australia for nine months, and by the Aid Association for Lutherans, Appleton, Wisconsin, for cartographic expenses and travel to Canada.

Librarians and archivists were most kind to me, and I remember especially Dr. F. J. H. Blaess and Rev. H. F. W. Proeve of the Australian Lutheran Archives, Rev. Reinhart H. Wuensche of the Texas District Archives of the Lutheran Church, Dr. Frido Mětšk of the Sorbian Ethnological Institute in Bautzen, and Mrs. Gladys Guebert of Concordia, River Forest, Illinois. Scores of Lutheran pastors in Australia, North America, and Europe made congregational records available to me and received me with gracious hospitality.

I have also benefited from the advice and guidance of Dr. C. A. Price of the Australian National University, Dr. Max Lohe of the Lutheran Church of Australia, and Dr. Henry L. Letterman of Concordia. The editor of the first edition of this study was Dr. Gerald C. Stone of the University of Oxford. He painstakingly examined the manuscript and corrected many shortcomings. Mr. Bill Biar of Denver and Dr. Dick Dalitz of the University of Oxford provided me with important documents, and Mrs. Edith Morison of Concordia, Mrs. R. J. Dohler of Adelaide, and Rev. J. C. E. Riotte of Toronto were most helpful as translators. And finally, I remember with particular appreciation Dr. Jan Cyž of Bautzen, whose assistance as translator, researcher, consultant, and source of encouragement was indispensable.

In Search of a Home

1

The European Background

LUSATIA

Lusatia (*Lužica* in Upper Sorbian), the homeland of the Wends (Sorbs), is not an administrative unit with fixed political boundaries, but a vaguely defined region in southeastern Germany, approximately fifty miles (eighty kilometers) southeast of Berlin. Already in ancient times geographers and historians used the term to identify an area of varying size and shape, but always in the same general section of Europe. Its southern limit has been the most specific, in that it shared a boundary with Czechoslovakia along the Lusatian Mountains. The less precise eastern limits in an earlier period extended as far as the Bober River, but in recent times the Neisse and Oder rivers, which presently separate Germany from Poland, have served as the eastern boundary of Lusatia. The western and northern boundaries are the most ill-defined and had previously extended north to Frankfort/Oder and west to the Schwarze Elster and Dahme.

The Lusatia of this study is the Lusatia of the nineteenth century, when its size was approximately fifteen hundred square miles within a tract thirty miles (forty-eight kilometers) wide at the farthest points east and west, and sixty miles (ninety-six kilometers) long from north to south. (See Map 1). While all Wends of the study originated from Lusatia, many non-Slavic people now live there and have for centuries. Lusatia, therefore, serves as a geographic term but not as a term to identify its inhabitants, who could be either German or Slavic.[1]

The southern portion, called Upper Lusatia because of its elevation and proximity to the Lusatian Mountains, is an area of rolling terrain and contains comparatively fertile soil. Although the eastern portion of Upper Lusatia is on the Oder watershed, the primary drainage of

Lusatia is through the Spree (Sorbian: Sprjewja) River that rises in the mountains to the south and flows northward through the center of Lusatia and the major cities of Bautzen (Budyšin) and Cottbus (Chośebuz). Bautzen, the largest town of Upper Lusatia, originated as an ancient Slavic fortress, but became German and was chartered as a town in the eleventh century.

Midway between Bautzen and Cottbus, but primarily part of Upper Lusatia, is the Heath. Its sandy soil of low fertility discouraged forest clearing so that the land was neither intensively cultivated nor settled. This area is now heavily industrialized because of its deposits of lignite and supports the Schwarze Pumpe (Black Pump), one of the largest coal, gas, and electricity producing combines in Europe.[2]

The northern portion, Lower Lusatia, is generally level, with a leached, sandy soil. The major city, Cottbus, now the largest in Lusatia with a population of 100,000, was mentioned in history as early as 1156. After the Spree River flows through Cottbus, it loops to the west and divides into a maze of small streams, forming a swampy area called the Spreewald (Błota). Of all Lusatia, the Spreewald is best known because it is a favorite vacation place for Germans, especially those from nearby Berlin, and the few people who have heard of the Wends usually identify them as occupants of this picturesque region. Only a small number of individuals examined in this study actually originated from the Spreewald.

Even though terrain and soil fertility in Lusatia vary, there is little difference in rainfall and temperature. Rainfall is ample with an annual average of twenty-four inches. Temperatures are moderate, with the January mean standing at 1°C (30°F) and the July mean at 17°C (63°F).

The People and Their Language

The ethnic group forming the subject of this study has been identified in English by the terms Wends, Serbo-Lusatians, and Sorbs. The most familiar name in the United States and Australia is Wends. This is not a particularly good term because the German equivalent, Wenden, was originally used to designate Slavic people in general and only in the last centuries have the Germans applied the word in a specific way to the Slavs of Lusatia.

Another reason for discouraging use of the term Wend is that it can take on a pejorative meaning. It was, for example, the subject of puns based on the plural of *Wand* ("wall"), *Wände*, in ethnic jokes.

Four Wends, according to one story, walked into a tavern, when a German patron quipped, "Mit vier Wenden baut man einen Schweinestall" (With four walls [Wends] one can build a pig sty). One of the Wends replied, "Dann steckt man einen Süddeutschen rein and dan hat man ein echt deutsches Ferkel" (Then one can place a south German in it, and he will have a genuine German piglet).[3]

"Serbo-Lusatian," another alternative, is certainly a descriptive term in that it identifies specifically the Slavs in Lusatia, but it is somewhat awkward. The third choice, Sorb, has greater simplicity and because it is derived from the ancient Slavic word *Srbi* it is in harmony with feelings of ethnic consciousness. "Sorb" is somewhat confusing in that it is similar to the name of the Serbs of the Balkan region, but it is nevertheless the official word adopted for use in the German Democratic Republic and has become the accepted term among scholars for the Slavonic population of Lusatia. It does not form part of the Wendish tradition in the United States and Australia, however, and is not used in that context.

The Sorbs have not attained the global recognition of other Slavic peoples because of their limited numbers and because they have never formed an independent state. They do possess their own language, history, and culture, however, and harbor a sense of their own nationality. For the last thousand years they have always lived under foreign governments and at present they constitute a minority in East Germany. Their isolation, moreover, has been accentuated because they were separated from their nearest Slavic neighbors, the Poles and the Czechs, by narrow bands of German-speaking people.

The small area of Lusatia supports two main dialects, Upper Sorbian and Lower Sorbian. Conversation in the two dialects, though difficult, is not impossible. Variations of the two main dialects exist in the center of Lusatia, which is considered a transitional zone. Formerly both Upper and Lower Sorbian were written and printed with Gothic letters, but in the nineteenth century the Latin alphabet gained popularity and since 1937 there has been no Gothic printing.

HISTORY OF THE SORBS (WENDS)

While the specific geographical origin of the Slavs has not been determined to the satisfaction of all scholars, it is possible to place the early Slavs to the east of Lusatia, generally between the Vistula and the Dnieper rivers. In the period when the Slavs occupied this eastern area, the region between the Oder and Elbe rivers, which included

Lusatia, was only sparsely settled by Germanic tribes. During the fourth century, however, these Germanic peoples drifted westward as the Roman Empire declined, leaving the areas between the two rivers largely unoccupied. Very slowly, the Slavs also began expanding westward and, encountering no resistance, they took over the lands west of the Oder, so that by the end of the sixth century, they held the heart of Europe. Among the many Slavic tribes were the Milceni who occupied Upper Lusatia and the Luzici of Lower Lusatia. These new occupants are considered the ancestors of the present Sorbs.

Economically the Slavs were a forest people and lived by hunting, fishing, and fowling. They also raised livestock and engaged in primitive farming, clearing fields by burning the trees and abandoning a plot when its fertility declined. Their trade items were also forest resources—honey, wax, and furs. Because the Slavs did not occupy the lands intensively, the Germans began to expand eastward once more and colonized regions beyond the Elbe. The German economy was largely agricultural and therefore on occasion was complementary to rather than competitive with that of the Slavs.

All too soon the area between the Elbe and the Oder became a battlefield and the westernmost wave of Slavic migrants felt the first counter-thrusts. German armies cleared the Elbe basin of Slavs and the Sorbs soon discovered they were under attack. In 806 Carl, the son of Charles the Great, defeated the Milceni and burned their fortress, Budyšin. The victory, however, was not conclusive and conflict continued until 932, when the Saxons, led by Henry the Fowler, again defeated the Slavs including the Lusatian tribes. Complete control of the Lusatian Slavs, however, did not follow Henry's victory, and not until 963 did the forces of Otto the Great totally subdue them. It was under Otto that the Margrave Gero invited thirty Sorbian princes to a banquet to talk peace and then had them murdered. Mato Kosyk before he migrated to America, commemorated the massacre in the epic poem, "The Treachery of Margrave Gero."

During this time of conflict the Transelbian Slavs experienced enforced conversion to Christianity. The Christian missionaries were motivated not only by religious conviction but also by economic advantages such as the collection of tithes. Because the Christianization was by force and not persuasion, it was not an inward change and the Slavs observed only the outward forms of Christianity. The double oppression from the Church and the German nobles did not generate loyalty and the Slavs responded with sporadic rebellions. Complete conversion to Christianity was not accomplished until the twelfth century.

In 1002 Bolesław the Brave, utilizing the growing power of Poland, seized the area of Upper and Lower Lusatia and confirmed the conquest in 1018 with the Treaty of Bautzen. The Germans regained the territory in 1032 and later partitioned it between the Margraves of Meissen and Brandenburg. The Germans could not stabilize their authority either, and beginning in 1136 German control of Lusatia alternated with that of the Bohemian crown. Finally in 1329 the King of Bohemia gained Upper Lusatia, and in 1367 he purchased Lower Lusatia. Bohemia, in turn, lost Lusatia temporarily to Matthias Corvinus, King of Hungary, but when he died in 1490, the area reverted to Bohemia. Brandenburg, on the other hand, had gained control of Cottbus and vicinity in 1462 and held it from then on, with the exception of a brief interlude from 1807 to 1815.

The Germanization conducted in the eleventh century during the period of intensive German colonization did not cease even under Bohemian and Hungarian rule. Control by Bohemia and Hungary did not mean the elimination of the Germans from the population or the expulsion of German nobles from local administrative posts, but only that there was a different governing head. The Germans remained in the cities and dominated the guilds and mercantile activity at the expense of the Slavs. Slavs were permitted to live in restricted sections of the cities or outside the walls, but they performed the least desirable tasks and possibility for upward mobility was slim. Even after the Wends became Christian, they were segregated and St. Michael's church, which still stands today, was the church for the Wends and was constructed outside the Bautzen city walls. Knowledge of German was a prerequisite, and a Slav who hoped to advance would be forced to learn the language and join the German community. In the countryside the German noble remained entrenched and Slavic peasants continued as serfs, working for the lord and paying dues for the very land they had previously owned. Life was doubly hard on the Sorbs at this time because besides being subjected and deprived in the same ways as German serfs, they also were Slavs in a society dominated by foreigners.

Much of the motivation for German colonization was economic, but some was stimulated by the Sorbs' hostility to the Christian faith. Because of the potential for violence, Christian churches could exist only in fortified places, and only Germans attended Mass. Replacing the Slavic leaders with German knights and nobles and planting German colonists in the community broke the unified resistance and allowed Christianity to prevail. Because Poland and Bohemia had been converted before they owned Lusatia, their leaders approved of

Bautzen, showing the ancient water tower and St. Michael's church, home of the Wendish congregation. *Courtesy Lothar Wlocka*

Christianization, but by encouraging it, they aided in the process of Germanization.

Bohemia held Upper Lusatia during the Reformation in Germany and also during 1581 when Lutheranism became the Sorbs' dominant religion. The Reformation was an important event for the Sorbs because Luther's emphasis on the vernacular encouraged religious people to translate materials into Sorbian. Prior to that time the Catholic church had used Czech on occasion, but with the Reformation both Catholics and Lutherans translated religious material into their language which previously had been only spoken. The earliest published work in Sorbian was the *Hymnbook and Catechism* translated by Albin Moller in 1574.

The Thirty Years War that followed the Reformation devastated much of Europe, including Lusatia. Armies marched across the country, and Christians on both sides burned buildings and robbed and killed civilians. So complete was the destruction that few local church records of the sixteenth century exist in Lusatia today, and most parish books presently available begin in the period after the conflict had ended. Bautzen, a fortified city, was also burned in 1634. The next year, in 1635, at the Peace of Prague, the King of Bohemia ceded the area to Saxony although he continued as protector of the remaining Lusatian Catholics.

The Thirty Years War was a blow to Sorbian society in that its small population could not absorb such a heavy loss of life and failed to repopulate the devastated areas. As a result the sparsely occupied lands filled with Germans and the Sorbian cultural boundary was again constricted. The transfer of Upper Lusatia to Saxony, however, was opportune in that it prevented the bloody counter-Reformation experienced in Bohemia and with it a further loss of Sorbian lives.

Saxony added Cottbus in 1807 and held the entire Lusatian area until 1815, when the Congress of Vienna drew new boundaries and distributed territories. Saxony had allied itself with Napoleon and as punishment was forced to transfer all of Lower Lusatia and a large part of Upper Lusatia to Prussia. The northern portion was replaced under Brandenburg administration and the middle under Silesian (see Map 1).[4]

Shortly after this boundary realignment an event took place that would have a direct bearing on the Wendish migration. The ruler of Prussia, Frederick William III, a Calvinist, initiated a program whereby both Protestant bodies, Lutheran and Calvinist, would be unified into a single state church. Many Sorbs, including the Lutheran clergyman Jan Kilian, eventually found this religious policy unacceptable and added this cause to the list of reasons for leaving their homeland.

Even though Sorbian nationalism intensified in the nineteenth century, the cultural boundaries shrank. In 1871 the German provinces were unified under Prussian leadership and German nationalism clashed with Sorbian nationalism. Prussia's Germanization before 1871 had been more intense than that of Saxony (under Saxon administration Sorbian was permitted in schools and religious instruction), and Prussia's point of view prevailed after unification. Sorbs, nevertheless, fought in the Prussian army in 1870 and again in World War I and demonstrated their loyalty to Germany. But they also dreamed of independence. The National Committee, following German defeat in World War I, presented a demand to the Paris Peace Conference to

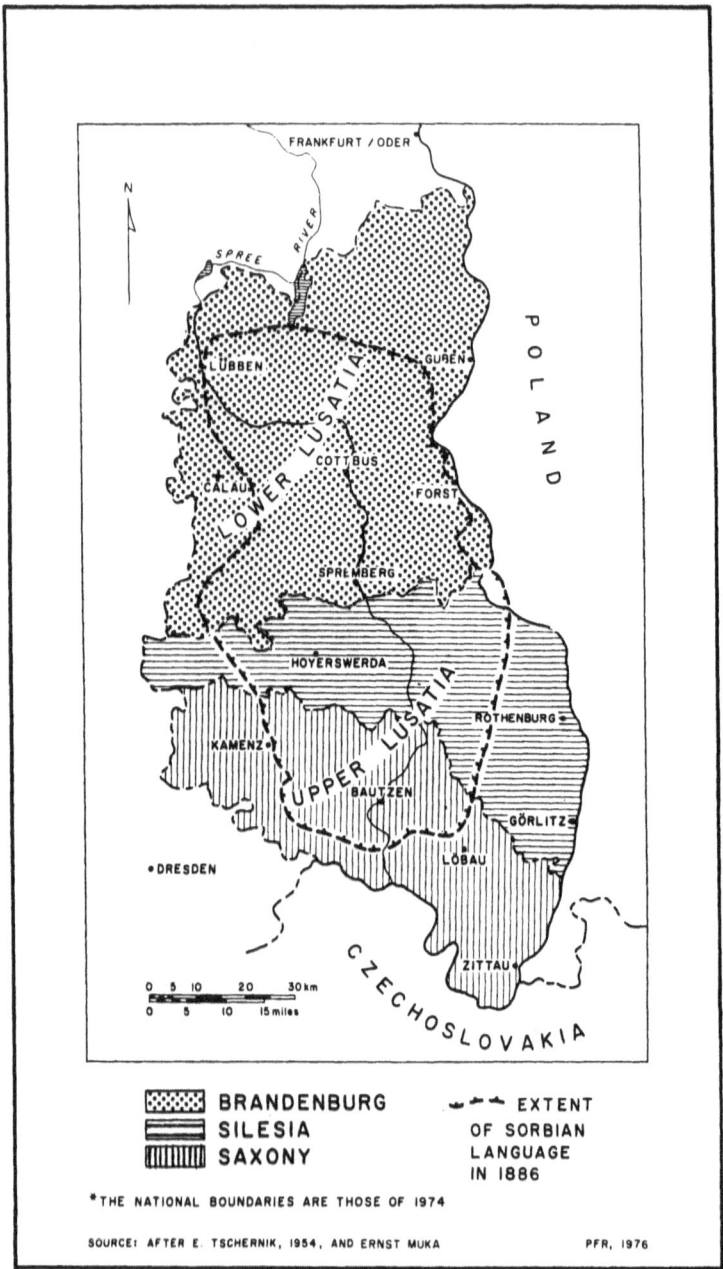

MAP 1 Administrative Divisions of Lusatia and Extent of the Sorbian Language in 1886

extend to the Sorbs the right of national self-determination. It was never granted, and they remained under German control.

Under the Weimar Republic, Germanization continued unabated, just as it had under the monarchy. The Nazi dictatorship that followed the Republic continued and eventually intensified the program. It disbanded Sorbian organizations, including the *Domowina* (Homeland), the main national body, which had been set up in 1912. It outlawed the publication of practically all Sorbian printed material, confiscated property, and arrested Sorbian leaders. The effectiveness of five decades of the policy was reflected in the marked decline of the Sorbian language. Use of the language is the surest indicator of the extent of Sorbian culture, and the boundaries delineating use of Sorbian shrank appreciably between 1886 and World War II.

The treatment of the Sorbs changed abruptly when the Soviet armies reached the area in World War II. The Russians were aware of their fellow Slavs, and the Sorbs brought out their blue, red, and white flags to welcome their liberators. The Sorbs re-established the *Domowina* and following the war asked for political independence. The request was unrealistic, however, and the Sorbs remained within Germany.

Under the newly created German Democratic Republic, the Sorbs have been viewed as a significant minority and have received favorable attention. Some of the changes, such as land reform, were motivated by Communist ideology, but whatever the motivation, many Sorbian families benefited. Among measures adopted with the express purpose of revitalizing Sorbian culture was government action to revive the Sorbian press and to make Sorbian language study in schools available for those who desired it.[5]

The relationship between the history of a people and its common characteristics is an intriguing question. To what extent did the historical experience of the Wends generate certain characteristics? Many references have identified them as conservative, clannish, convivial, or stubborn.[6] Any generalization along these lines remains nothing more than speculation. Nevertheless the centuries of resistance to foreign threats must have left some legacy.

How much longer the Sorbs will exist as an identifiable unit is also a matter for speculation. Too many people have set a date for the disappearance of the language and culture, and have been wrong. The Sorbian-speaking population has steadily declined, however, and the smaller the group, the faster its decline. In 1840, for example, shortly before the overseas migrations, the population stood at 164,000; in

1930 it was 120,000; today it is approximately 60,000.[7] The trend may be reversed by the new government policy, but the shift may have come too late. There is also a distinct possibility that survival of the culture will be more difficult under a friendly government, where there is association between majority and minority, than in a society where the minority was isolated and forced to look to its own for help.

2

The Australian Wends

Migration from Lower Lusatia

Migration, by its very nature, is intensely disquieting and bewildering at any period of time. Especially in the era before rapid transportation and mass communication, when knowledge of the world beyond the immediate country was limited, few ventured into the unknown. Leaving the familiar behind forever in order to live in a strange country with a different language was not a step to be taken lightly by a slightly educated and insecure peasant. No matter how objectionable his lot in life might be, it was one thing to be discontented, but quite another to exchange the familiar for the unknown.

People had been unhappy before and there had been migrations before, but how repulsive must conditions be for inertia to be conquered and people to leave their homeland? In the mid-nineteenth century three factors encouraged an exodus of people, including the Wends, from Europe. The first was the problem of earning a living; the second was an improved transportation system; and the third was an available destination. The Wendish migration took place in a setting where the irritations were galling enough and the alternatives enticing enough to cause people to break loose and move. The migration would never have reached such enormous proportions had not the destination seemed so appealing and the methods of transportation promised speed and safety.

To identify and isolate each motive for each individual is impossible, and in many instances there were undoubtedly several causes of discontent. One person may emigrate in search of better economic conditions, while another may wish to escape an unbearable domestic situation. Another may be motivated by both reasons and in addition possess the urge for adventure. Migrants may not even understand the complexity of their own motivation, or may never tell anyone what actually prompted them; instead they may give a motive that is noble or one the audience would like to hear, such as desire for religious freedom or avoidance of military service.

The primary cause of migration from the Cottbus area, as stated by the migrants and supported by historical accounts of existing conditions, was economic. The area suffered from shortages of food, employment, and land. Contrary to the romantic view of a peasant's life, there was little security or predictability. The peasant was subject to the whims of the weather, price fluctuations, and government disinterest.

The harvest of 1844 in Germany had fallen short of needs, and the shortfall was repeated in 1845 with the additional tragedy of potato rot making this staple food unpalatable. The excessive heat of a third bad year, 1846, caused the grains to dry before the kernels could form, and the potato rot continued for a second year. Prices of food increased 50 percent between 1844 and 1847, with food shortages peaking in May, 1847, shortly before a better harvest.

In addition to the inadequate supply of food, there was also the problem of land shortage and land hunger. The German states ended feudalism by stages between 1807 and 1860, and this directly influenced the Wends (Sorbs), who were predominantly agricultural. Under feudalism peasants lived on the land and paid the nobility with dues in commodities and services. In return they received the right to farm the land and were given the protection of the lord.

While the elimination of serfdom sounds like positive reform, the peasant did not gain. Instead of taking the land from the nobles with or without state compensation, the reform laws stated that to get clear title to land, a peasant would be required to pay for it with currency or give a portion of the land back to the noble as payment. The noble then became the large landowner who made a profit hiring workers for the fields and selling the harvest. The peasant, farming smaller plots, lost the security of the earlier period and was forced to compete with the agricultural entrepreneur, whose costs were lower and whose operation was more efficient. During the transition from manorialism to capitalism, the peasants lost approximately 10 to 15 percent of the land they had previously tilled.[1]

While the number of arable acres held by peasants remained fixed or declined, the population increased, and the peasants discovered that the productivity of the soil could not keep pace with that of their wives. Some German states placed restrictions on marriage in the hope of controlling population. Prussia and Saxony did not, and restrictive policies in other states were understandably ineffective. The population of Werben, for example, was 903 in 1806 and had almost doubled, to 1,783 by 1846. Drewitz had 153 people in 1816 but 430 in 1846. Jänschwalde had a population of 315 in 1816 and 590 in 1846.[2] Unfortunately, the available land did not double.

Although there were too many people and not enough food, and something had to be done, the conservative nature of the government precluded economic assistance or land redistribution.[3] The two alternatives for the Wendish (Sorbian) peasant were migration to the city to seek employment in the growing industrial sector, or migration to a country that still had lands open for agriculture.

The transportation and communication system that grew with industrialization first influenced the Wends through the dissemination of knowledge of the world. In their isolation, they did not have direct access to lands outside Germany, but were dependent upon information from their German neighbors, newspapers, and writings. The first weekly newspaper written in Wendish was *Jutrnicka* (*The Morning Star*), which appeared in 1842. Development of a Wendish press both reflected growing ethnic awareness and stimulated it, but the rarity of newspapers until then explains Wendish dependence on German information sources.[4] Thus Wendish migration out of Europe was understandably associated with German migration and no Wends went where Germans had not gone earlier.

Once Germans had migrated to Australia, the United States, Canada, and Africa, the Wends learned of these lands and how to get there. Published accounts described in detail all aspects of the trip, including routes, menus on board, and the speed of transport. The industrial revolution had drastically changed land transportation. Having left the wagon and boarded the railroad train, a migrant could be in Berlin in one day and on the coast in two. The ships were still sailing ships, but the hazards of ocean travel had diminished and the voyages were routine.

Freighting was the chief function of shipping companies, but passengers also brought revenue, and shipping agents scoured the countryside trying to dislodge peasants from their entrenched life. The agents advertised in newspapers, talked to individuals, answered questions, and helped organize people into groups. They were the facilitators, telling prospective migrants about the route of travel to the seaport, costs, and baggage and offering security for the journey. Without modern transportation systems and their publicists, the complexion of the Wendish migration would have been different. Wends could plan their travel in advance and leave their hearths secure in the knowledge that risks had been minimized.[5]

Australia, one of the goals for European migrants, may have been forbidding because so little information was available, but the peasant knew that it was a continent with few people, and stories of how good farmland was being distributed without cost roused considerable interest. While the first wave of migrants landed in Australia without much accurate information, they soon wrote letters home describing the new area and way of life. Letters to the immediate family were often printed in newspapers and thus educated the entire community. The impact of the letters in setting up an image of Australia as the place to live must not be underestimated, and although months elapsed between the posting of a letter and its publication, many people were infected with the desire to follow. Martin Teschner, for example, left his Lusatian home in 1848, wrote letters in 1849 that were published that same year, and in 1850 welcomed more migrants to Australia from his old neighborhood. Mato Nowka, editor of the *Bramborski serski Casnik,* sent Teschner the newspaper and asked for more news from Australia, but Jan Smoler in the *Tydźenske Nowiny* published largely negative letters and lists of fatalities on board ship.[6]

Some letters described the conditions favorably and included money because the migrants had indeed improved their lot in life; others painted a rosy picture in order to lure friends and relatives who in turn would relieve the isolation of the Wends already in Australia. One unhappy migrant, Carl Traugott Hoehne, claimed he was warned by others not to write the truth or no more would migrate and his loneliness would continue.[7] Newspaper editors could thereby influence migration by printing the negative or positive letters.

Although extensive migration took place from southwestern Germany in the early nineteenth century, Prussia did not witness largescale emigration until the mid-1840s, and Saxony not until the end of the decade.[8] The Wendish migration was therefore a delayed reaction to what the Germans had started, and began just as the German migration was dropping off. German migration slowed in the late 1840s because land prices in Germany had declined to reasonable levels as a result of the crop failures of that decade and the loss of population through migration. Moreover, risks in travel were compounded by Danish warships that harassed the ports of Hamburg and Bremen and posed a threat to safe transportation.[9] It was just at this time that Wendish migration to Australia got under way.

The beginnings of Wendish migration from Lower Lusatia were associated with the recruitment efforts of a Britisher, George Fife

Angus. He had purchased land in South Australia and formed the South Australian Company in the hope of transporting settlers to his new holdings. In 1837 he had come to the rescue of the Reverend A. L. C. Kavel, who was unhappy with the church in Prussia, and financed the travel of the pastor and his flock to Australia. In need of more settlers, Angus decided to recruit more Germans. One of his Lusatian agents, named Hakert, succeeded in signing up individuals from the villages of Tauer and Turnow, eleven miles northeast of Cottbus in the Peitz parish.[10] They left in 1848 and at Hamburg met a group from Upper Lusatia also bound for Australia. Together they boarded the ship *Victoria* and began the Wendish exodus to Australia.

No Wends migrated in the following year, 1849, but favorable letters sent from Australia convinced more to migrate from the Peitz district and from the neighboring Jänschwalde. Harvests were bad again from 1850 to 1853, and German migration accelerated. Fewer Wends migrated between 1851 and 1853 than had left in 1850, but then in 1854 the migration spurted. Already in 1852, Christian Duschka had migrated from Werben, a village northwest of Cottbus, and in 1853 Friedrich Konzag and Matthes Matschka followed.[11] The bulk of the 1854 migration continued the trend and came from the area west of Cottbus. Migration dipped again in 1855 but then came the peak years of 1856 to 1860 with the zenith in 1858. Migration to Australia was sporadic after that, as the figure on Lusatian migration shows, with 1865 and 1877 as years of higher migration than the intervening years. (See graph, page 18.)

The typical emigrant parents from Lower Lusatia were thirty-four years old and left Germany with three children. Nevertheless several widows, such as Agneta Altus, migrated with their children, and some families such as those of Christian Marschall and Matthes Modra, had as many as eight children at the time of emigration. The oldest person to venture on the long voyage was seventy-one-year-old Anna Baschzisch who accompanied her son-in-law Christian Jarick.

Most of the migrants were employed in agriculture, but not all were equal in economic wealth or status. According to Gerhard Krüger who studied the passport records for all migrants from Kreis Cottbus, both German and Wend, 76 adult males were classified as *Häusler* (owners of a cottage and less than five *Morgen*—a Morgen being the amount of land a farmer could plow in a morning or generally .6 to .9 acres of land), 26 craftsmen, 24 laborers, 19 tenant farmers, 13 *Büdner* (owners of a small cottage and from 5 to 30 *Morgen*), 13 *Kossäten* (owners of a house, from 30 to 200 *Morgen*, and draft animals), 12 servants, 7 farmers' sons, 5 colonists, 4 retired farmers, and 4 *Bauern* (owning

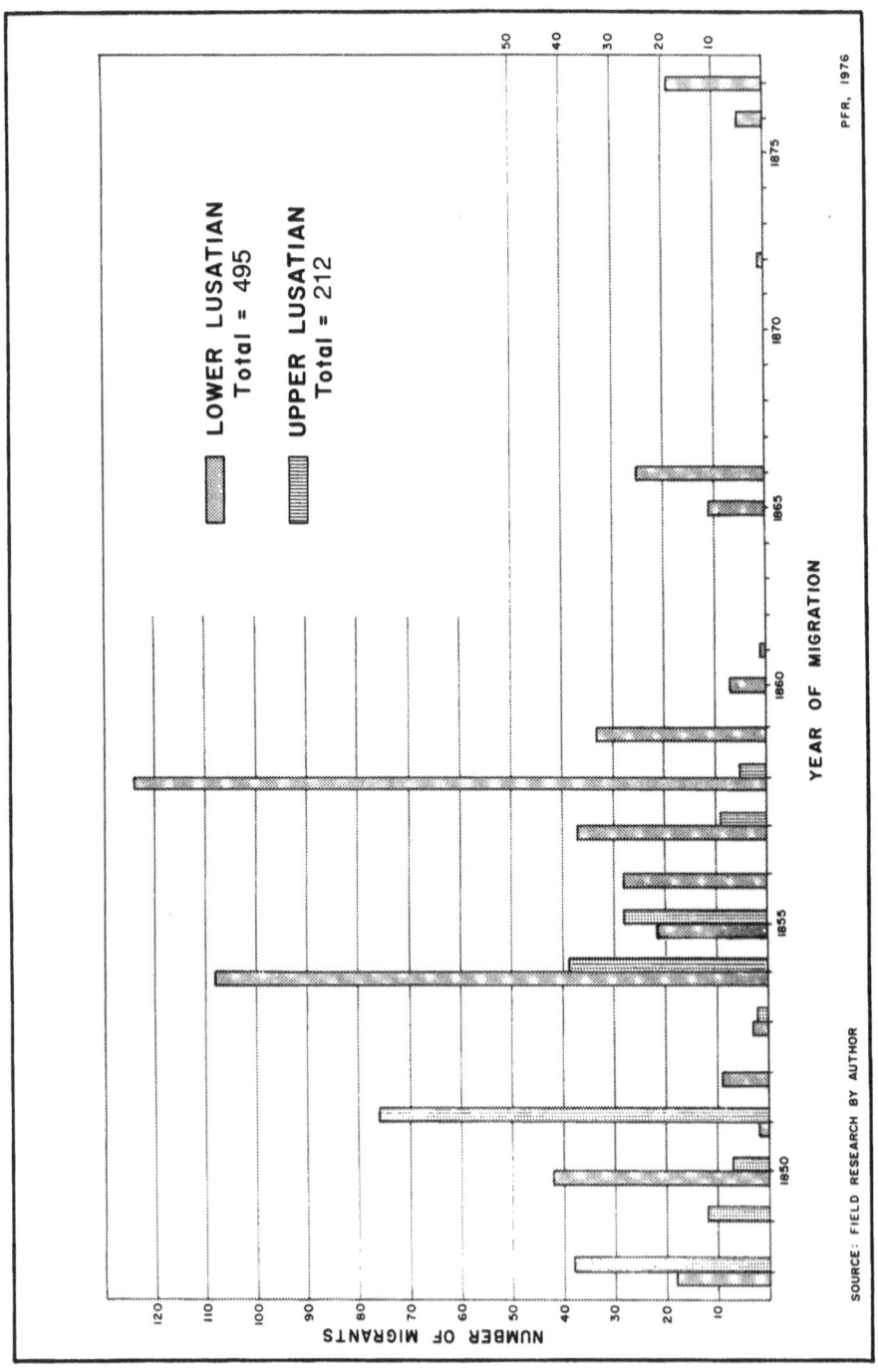

Migration from Lusatia to Australia by Date of Departure: 1848–77

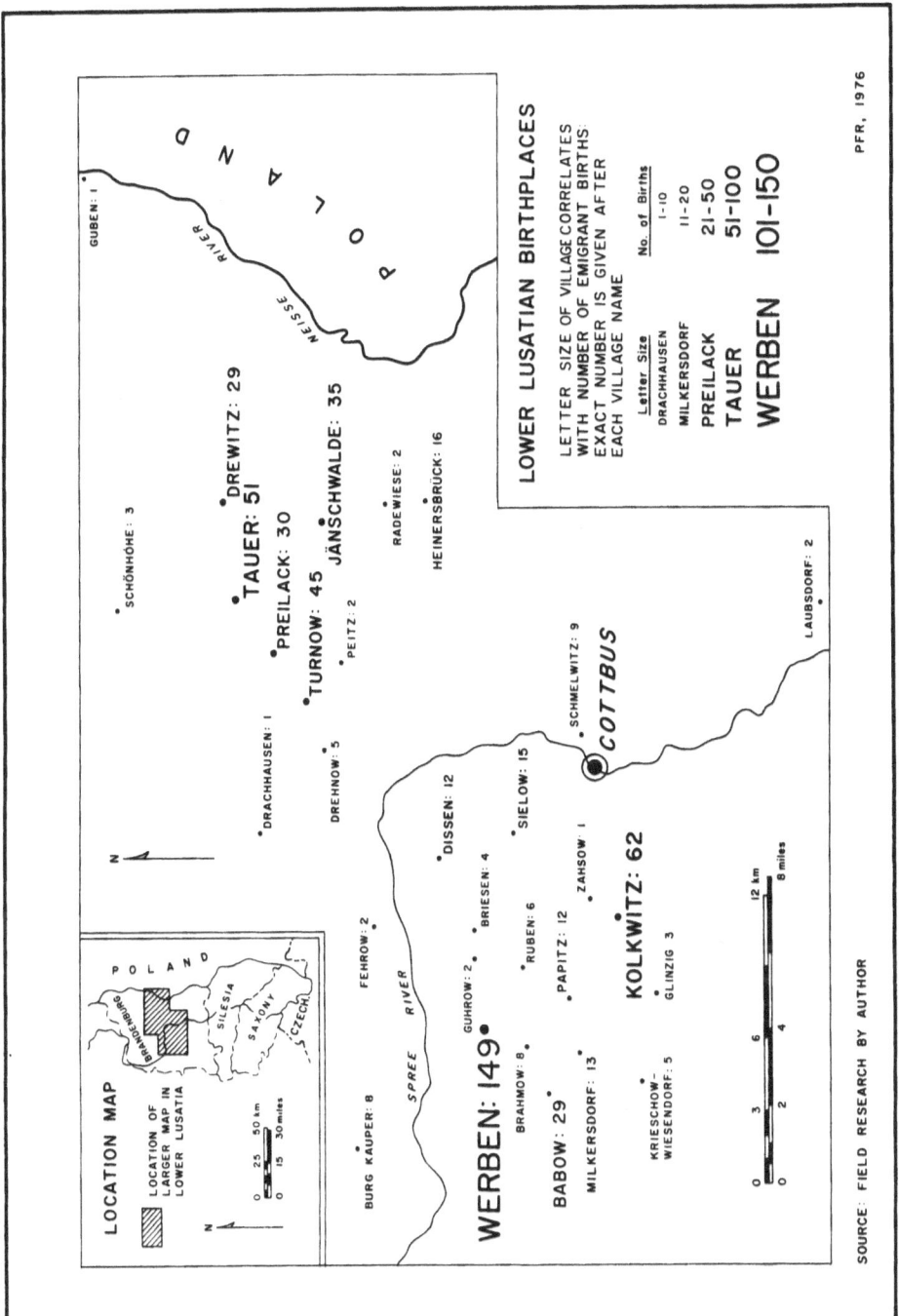

MAP 2 Lower Lusatian Birthplaces of Australian Wends

100 to 300 *Morgen*).¹² The majority of the migrants were from the poorer categories of agricultural rank, but most had some property to sell in order to pay for migration expenses. Christian Marschall, for example, received only fifty-five *Taler* for his property, enough for half a fare, so he borrowed the remainder. Martin Poesch, on the other hand, sold his holdings for five hundred *Taler*. Many who had no money at all became the indentured servants of anyone who could pay the fare. It is safe to assume that in general the findings of Krüger's study apply to the Wends as well, because so many records he examined were for Wends. If any discrepancy existed between his conclusions and the actual status of the Wends, their average economic level was probably lower than that of the group he studied.

Once the economic affairs were settled, the major obstacle was passed. Prussia placed no restrictions on emigrants in time of peace, except on those individuals who performed special service for the state. Even young men who had not met their required military service were permitted to go provided they were not leaving for the purpose of avoiding their military obligation. While most of the migrants faithfully applied to the state officials for permission, some did not even bother to do so.¹³

Migration from Upper Lusatia

The motives for the Upper Wends are more complex because in addition to the economic motives, social and religious aspects must be considered. The crop failures and potato rot also hit Saxony, subjecting its citizens to poverty and hunger. As early as 1842, Johann Dallwitz, father of one of the later migrants, wrote to his son, serving in the Saxon army, that the drought was so severe that the flax had failed to produce and the potatoes were threatened. His wife, helping to earn money for the family, worked for the local lord, but the pay was extremely low.¹⁴

Compounding the difficulties resulting from crop failures was social dislocation. When Saxony ended serfdom in 1832 society began to reshuffle. Johann Kilian, future pastor of the Texas Wends, reported in 1840 that the population of his village of Kotitz was increasing in both Germans and Wends, but too many came from different regions and divergent family backgrounds. In the same bittersweet view, he maintained that conditions improved for those who owned land, but that many held none at all, and that this group prevented the overall improvement of the community. In 1845, five years after he made his original report, he noted that poverty and indigence had increased in spite of the improved employment opportunities. In the hope of upgrading economic life he founded The Society for the Poor, which distributed money, but also encouraged citizens to admonish all those who were drunkards and lazy.[15]

Although the documentation for the religious factor is thin, there was a qualitative difference between the religious views of the Lower and the Upper Wends. The Lower Wends viewed the church the same way as they did the air. It was necessary, but not something you changed or reformed. The Cottbus migrants gave no indication that religion was a motive for their migration, and once in Australia, they did not reflect any doctrinal concerns, but readily associated with the Lutheran church in Australia.

The Upper Wends who went to Australia also did not specifically state that they migrated for religious reasons. In fact, the records that remain supply no statements on motivation at all. The religious cause must be considered, however, because these migrants were the neighbors and relatives of the Wends who migrated to Texas primarily for religious reasons and also because the Upper Wends, once in Australia, reflected more of an involvement in religious concerns.

The only Lutheran pastors to leave Lusatia were from Upper Lusatia—Andreas Kappler and Andreas Pjenck left for Australia and Kilian for Texas (Mato Kosyk was ordained only after arrival in the U.S.A.). Kappler migrated in 1848 and landed in Adelaide, but Pjenck, who left in 1849 with the group which was to travel on the *Pribislav*, died in Berlin. Besides pastors, active lay leaders were associated with the Upper Wend migration. One devout lay leader, Johann Zwar, went to Leipzig in preparation for the *Helena* migration to purchase crosses, religious books, and a church bell. He also interviewed Korla August Jenc, then a theology student, in the hope that he would become their pastor when his studies were completed and the congregation in Australia became organized. Jenc, who was later to become a prominent figure in the Sorbian national movement, never did migrate, and Zwar served as a lay religious leader for the remainder of his life. The Upper Wends were thoughtfully discriminating in their religious affairs, and migration may have been prompted by their religious views.[16]

The Upper Wends were also involved in, or at least exposed to, the Pietism and Old Lutheranism movements. Pietism, established by Philipp Jakob Spener in the seventeenth century, stressed Bible study and personal involvement. The Moravian Brethren, a Pietist group, designated Herrnhut, a few miles southeast of the Wendish area, as its

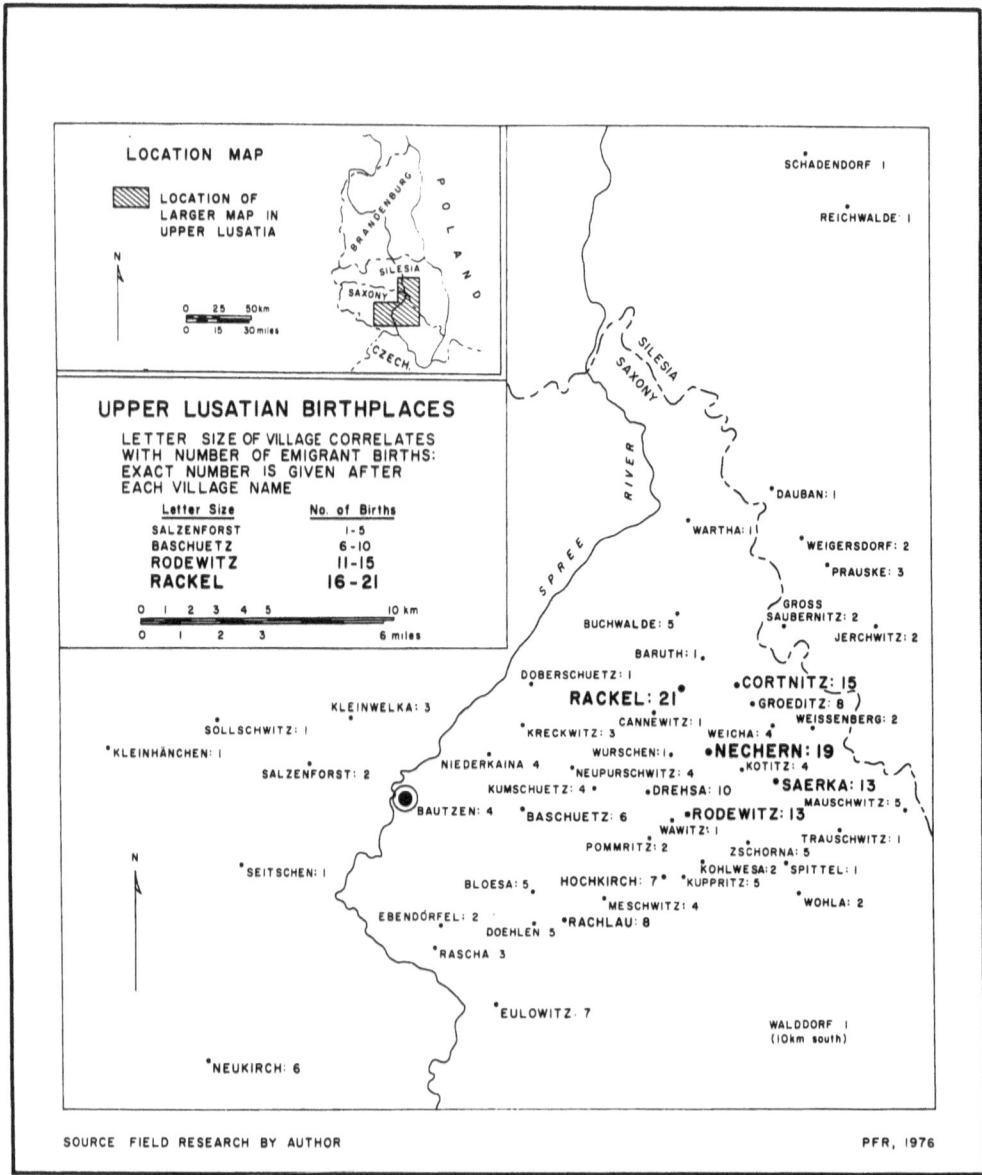

MAP 3 Upper Lusatian Birthplaces of Australian Wends

headquarters, and founded a congregation at Kleinwelka, just north of Bautzen.[17] The Pietist attitudes appeared later both in the congregation at Tarrington, Victoria, and in Serbin, Texas.

Old Lutheranism, a protest against the union of the Lutheran and Reformed churches by the Prussian monarchy, was a vibrant movement, especially in neighboring Silesia. Although the Calvinists in Saxony were too few to form a union, the common people were not happy with the liberal views of the clergy and educators. Many Wends instead identified with the Old Lutherans and one of the frequent requests of the Australian Wends was for the Breslau Hymnal of that conservative body. To what extent dissatisfaction with the Saxon church encouraged migration to Australia is a matter for speculation, but it must not be ignored.[18]

The migration of the Upper Wends also began in 1848 with a small group that accompanied Pastor Andreas Kappler. While no Lower Wends left in 1849, the migration continued from Upper Lusatia. The largest group departed in 1851 under the guidance of Johann Zwar, but then the momentum declined. In 1854 about twenty-five left for Australia but the vast majority went to Texas with Kilian. The next year twenty-eight more migrated to Australia, but after that only the Biele family and the Altus families followed.

Even though fewer Wends migrated from Upper Lusatia than from Lower Lusatia, the complexion of the emigrant family was not very different. The typical couple also was agricultural and averaged thirty-four years of age. Fertility was lower, however, with only two children per family compared with three for the Lower Wends.

The migrants from both parts of Lusatia were more interested in conserving what they had than in building something new. Suffering from insecurity and lack of predictability, they wanted to go where they could be secure and predict their future.[19] Migrants were certainly more daring than those who stayed behind, but they did not reject the values and institutions of the old society. The Wends had been cautious and conservative in Europe and continued to be so in the new land. The industrialization of Europe and the famines had undermined the old security, and the Wends changed to remain the same.

Arrival in Australia

Prior to 1848 only isolated Wends, undoubtedly part of the German migration, had set foot on Australian soil. The very first Wend to go to

Australia was Jan Rychtar, a Moravian Brethren missionary who settled in Sydney in 1844. Teacher Peter Bryl followed in 1847 but turned to farming in the Lyndoch Valley of South Australia.[20] The German migration, in all probability, rather than the migration of these two men from the Bautzen area, set the stage for the exodus of the Wends in 1848.

Although some of the German migrants bound for Australia embarked from Bremen, the majority sailed from Hamburg. One reason for this was the concerted recruitment efforts of the company of J. C. Godeffroy and Son that shuttled nine ships across the waters from Hamburg to Australia. The ships ranged in size from the *Alfred* of 450 tons to the *Australia* of 750 tons to the *Peter Godeffroy* of 1050 tons.[21]

One route to Hamburg took the migrants from Lusatia to Berlin by train and was used by the *Alfred* migrants in 1848. The train stopped in Berlin for the night and those peasants migrating in 1848 saw the shambles left by the 1848 Revolution. Eight-year-old Christiane Petschel sensed the tension in Berlin as well as the migrants' relief when the night was over and they were able to leave for Hamburg.[22]

Another route to Hamburg was that used by Johann Zwar and the *Helena* group in 1851. They rode the train from Bautzen to Dresden and then to Leipzig and Hamburg. This route made it possible for pious Lutherans to visit Halle and Wittenberg, cities of the Reformation. Travel in a large group was an advantage: not only was Zwar able to obtain half fares for the adults and free passes for the children, but they bolstered their spirits singing Wendish hymns when they missed the train and were forced to spend the night in Dresden.[23]

Once in Hamburg the migrants waited and lived as cheaply as possible while the ship was loaded and final arrangements were made. The *Alfred* group remained in the city for ten days, during which all the families lived in one large room, sleeping in their clothes on a straw-covered floor.

When the ship was fully supplied, the passengers were shown their berths. Captain H. E. Decker, of the *Alfred*, in the hope of reducing the tension of a four-month voyage, segregated the 275 passengers into provincial groups with Silesians in the bow; Saxons, including Michael Deutscher and the Wends, in the center; and the Berliners and Hamburgers in the rear. The shiplist noted that the Saxons were of "ordinary circumstances" but most respectable persons.[24]

Although many emigrant ships provided no partitions on the passenger deck, both sides of the *Alfred*'s 'tween deck were lined with compartments, each large enough to accommodate four people. While each section had beds, there was no furniture, and traveling trunks were utilized as tables and seats. The Zwar group on the *Helena* had been led to believe that all their baggage would be placed in their quarters, but they discovered that much of it had been stored in the hold. Zwar insisted that the baggage be brought up and cited legislation protecting the passengers' rights. The ship's agents, on the other hand, stated their policy, and threatened to assess additional fees for any baggage in the compartments exceeding the twenty-cubic-feet limit. Finally, while Zwar was writing a letter of complaint to the police, an official of the company arrived and made concessions. After everyone had found a place on board, final farewells were exchanged with relatives who had accompanied the migrants to the coast, and the ship cast off.[25]

From Hamburg the vessels sailed down the Elbe for nineteen miles to Cuxhaven, where a doctor boarded for an inspection, and then the ships moved into open water. The two ships leaving in 1848, the *Victoria* in June and the *Alfred* in August, were significant not only because they carried the first Wends to Australia, but also because they faced the Danish blockade. Both ships penetrated the blockade successfully, although the *Alfred* was pursued by the *Meander* for eight hours and remained undamaged by the eight shots directed at her. One of the passengers, a German blacksmith named Ernst Kaulvers, credited Captain Decker's sailing ability as well as the speed of the three-masted *Alfred*. The *Victoria*'s captain, J. Meyer, was apparently equally impressive; at the end of the voyage, the passengers placed a notice of thanks in the Adelaide newspaper.[26]

On board both ships were passenges who would be active in the Wendish community for many years. The Saxon Wends included such individuals as Charles Duschke, Adam Bartsch, Andreas, Peter and Traugott Preusker, Andreas and Michael Deutscher, and Pastor Kappler, while the Prussian Wends included Martin Teschner, George Miatke, and George Proposch. Ernst Kaulvers subsequently returned to Germany to write an account of his travels and offer advice to prospective immigrants. Another traveler with literary talents was the eight-year-old Wendish girl, previously mentioned, Christiane Petschel. Wide-eyed and impressionable, she was awed by the world unfolding before her and later in life recorded the journey with amazing accuracy and detail.[27]

According to her account, seasickness, the most frequent problem, was worst at the beginning of the voyage. When the nausea eased and appetites returned, new ways of preparing food had to be learned. The chief utensils were a wooden basin eighteen inches wide and six inches deep, tin buckets, and tin cups for tea and coffee. Meat was on the menu for each day except Sunday, when a pudding with dried plums was substituted. The meat dishes, pickled pork and corned beef, alternated on the remaining six days. Shortly after breakfast a barrel of meat was opened and a person from each double cabin, occupied by four people, went to receive a piece of meat weighing two to three pounds. The meat was washed with sea water, trimmed, tagged with a metal disk bearing the number of the cabin, and prepared by the cook.

The same regimented schedule applied to the vegetables: Monday—peas; Tuesday—pearl barley; Wednesday—sauerkraut and potatoes; Thursday—lentils; Friday—beans; Saturday—rice; and on Sunday the pudding replaced the vegetables as well. There was coffee in the morning and tea in the evening, and twice a week ship's biscuits, butter, and sugar were distributed. Water was stored in barrels on the deck and as the travelers neared the tropics, it became foul and stank. The barrels had generally been used for storing other liquids such as beer, wine, and vinegar, and these tastes flavored the water.[28]

The 1855 diet was similar: Sunday—half a pound of beef, flour for pudding, dried fruit, and one bottle of wine for eight persons; Monday—pork, sauerkraut, and potatoes; Tuesday—beef and dried beans; Wednesday—fish, dried beans, and potatoes; Thursday—beef, thick rice with syrup and raisins; Friday—pork, dried beans, and potatoes; and Saturday—barley with syrup and dried fruit. The weekly allotments per person were two ounces of coffee, three-quarters of an ounce of tea, four ounces of sugar, eight ounces of butter, and five pounds of white and dark bread.[29]

Comforts were lacking in the close quarters and each day had its little irritations and agonizing heartaches. There were fleas and lice, and Pastor Kappler was ill the entire voyage and close to death on two occasions. Four children died on board the *Alfred* and five were born. One of the children who died on the *Helena* was Marka, the daughter of Johann Mirtschin. He later recounted that all the passengers appeared on deck for the funeral service and sang the hymn "*Štož čini Bóh, wšo dobre je*" ("What God Ordains Is Always Good"). Peter Doecke then spoke a religious message in both Wendish and German and the captain followed with a statement of sympathy. Two sailors lowered the body, wrapped in white cloth and tied to a board, into the water, and the short service was over.[30]

The ship's first stop was Rio de Janeiro, where Christiane Petschel's parents went ashore and returned with tropical foods such as oranges. After a short stay at Rio most ships sailed directly for Adelaide while some scheduled another stop at Cape Town.

The port at Adelaide had improved since the early days of "Port Misery" when the sailors had to carry passengers ashore, but in 1848 the harbor facilities were still limited. Each passenger climbed down the ship's ladder into a rowboat and then, with bedding and small parcels in tow, was taken to the pier. After four months of travel the migrants finally arrived at their land of promise. They gave up the unsettled revolutionary Europe of 1848 and gained instead a new country where the social problems included such legal niceties as one George Rivett being charged with stealing a purse, and Edward Nettleship with being drunk.[31]

THE PERIOD OF ADAPTATION

With terra firma underfoot once again, the farmers turned their backs on the sea. The women and children were taken inland by ox-drawn drays to homes in the German community, while the men stayed briefly near the ship to look after the trunks and to earn money unloading freight. The *Victoria* and the *Alfred* also carried a limited amount of cargo such as wine, paint, cigars, pianos, furniture, nails, tools, and seltzer water.[32]

The week during which the Petschel family was separated was a difficult one, especially for the women and children, and Christiane recorded the loneliness of the new land and her mother's tears as she learned the new ways. One of the first lessons was about the danger of bush fires in the dry Australian summer. The dray had taken them ten miles east to Klemzig, where they shared a little house with three other families. Outside the building was an oven, but when Mrs. Petschel, happy to be able to bake bread again, lit the fire, the neighbors rushed over and graphically warned her of the fire hazard. The baking was completed as the new Australian stood guard with a bucket of water.

Five days after landing, and with clothes newly washed in the River Torrens, the women and children were taken by wagons to Tanunda, approximately forty miles northeast, where they were reunited with the men of the family. Tanunda, like Klemzig, was a thoroughly German community and at least those Wends who knew German could communicate. The accommodations at Tanunda being adequate, the Petschel family stayed in a partially completed school for the next six weeks.[33]

During this period the six Saxon families who had come on the *Alfred* purchased land in a frontier area ten miles away from Tanunda, in the direction of Adelaide, and named it Rosenthal (Rosedale).[34] Once again the teamster came to pick up their goods, but this time there was no shelter waiting for them at the end of the ride. With goods simply stacked in the open, the men took their axes and saws and went into the bush looking for suitable timber. They rammed the trimmed logs into the ground and then built a framework for the roof. One of the earlier settlers at neighboring Hoffnungsthal (Karrawirra) offered them the straw for the roof if the men would thresh his wheat, so the men made flails and became threshers. While at Hoffnungsthal, Christiane's father purchased a wagon and bullocks (oxen) and after two loads of straw and a few more days of work, the family was again under a roof.

The next step in house construction was building the walls. The upright timbers had been set in place as closely as possible, but there were spaces in between and Christiane thought the house looked like a bird cage. The gaps had to be filled with a plaster-like material called pug. To make this the builders needed water, so they made a sled out of an old tree, placed a barrel on it, and pulled the water to the building site. There they mixed water, clay, and soil and applied it to the walls, completely concealing the timber. Finally some calico was attached to the windows and doors and the two-room pug house was completed. In later years homeowners whitewashed the outside walls and papered them on the inside. A calico ceiling held back dust, and corrugated, galvanized roofs eventually replaced the straw.

Another building variation described by Christiane Petschel was wattle and daub construction. With this method, branches an inch or two in diameter were fastened to the widely spaced wall supports and then clay, water, and straw were mixed and applied to both sides of the wattle walls. Both types of construction were generally used in Australia before the Wends arrived and were well suited to the environment. Sufficient and suitable timber was not available for log cabins as on the American frontier, yet for these homes the settlers could use the building materials readily at hand. In addition to being inexpensive, the earthen walls were good insulators against the summer heat and could be easily maintained because of the scant rainfall.

The next building project on the Petschel farm was a two-room house for Christiane's bachelor uncle, Wilhelm Petschel. One of the two rooms was used as a carpenter's shop where he built windows, doorframes, and bedsteads out of native pine trees. Instead of buying boards, he dug a pit and cut the boards himself. Other smaller projects included building an oven out of flat stones and pug, constructing fences for their animals and garden, and digging a well. The well was a disappointment because after striking water at sixty feet, they found it to be salty.

As spring approached, they set aside building and prepared the land for cultivation. Like everyone else, they grew wheat, but unfortunately because seed was scarce, their first crop was small. They guarded their first crop and harvested it with utmost care because it was needed to feed the family and also for sowing a larger acreage the following year.

The remaining concerns at the Petschel farm centered around the animals. Besides his bullocks, Petschel bought some goats to provide milk for the family. The fences were not goat-proof, so he sold the goats and purchased two cows. They had no greater respect for their enclosure, however, and escaped, but one was recaptured and slaughtered. Although the Petschels kept no sheep they ate mutton because a neighboring squatter (grazier) was forced to sell his sheep very cheaply when grass seeds ruined the wool and even penetrated the flesh.[35]

During all this time religious matters were not neglected. First the small group attended church services at Hoffnungsthal, then in Michael Deutscher's barn, and finally in 1852 they built a small church of sun-dried bricks on the Petschel land. They had no resident pastor, so either a neighboring pastor would visit them at times, or a layman such as Michael Deutscher conducted services. Deutscher also opened his home every Tuesday and Wednesday for Bible study.[36]

After three years in Rosenthal, the Petschels and several other families began to consider still another move. The majority of the new settlers at Rosenthal were from Magdeburg, and the Saxon Wends were not comfortable with them. The soil was not suited to raising vegetables and the brackish well water did not please them. When a friend from Melbourne wrote that the soil was fertile in Victoria and the temperature moderate, one man decided to see for himself. No ship from Adelaide to Melbourne being available, he took one to Portland, halfway. There he consulted Thomas Henty, a political leader and economic developer, and was convinced of the desirability of the western district of Victoria. He returned with a favorable report and nine families decided to make the trek in 1852.[37]

The Preusker brothers, Andreas and Traugott, had landed in 1848 and not followed the same settlement pattern as the Petschel group, but remained in the German community. First they earned money helping with the harvest, and then rented some land near Light Pass. During their first season they sowed thirty-three bushels of wheat seed and found a ready market for their wheat, as well as melons, potatoes, fruit, with the copper miners at Kapunda. Highly satisfied with the land, they settled permanently among the Germans.[38]

Even though each immigrant ship was met by countrymen offering them shelter and employment, the Wends had to adjust quickly to a new way of life. The most perplexing demands were those of language. One immigrant observed that anyone who did not know English was deaf and dumb, and even if he were highly intelligent, the lack of English skills made him into a servant. Michael Zwar bemoaned the fact that he had not studied English on board ship and did not even know the difference between "yes" and "no." As a result he was cheated, misinformed, and unable to get a good paying position. The English language was less of a problem for those who lived in a larger German community such as South Australia, for many of the Wends could speak German. Very often a German who spoke English could be called on to make the necessary contacts and arrangements, and many Wends never learned English. Martin Hondow, a Wend who learned English readily, was one of the spokesmen for the Peter's Hill community.[39]

Most of the Wends became farmers and all quickly adapted to the seasonal schedule of the southern hemisphere. Some fruit ripened at Christmas and preparations for planting were made at Easter in autumn. The climate of South Australia was Mediterranean with a dry and wet season, so plowing and sowing were carried out in May and June with the coming of rain, and the grain harvested from November to January. After generations of their forefathers had grown rye for their bread, the Australian Wends accepted the Australian agricultural practice and changed abruptly to wheat.

Those Wends who had trained as builders and craftsmen had to learn new measures and new ways of doing things. Money, blueprints, sizes, and bills were all in English. None of the Wends was receptive to the English system of buying licenses. Any merchant or person selling goods was required to obtain a license that could be invalidated if he did anything illegal. To the Wends it was a form of taxation, and they had been led to believe that they were leaving taxes behind in Europe. Andreas Albert, for example, had to buy a license for selling firewood in the city, and all the Wends in the goldfields paid thirty shillings per month for their licenses.[40]

Because Australia was itself a developing area, commodities that the Wends took for granted were often unavailable or of inferior quality. In their letters back home, they asked friends in Germany to send such items as scythes, canvas, blue and green linen cloth, warm furs, deerskin trousers, boots, beds, good knives, and the Breslau hymn book.[41]

Some Wends regretted their migration to Australia and the *Tydźenske Nowiny* happily printed the negative letters so that others would be discouraged from migration. Carl Traugott Hoehne considered the Wendish migration equal to Napoleon's mistake in invading Russia. After one year in Victoria, he believed Australians to be thieves and cheats. He and others such as Michael Zwar complained about inflated prices, high interest rates, the heat, the sterile soil, scarcity of water, and widespread drunkenness and sin. The immigrants missed the Lutheran churches and schools and criticized the secular tone of the entire society. The villain in Hoehne's mind was a certain Hartig, the travel agent, who had filled his mind with lies in order to sell him a ticket. Almost everyone, in the early days, talked of returning to Lusatia, even if only for a visit, and some—like Hoehne—went back to stay.[42]

Most of the letters of complaint came from people who had settled at Melbourne with its smaller German and Wendish community, while those who wrote favorably of Australia and challenged the attacks on the new homeland came from South Australia. Most neutral individuals who balanced the gains with the losses advised their friends to remain in Germany if life did not become intolerable, because making a living in Australia was almost as difficult as it had been in Germany. No one, they all emphasized, should migrate unless willing to work hard.

Homesickness was widespread and in the early days the Wends sought each other out. John Ponich, for example, was digging gold in the Alexander Hills, eighty miles from Melbourne, when he heard of the arrival of the *Helena* at Adelaide. He left immediately and spent five weeks with the new arrivals. In letters home to Lusatia Wends often listed the names of fellow countrymen in their vicinity and said what they were doing. They yearned for replies and searched the newspaper notices of newly arrived letters for their names. Hoehne took his letters to a hill, and there, his eyes brimming with tears, envisioned the beautiful woods and birds of Lusatia. With less emotion and more humor, Carl Hempel, who had become a kangaroo hunter, one day spotted the familiar rabbit among all the strange marsupials, so he doffed his hat and greeted him with "*Hejda, krajano*" ("Hello, fellow countryman").[43]

In spite of the emotional depression from failures and the difficulties of learning new ways, conditions improved for the Wends.

Even Ponich, who migrated to Melbourne in 1849 and complained about Australia, had been mellowed with success by 1852. He had paid off his debts and purchased land with the £250 he earned after only four months in the goldfields. He still advised caution about migration, and confessed that he had been lucky. Prosperity did not endear Australia to George Boback and Jacob Prochno. After fourteen years in Australia they sold their possessions for a handsome profit and returned to Lusatia to purchase land.[44]

Wendish Settlements in South Australia

All the *Alfred* Wends originated from Saxony and settled initially on farms at Rosenthal. The *Victoria* migrants, on the other hand, came from both Saxony and Prussia and included not only agricultural families but a schoolmaster, pastor, cabinetmaker, wheelwright, and soap-boiler. Those *Victoria* immigrants who decided to try farming regardless of their earlier training generally settled in Hope Valley, near Adelaide, and then, after several years, moved to Hoffnungsthal. The extent of contact and social exchange between the two Wendish groups located only twenty miles apart has not been documented, but no attempt was made at forming a central colony. There evidently was some communication, however, because one of the *Victoria* migrants from Prussia, Karl August Krueger, joined the Rosenthal settlers in Victoria in 1851 and his father, Johann, the organist and organ builder, followed in 1855.[45]

The next major migration took place in 1850 when the *San Francisco* and the *Pribislav* sailed for Australia. The *San Francisco*, which docked at Adelaide on October 14, 1850, carried Prussian Wends, while the *Pribislav*, arriving at Melbourne in February, 1850, brought Saxon Wends. The *San Francisco* settlers first joined their friends at Hope Valley and then, beginning in 1864, migrated fifty miles north to Peter's Hill.

The *Pribislav* brought approximately fifty Wends, of whom five families including Graff, Gruetzner, Rosel, Wuchatsch, and Zimmer found land at Thomastown, near Melbourne. Michael Zwar, however, became a tanner at Beechworth, sixty miles from Melbourne, and Johann Stephan eventually joined the Rosenthal Wends in western Victoria.[46]

The Wends who migrated prior to 1851 traveled as individuals, single families, or in small groups. Those in small groups had leaders and spokesmen, but the settlement patterns show that there was no

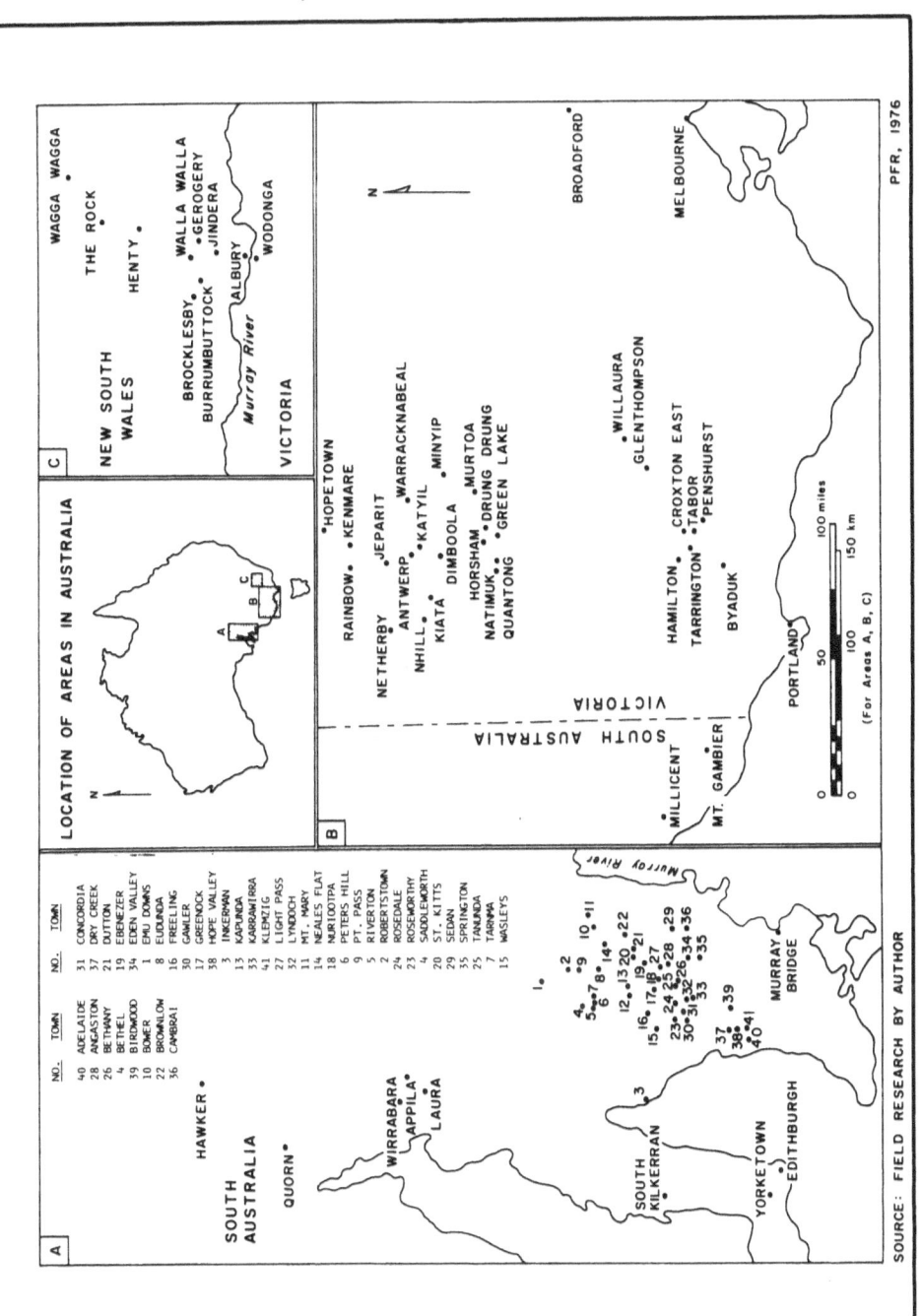

MAP 4 Australian Location of Wendish Settlers

attempt to establish a Wendish community, and the little cohesion that existed was the result of family ties or a personal desire for security.

The one person who could have provided the leadership and focus for a Wendish colony was the only Lutheran pastor able to preach in Wendish, Andreas Kappler. Kappler was born at Kleinhänchen, west of Bautzen, and served the parish at Weissenberg from 1848 to 1853, at about the same time that Kilian was the pastor at Kotitz. Even though Kappler was Lutheran, he did not join the formal association of Lutheran pastors who had migrated earlier, but established congregations of his own in the Adelaide–Hope Valley area. He preferred the freedom of the Saxon church to the restraints of the Old Lutherans, who themselves had already split over the issue of chiliasm. In 1851, three years after his arrival, Kappler unhappily admitted that a unified Wendish colony was not possible. Not enough Wends had migrated, and among those who had, ethnic considerations had been subordinated to the economic, as people scattered to make a living.[47]

There must have been additional problems, however, because reference was made to Kappler's failure to keep the trust of the Wends. Another suspicious sign is that during his ministry he never performed baptisms, marriages, or burials for the Saxon Wends who had been his European neighbors and spoke his dialect, but only for Germans and Cottbus Wends. Furthermore, in December, 1851, when the Zwar group landed with ninety-eight Wends, they chose an Old Lutheran as their pastor. Then in 1852, Kappler, discontented with Adelaide, left for Melbourne to examine the possibility of starting a parish either in the goldfields or among the Wends of the city, but he soon returned to South Australia.

The most reasonable explanation is that the Wends were not impressed with Kappler's religious views and his attempt to follow the practices of the Saxon state church. Because of either Pietism or Old Lutheranism, the Wends preferred a German whose beliefs were their own to a Wend whose theology was too unionistic and liberal. Even the Cottbus Wends, who accepted him when they lived in the Hope Valley area, did not try to make him their pastor when they moved to Peter's Hill. Kappler took a parish at Mt. Gambier in 1860, where he served Germans and some Wends until his death in 1877.[48]

With no pastor or politician to lead them, the Wends either separated themselves completely from their countrymen or settled in small Wendish communities beside Germans and Englishmen. One of the larger Wendish concentrations was that of Ebenezer, established by Johann Zwar. While still in Germany, Zwar had envisioned the founding of a colony and had tried to recruit a pastor for the congregation, but his plans would not materialize either.

The moment the Zwar group disembarked from the *Helena,* Andreas Polnich, a member of the group, was sent ahead to notify the Wends at Rosenthal. Since the wheat harvest was under way, the new migrants stored their possessions in Adelaide and settled temporarily at Rosenthal and the Lyndoch Valley for the remainder of 1852. They not only earned money working in the fields, but they discussed theology with the Lutherans in the area and, after arriving at mutual understanding, were admitted to communion.

Finding good land near Adelaide was more difficult, and they considered taking the *Helena* on farther to Portland, Victoria. The Rosenthal Wends, however, needed help with the harvest and talked the newcomers into letting the *Helena* go, it being agreed that if they located no land by the end of the harvest, all could join the Rosenthal settlers and travel overland to Victoria together. The harvest and profits must have been good: Andreas Albert threshed 375 bushels of wheat and sold it at a pound per bushel. Zwar kept looking for land in the meantime, and the majority—including Dallwitz, Doecke, Kleinig, Lischke, Lowke, Mickan, Pannach, Schneider, and Wenke—migrated with him to the Upper Barossa Valley and settled at Ebenezer, five miles from Nuriootpa. Other families such as Burger, Hundrack, Mirtschin, Rentsch, and Urban, however, decided to join the Rosenthal group in their migration to Victoria. One of the Wends, bachelor Johann Gude, also went to Victoria in 1853, not to farm, but to dig for gold.[49]

The first services of the Ebenezer congregation were held in Andreas Schneider's home on section 3005, east of the present church. The Reverend Heinrich A. E. Meyer, the German pastor of Bethany and Rosenthal, served the new congregation until 1854, when he was replaced by a Moravian Brethren minister, Christoph S. D. Schondorf. Schondorf, also a German, was stationed at Bethel, fifteen miles northwest of Ebenezer, and could preach in German, Wendish, and the language of the Aborigines. Obviously Zwar and many of the congregation preferred the Wendish language in the pulpit, and possibly Schondorf's pietism was not that objectionable.[50]

Not all members of the group were pleased with Schondorf, however; several left and joined some Germans in forming a new congregation at Neukirch, only two miles away. Pastor Meyer became Neukirch's first pastor and conducted services in the home of Adam Bartsch, a Wend who had landed in 1848 and moved to the Ebenezer vicinity in 1853. Both congregations, composed of Germans and

Wends, built and dedicated churches in 1859. Ebenezer released Schondorf that same year and joined the Lutheran Tanunda–Light Pass Synod, while Neukirch affiliated with the Lutheran Bethany–Lobenthal Synod.[51]

The splitting of the Ebenezer congregation highlights the problem of establishing a Wendish community. Some members were comfortable with the German language and considered Lutheran doctrine more important than the Wendish language, while others initially cared more about the language. In either instance, both congregations were becoming part of the German community in Australia and by 1859 even the Ebenezer services were in German. Family devotions and prayers were conducted in Wendish, but it was only a matter of time until Wendish was forgotten. There was neither unity among the Wends nor any intense desire to preserve Wendish ways. Wendish culture came after economic need and doctrinal concerns on the list of priorities.

The next sizable migration took place in 1854, the same year that Kilian led his group to Texas. The *Steinwarder* carried Saxon Wends to Australia with such families as Biar, Gersch, and Zschech, names that also appear in Texas. The *Malvinia Vidal*, however, transported Wends from the Cottbus area—a region that sent few settlers to Texas. The Prussian Wends settled first in the Hope Valley–Hoffnungsthal vicinity and then moved north to Peter's Hill, while the Saxon Wends went directly to their friends in the Ebenezer-Neukirch area and then bought land in the nearby hills and established St. Kitts. One of the Saxon Wends, Johann Zschech, moved to Victoria the same year he landed in Adelaide.

These two settlements, Peter's Hill, sixty miles north of Adelaide, and St. Kitts, forty-five miles from that city, are significant to the history of the Wends. Peter's Hill (Lower Wends) was the one congregation other than Ebenezer to conduct religious services in Wendish, while St. Kitts (Upper Wends), because of its isolation, kept the Wendish families and tradition together a long time.

The Hundred of Gilbert,[52] the survey unit for Peter's Hill, had been proclaimed on August 7, 1851, and surveyed in 1853. The region was described by Burrows as "typically savannah woodland, well grassed, plenty of trees (peppermint gum and blue gum) and wide open spaces." Martin Teschner, the 1848 migrant, was among the first to buy land in the area, and he was followed by Martin Hondow in 1854 and Johann Duldig in 1856. They selected the western slopes of the small range of hills where there was some timber, evidently in the belief that land supporting trees would be better suited for agricul-

Biar homestead, St. Kitts, 1969. The original building was wattle and daub with a thatched roof. The corrugated metal on the end wall was added after that side of the building had been weathered

ture than the treeless plains. The settlers purchased small tracts of land and lived in hillside dugouts while they cleared land and planted crops.[53]

Pastor Meyer served the congregation from its founding in July, 1856, until his death in 1862, but because of the distance from Bethany he traveled the distance only once a quarter. In 1860 a railroad was completed to Kapunda, fifteen miles away, and the journey's cost in time and money was greatly reduced. Meyer's chief function was to administer the sacraments, and because of responsibilities to his other congregation, he conducted worship at Peter's Hill during the week. Both Teschner and Matthes Borrack possessed books of Wendish sermons, with which they conducted reading services on Sundays between the pastor's visits. Martin Hondow served the congregation as lay reader and elder for fifty years. Because of the poverty of the people and the efforts required simply raising food, they built no church until 1856, but worshipped in the home of Johann Noack.

Once the congregation was officially organized in July, 1856, members began construction of a small building that served as church, school, and teacher's residence. About a year later they erected another church one mile west of the original and finally in 1864 they built a new and larger church which still stands. For the dedication of one of these buildings, the Sorbian poet Kito Šwjela sent a hymn he had written for the occasion.⁵⁴

The congregation was not blessed with concord, however, and controversy raged as early as 1860. While Ebenezer's division was theological, much of the trouble at Peter's Hill centered around personal relations. Friedrich Semlin, the German schoolteacher who also served as elder, blamed this on the fact that the people were Wends. One argument was concerned with the administration of church activities. When Martin Lehmann led evening worship, Christian Jarick would not attend, and if Jarick served as leader, Lehmann was absent. Personal clashes are also demonstrated in the existence of two cemeteries, the larger for the congregation and one called the Huppatz cemetery. This arrangement evidently was the result of another disagreement, and in 1860 a father whose children had been buried in the Huppatz cemetery removed the remains to the larger cemetery.⁵⁵

While the laymen failed to maintain goodwill with each other, they also were not successful in cultivating the happiness of their teachers, especially E. von Plönnies. He complained not only that his annual salary of fifty-two pounds plus wheat compared unfavorably with that of an ordinary shepherd in Queensland, but that his room, which evidently doubled as the school on weekdays, was not sufficiently private. The young people jammed mud into the lock, and some of the youths occasionally went into the room during the church service and smoked their pipes without first removing their hats. As a result he stayed in his room and attended services only on Sunday as his contract required.⁵⁶

The attitudes toward the pastor showed a great deal of independence. The congregation had been satisfied with Pastor Meyer and had paid him twenty-five pounds sterling a year in addition to travel expenses. He in turn visited them once a quarter, preaching and teaching the entire day. After Pastor Meyer's death in 1861, the Peter's Hill congregation asked the synod for the names of several pastors, so they could hear them preach. If the synodical leaders did not agree to this procedure, the "mission congregation without strong church members" would look elsewhere for a shepherd.

The scarcity of pastors ruled out their demands, however, and after two years of waiting they finally agreed to accept the services of the Rev. C. G. Teichelmann. Teichelmann, a veteran pastor and missionary to the Aborigines, who had arrived in Australia as early as 1838, agreed to live at Peter's Hill for two weeks out of every six, preaching and instructing the confirmands. After three years the congregation

School children in front of Peter's Hill Church, circa 1890. The building was constructed in 1864. *Courtesy Don J. Wells and the Dreckow-Stubing Family Committee*

dismissed him, either because people did not like his approach or because the expense was too great. They joined the parish of Carlsruhe for a while and then in 1876, with a membership of 132 souls, joined the Eudunda parish.[57]

Internal quarrels and splintering were not unique to Peter's Hill and Ebenezer, but occurred in many Lutheran communities in Australia, Canada, and the United States, among both Germans and Wends. The position of the church in the life of the immigrant was most important because it constituted one aspect of the new existence that could be controlled. Immigrants adjusted their farming methods, their building techniques, and their speech, but the church provided a link with the past and the point of reference people needed to stabilize their lives. In Europe the church had always been there and had been administered by the state. In Australia the church would not exist if the members did not desire it, and they tried to make it conform to the image of what they thought it should be.

The Wends did not look upon the Lutheran church as the church for Irish and Englishmen. Those people belonged to the Catholic and Anglican churches, and each denomination should evangelize the people from which it sprang. Internal controversies and splits, in their view, did not therefore weaken the message of the church or hinder its mission because each ethnic group had its own church, which did not need to appeal to others. Quarrels and divisions were

Johann Herman Gersch and Maria Magdalena Kleinig, St. Kitts, 1883. *Courtesy Eric Borgas and the Gersch Reunion Committee*

frequent because the laity, for the first time, were managing their own church. In the process of gaining experience they made many mistakes and too often manipulated the church to suit their own needs.

In 1855, one year after the Peter's Hill settlers arrived, another somewhat diminished migration took place from Upper Lusatia. These twenty-eight Wends traveling on the *Bielefeld* settled fifteen miles west of St. Kitts, near the Schondorf settlement of Bethel. Two of the families, Schlemmer and Zieschang, continued to Victoria because their wives were related to the Gude and Rentsch families. From 1855 on, with the exception of the Altus and Biele families, the Wendish migration to Australia was completely of Prussian provenance.

The heaviest migration from Lower Lusatia took place in 1858 when the *Victoria* and *Bielefeld* returned with 124 Wends. They scattered to all the earlier settlements including Hope Valley, Hoffnungsthal, and Peter's Hill, and many went to Victoria and New South Wales. Assessment of shipping and family records indicates that migration after 1858 was insignificant, and those who came were generally friends or relatives of earlier settlers.

South Australia, the state to which the Wends migrated, was a planned colony. It was distinct from other early Australian settlements in that there were no prisoners, only free inhabitants. The administration of the colony, moreover, was to be enlightened and reflect the centuries of British experience with colonization. In 1836 Colonel William Light selected the location for Adelaide and began to lay out the design for the city and surrounding area. In 1842, six years prior to the Wendish migration, the population of South Australia was only 16,000, with half of the citizens living in Adelaide. But following the discovery of copper at Kapunda in the 1840s and gold in the neighboring state of Victoria, demands for wheat rose, and more people turned to agriculture. Technological developments such as John Ridley's stripper in 1843 also brought wheat to a competitive price on the overseas market. The Wends, therefore, arrived when the colony was sparsely populated and the demand for labor in the production of foodstuffs, especially wheat, was rising. By the time Wendish migration declined, the population of South Australia stood at 125,000.[58]

One of the ways in which the careful planning of Australian administrators influenced the Wends was in the sale of land. The blueprints first called for the sale of land at a "fixed minimum price or more and that the revenue obtained should be used to assist the emigration of new settlers."[59] A second principle was that frontier expansion not proceed helter-skelter, but in a systematic manner that opened tracts of land for purchase, thereby regulating the advance of settlement and simultaneously keeping the land in short supply in order to maintain a good price.

The Australian Land Sales Act of 1842 reflected efforts to concentrate the population and advance the frontier in an orderly fashion. Once a county was established, the governor declared an administrative unit called a hundred and instructed the surveyors to mark off tracts of eighty acres each. Proclamation of hundreds was usually in areas contiguous to older settlements. Land sales were conducted quarterly at cash auctions where bidding generally started at one pound an acre although the government could set a higher base depending on the quality of the land.

The system had a negative impact on the Wends. Limited surveys, bidding procedures that kept prices high, and the policy requiring payment in advance greatly reduced the chances of the poor for becoming land owners. Considering the price of land and the level of wages, the average laborer had to work and save for three or four years before he could afford to purchase land.[60]

The land put up for sale was generally overpriced because it had inadequate water supply and was situated a long distance from transportation. If it were mallee land (eucalyptus scrub), the vegetation had to be cleared at the additional cost of between two and five pounds per acre. As a result the immigrants often became tenants or worked for wages in an effort to buy land or, when they did buy, purchased small amounts. This procedure was acceptable when labor was needed to clear and prepare land, but not when wheat production became a large-scale operation. Life on a small farm became further complicated as the large families matured and the sons could not find enough to do. As a result the farmers kept looking for new lands and waited patiently for more land sales in South Australia, or they migrated to Victoria where the policy was different.

South Australian officials noticed the loss of population to Victoria, and in January, 1869, passed a new land law, called the Waste Lands Amendment Act or the Strangeways Act, which for practical purposes destroyed the colonial blueprint. The new act designated land suitable for cultivation, even if it was not contiguous to settled lands, and placed plots of up to 320 acres for sale through bidding. A credit system was also introduced that required a down payment of 20 percent and the remainder at the end of four years. In 1872 the down payment was lowered to 10 percent and the date due for the balance extended to six years.[61]

The Wends moved with this expanding frontier, and some first-

Fred Dreckow's team carting wheat, Cleve, 1912. *Courtesy Don J. Wells and the Dreckow-Stubing Family Committee*

and second-generation migrants left their earlier holdings and built new homes and farms. In the 1870s the settlers who had taken land at Springton, including the Schuppans, Eckerts, and Kielows, migrated north along the east side of the hills to Emu Downs. The surplus population from St. Kitts, including the Doecke, Noack, Freund, and Biar families, traveled a short distance eastward and purchased land around Neale's Flat and Brownlow. Family records indicate that the Wends around Gawler and Birdwood—Geitz, Grabia, Modra, Twartz, Domachenz, Teschner, Kossatz, and Kollosche—crossed the Gulf of St. Vincent and occupied the lower portion of Yorke Peninsula. The Peter's Hill settlers migrated in all directions, especially to Victoria and the areas adjacent to Peter's Hill. From then on the Wends spread to Appila and Booleroo Center, later to Quorn and Hawker, and eventually to the Eyre Peninsula.

Other Wends settled away from the larger Wendish communities in places like Robe, Kangaroo Island, and Point Pass. Many never became farmers at all but remained in Adelaide. South Australia was the first new home of the Wends, and their internal migration within the colony illustrates the growth of the South Australian agricultural frontier.[62]

THE WENDS IN VICTORIA

Migration of free, or non-convict, settlers to Melbourne, the first location in Victoria to receive Wendish immigrants, was stimulated by William Westgarth, an Englishman who traveled to Germany and wrote a pamphlet encouraging migration to the city, then known as Port Phillip. He especially pointed out the need for workers, and Edward Delius, an agent of George Fife Angus, brought 350 Moravians to Victoria in 1849.[63]

By 1851 there were 23,143 residents in Melbourne, and included in this number were the Wends who had migrated on the *Pribislav* in 1850.[64] The period when the first Wends landed was notable, because 1851 was an extremely hot year and also the year gold was discovered. The Wends had never experienced such heat and learned quickly about fires and the inconvenience of acquiring water from great distances. The gold rush raised food prices, complicating finance, but at least jobs were more easily obtained and many Wends also found gold. Johann Ponich was in the fields for fourth months in 1851 and earned £250 sterling. Johann Mirtschin and his son went to the gold diggings too, but the inflated costs of food and shelter claimed one hundred *Taler* of the three hundred *Talers*' worth they found. Agnes Kaiser Stephan, following her brother's path to Melbourne in 1851, worked side by side with her husband, but after three months the couple had earned only eighty-three pounds. And tragedy struck the family of Johann Graff when his son was killed by a burning tree falling on him.

Those Wends who did not become miners shared in the prosperity nevertheless. They became the suppliers of vegetables, butter, and eggs, and the young men earned money hauling freight to the mines with ox-drawn wagons. By 1854, after only five years in Australia, the Wends at Dry Creek (Thomastown) had achieved financial stability and with their German neighbors constructed a church. Some Wends who stayed near the port provided reception services for new arrivals. Carl Hempel's home, which was one hour outside Melbourne, was the reception point in 1855. Hempel, for example, brought Maria Kaiser to his home for three days and then helped her find a job in Michael Zimmer's household at Dry Creek.[65]

While the Wends were adjusting to Melbourne, the Rosenthal group was planning to move to western Victoria. The investigators of the Victoria lands returned to Rosenthal with a favorable report, but because the pioneers had accumulated implements and livestock, a land trip was preferred to a voyage to Portland, on Victoria's south coast. The problem of the overland route was that the most direct way would take them through a desert. The migrants therefore sent two of their group with an experienced bushman, Wilhelm Blandowski, to blaze a trail. After several weeks they returned satisfied that they found a suitable route.[66]

In the meantime, the migrants who had not already done so applied for naturalization papers. Although many of the Wends never bothered to file applications, especially if they lived in the city, the Rosenthal group looked forward to full citizenship. The Deutschers had already been naturalized in 1848, the year of their arrival, but J. Rentsch, C. G. Petschel, and A. Albert filed in 1851; Burger, Mirtschin, and Hundrack followed in 1852.[67]

After the 1852 harvest was in, the Rosenthal settlers sold the South Australian holdings and prepared for migration to Victoria. Realizing that not all of their possessions and provisions could be taken overland, they shipped some freshly gristed wheat, furniture, and a few containers of equipment to Portland by sea. Johann Mirtschin and his family accompanied the shipment, but while the passengers arrived safely along with the flour, the furniture and cases were lost.[68]

The nine families to migrate overland apparently were those of Andreas Albert, Peter Burger, Johann Huf, Johann Hundrack, C. G. Petschel, William Petschel, John Rentsch, and the two Deutscher families. All were Saxon Wends with the exception of Huf, and the group was strengthened through intermarriage. Andreas Deutscher, for example, had married Agneta Albert, and Johann Hundrack's wife was Anna Rentsch.

According to Christiane Petschel's account, the party left on April 26, 1852, from Rosenthal with eleven wagons and a herd of fifty-two cattle. The wagons were covered with hoods to shelter them from the rain and sun and to protect the chaff (wheat heads and stems ground together for animal feed), the flour, and the bedding. The seat in front of the wagon also doubled as the tucker box (food container), and the coop of chickens was fastened to the rear of the vehicle.

Each morning women prepared bread dough while men worked with the animals. Dough was kneaded during the midday rest and replaced in the containers. In the evening when the wagon train stopped, children gathered enough firewood for a large fire, and after the flames had died, the mothers raked the coals into a circle and placed the camp ovens containing the dough among the coals. Bread, baked daily, was the staple food, supplemented with butter and tea.

With punctuality equal to that in the baking of bread, the immigrants observed the Sabbath. They had never missed a service since their arrival in Australia, and they continued the observance on each Sunday of their overland journey. On that day they rested their animals and gathered in a circle to listen to a reader and to sing hymns.

Near the end of their journey they amended their Sunday routine by traveling during one afternoon to gain some time and to reach a

Carting wool bales, 1928. *Courtesy Don J. Wells and the Dreckow-Stubing Family Committee*

camping spot that offered sufficient water and luxuriant grass. They soon discovered, however, that the area was packed with leeches, and all retired to the wagons for the night. The next morning the horses and cattle were nowhere in sight, and not until noon were they found, their noses and legs covered with leeches. It was considered an object lesson on the proper observance of the Sabbath.

Another problem that occurred tested the strength of the community bonds. One family's horses were exhausted by an extended period of hard pulling, so the family could not keep pace and fell behind. Every evening, however, when the eight families made camp, the younger Petschel retraced his steps with a pair of bullocks and hitched them to the lagging wagon to help the family keep up with the main body.

They traveled south from Rosenthal along the coast and through Mt. Gambier, which was nearly deserted, the people having rushed to the goldfields. Finally, on May 26, one month and four hundred miles later, they entered Portland and were met by the town children who ran behind the wagons yelling, "Germans." Portland being also largely deserted by goldseekers, the tired migrants easily found houses for rent, just in time to shelter themselves from the winter rains.

The reception from the settlers of British origin was negative, however, and Thomas Henty, the man who had encouraged the migration, had been elected to Parliament and had taken up residence in Melbourne. Most of the British settlers were squatters (graziers) and any influx of farmers would eventually force them off the unfenced range. The migrants were not abused, but when they inquired about available land, they were given the wrong directions and at times found their horses set loose and driven away. Only when the Wends offered rewards of a pound or two were the animals "found."[69]

The onset of winter prevented the purchase of land, so they decided to rent some land in the area for a year before making any investments. When Rentsch and two other families found sixty acres about twenty miles north of Portland, they quickly erected a slab hut with a stringy bark roof and set to work making butter which sold for 2s. 6d. per pound, and cutting hay that sold for two pounds per small wagon load.

In 1852, before the migrants left Rosenthal, they had sent a call to the Rev. Clamour W. Schuermann to become their pastor in Victoria. The call was signed by Albert, Burger, Johann Gude, Huf, Hundrack, Petschel, and Rentsch. Michael Deutscher, although highly concerned with spiritual matters, had not signed the call. Schuermann was born in Osnabruck, Hanover, and educated at the Dresden Mission Society. After graduation he and a classmate, C. G. Teichelmann, were commissioned for Australia to work among the German settlers and with the Aborigines.

Schuermann arrived in 1838, before the large wave of German migration, and immediately explored the unsettled area looking for a place to establish a mission. Eventually he chose the Port Lincoln area, where he worked for four years as a clergyman and also as a government official for the Aborigines. Although his wife liked the Port Lincoln area, Schuermann accepted the call of the Rosenthal people but waited for a successor and for the disposal of his property. He had been well paid at his first position, receiving £120 a year, a free house, and a garden, but his new parish promised less than £75. As he traveled from Port Lincoln, he stopped at Bethany to visit his friend Pastor Meyer, and from there he went to Adelaide where he boarded a boat for Portland. He arrived at his destination six days later on May 21, 1853.

Along with Schuermann on the boat were two more families, probably Andreas Urban and Johann Gude, the gold miner. Gude was not married, but his sister had married Mirtschin. When Schuermann arrived in Portland, he went to Michael Deutscher's house but discovered that Deutscher had moved to Mt. Clay two weeks earlier. Schuermann also discovered that the increased migration into the area had filled up the available housing and the house that had been selected for him had been rented. After visiting the Mirtschins and the Hufs, Schuermann was given shelter in the front two rooms of a home occupied by a German named Schneider. The cramped quarters, winter cold, and frequent visitors robbed Schuermann of his privacy. He nevertheless went to work and started a school for the nine children of his parish.[70]

Henty also returned from Melbourne, and he advised the land-seekers to migrate fifty miles northward to the Grange, near the township of Hamilton, an area opened by Maj. Thomas Mitchell in 1836. The first land sales had been held in 1851, but most of the occupants were squatters who had been grazing the land since 1839. The population of the district in 1851 was only 1,579. The Hamilton squatters also molested the Wendish land-seekers, but their attempts at releasing the horses were not as successful as those at Portland the year before, and the examiners found the land acceptable.

The next hurdle was the price of land. Only a limited amount of land was placed on sale at once, and competitive bidding drove the prices upward, as high as £10 per acre. By May 5, 1853, the Wends had purchased 640 acres and in the following month Petschel, Hundrack, and Deutscher bought another 230 acres for £1,359 17s. at rates ranging from £4 4s. to £8 12s. per acre. Then the land was divided for use among the families, and ten acres were purchased from Deutscher's tract for the church and school. The initial purchase gave them a footing, and once the Wends showed determination to stay, the price of land seldom exceeded £1 per acre.[71]

Eleven of the families migrated from Portland to Hamilton in August, but three remained in Portland and petitioned the government for more reasonable prices. When the land was opened near Mt. Rouse (Penshurst) it sold at the lower rate of £1 2s. 6d. per acre. Another Wendish settlement was formed when Burger purchased 150 acres, Mirtschin 178 acres, Stephan 20, and Urban 10.[72]

Once again the Wends were on virgin soil, but this time they were experienced and better equipped. Building a house could wait, so the Petschels put up a tent with a pugged chimney that served satisfactorily for a year. The first task was to fence the fields to keep out the squatters' sheep and to keep in the settlers' own livestock. The second task on the list of priorities, plowing the prairie, was complicated by a wet winter, but the settlers pushed on and sowed oats and wheat. Although not an enormous success, the first crop was satisfactory and a bushel of oats sold at 17s. 6d., wheat at a pound, and a load of straw at two pounds. The chief source of income in the early years was not grain, however, but butter, which sold at 2s. 6d. per pound, and eggs at 2s. 6d. per dozen. In addition to farming, Andreas Albert hauled wood to town for sale, Burger's sons assisted a surveyor, and Mrs. Mirtschin worked for four shillings a day and food while her husband

St. Peter's Lutheran Church, St. Kitts, 1910. The building with the thatched roof was the original church and school, built in 1869. *Courtesy Eric Borgas and the Gersch Reunion Committee*

went to the goldfields. Later Pastor Schuermann observed that the settlers were "working like lions" and should achieve prosperity in a few years.[73]

With the help of Hundrack, Pastor Schuermann in October, 1853, had followed his flock to Hamilton, where, one mile east of town, the congregation built a two-room manse with pugged walls and thatched roof. It was small and primitive and the pastor papered the walls with newspapers to keep out the wind. Next they built a small church of wood and clay with a thatched roof, twenty-eight feet by sixteen. Schuermann, in addition to ministering to the members, opened a morning school for six children; within two years it served thirty-four children. Confirmation instruction was held three afternoons a week, and evening worship two evenings. This brought Schuermann to church twice a day, and in addition he had to prepare for all his presentations, order and mend books, and visit his members. On free afternoons he cleared the land around the house and fenced and cultivated it. He also built a shed for poultry and a yard for cows. While he did not complain about his low salary, he was irked by the fact that the farmers did not realize how much work there was being a pastor and teacher.[74]

Schuermann's task was complicated by the settlers' desire for more and cheaper land. Almost immediately members went four miles farther east and bought eight hundred acres in the area they called Bukecy or Hochkirch (Tarrington), after the village in Upper Lusatia, and by September, 1853, six families had settled in the Mt. Rouse–Penshurst area, twenty-one miles away. This scattering meant that Schuermann would be forced to establish two congregations, and he was annoyed that so much of the good land around the church was being purchased by non-Lutherans. Schuermann recognized the value of the land and advised his members to buy. Although he bemoaned the scarcity of money among them, he did try to buy land for Pastor Meyer and the land map shows that Schuermann himself purchased several parcels at auction.[75]

The congregation grew rapidly in 1855 when eighteen more families traveled overland to Hamilton from South Australia. In 1858 the Lutherans, in an attempt to locate the church building more centrally, built a new and larger church of wood and clay at Hochkirch (Tarrington). In 1863 still another church was built of bluestone quarried on Schuermann's property. It measured fifty-three by twenty-six feet with walls fifteen feet high. The size of the congregation peaked in the 1870s with four hundred souls and then declined with the migration to the Wimmera.

While the settlement was growing in size and prosperity, its history was clouded with an internal controversy that eventually led to a split and to strained feelings that lasted into the twentieth century. On the one hand was Pastor Schuermann, an ordained clergyman, university trained, a firm believer in the formal, institutional church, an associate of the Old Lutheran pastors in Australia, and a German. On the opposite side was Michael Deutscher, a headstrong layman, poorly educated, intensely religious with pietistic sympathies, and a Wend. In itself the conflict was significant because it set up the traditions of two separate synods in Victoria, and it also provides a case study of the relations between the Germans and Wends. Did the conflict lead to a division along ethnic lines or was it primarily a matter of theology and personality?

Almost from the moment of Schuermann's arrival in Victoria, he experienced what he called "Deutscher's limitless pride and unbearable thirst for power." This, Schuermann believed, was the result of growing prosperity, which caused spiritual blindness and impenitence. An indication that Deutscher vexed him appeared in a letter to Reverend Meyer in which Schuermann asked for some books for himself and Deutscher. Schuermann commented that the books were for Deutscher "who in typical fashion wants something extra."[76] Evidently Pastor Meyer knew Deutscher from the days at Rosenthal.

Already at the time of his arrival in Australia in 1848, Deutscher was identified as a man of property and the leader of the Wends on the *Alfred*. Religion and the church meant much to him, and as the elder of the congregation and a vigorous man in his forties, he expected to play a major role. He in turn had been disappointed with Schuermann's performance in the new settlement. On July 14, 1855, Deutscher was sufficiently unhappy to write a letter of complaint to Pastor Meyer. Deutscher charged that Schuermann was preaching too much law and not enough of the New Testament message. Deutscher suspected that Schuermann was unable to preach the gospel because he himself had not experienced it. Many of the charges sound pietistic and apparently were supported by a person in the community called Schneider.[77]

There were two Schneider brothers, Kasper and Johann, one belonging to Schuermann's church and the other to a Moravian Brethren settlement headed by a man called Krummnow in the Mt. Rouse area. Krummnow had come to South Australia in 1839 along with the early German migrants and tried to convince members of Kavel's congregations of his idea of communal living. Although never enormously successful, he did convince a few people to attend prayer meetings at his house. Both Kavel and later G. D. Fritzsche, leaders of the Lutheran synods, spoke against him, and in 1853 he moved his small flock to Victoria. He apparently was a kindhearted, honest man who possessed a strong will and persistent nature. He was handicapped, however, by his humpback and short stature as well as by indistinct, nasal speech. In Victoria he bought sixteen hundred acres of land near Mt. Rouse for his following. The Schneider who belonged to Schuermann's congregation had belonged to the state church in Prussia but was attracted to the beliefs and practices of the Krummnow group. Schuermann knew Schneider well, because Schneider had opened his home to Schuermann at Portland and also tried to convince Schuermann of the necessity of experiencing conversion and being able to recount it.

Schneider and Deutscher soon found each other and sympathetically exchanged their religious views and their criticisms of Schuermann's sermons. Wilhelm Petschel agreed with them and believed that a person could not know he was saved unless he experienced an actual conversion. When Deutscher's child was born on September 4, 1855, he chose Schneider to be the sponsor. Schuermann objected that Schneider was unsuited because of his religious views and Schneider's expressed intention of joining the Krummnow settlement. The first aspect of the conflict, therefore, centered around pietism—not too different from what Pastor Jan Kilian was experiencing in Texas.[78]

Another point of contention between Schuermann and Deutscher was over adding new members. Schuermann did not know the method of adopting new members because it had not been clearly defined. When two people from the Krummnow settlement applied for membership, Schuermann asked them if they accepted the constitution of the congregation and admitted them when they did. When a Mecklenburg family came with certificates of baptism from the German Lutheran *Landeskirche*, he accepted them also. Deutscher was not there at the time and no other member raised any objections. When, however, a Wendish family and a South German family applied, Schuermann required an examination before the elders. This, to Deutscher, did not seem just and when the Wends did not perform well, they were embarrassed and Deutscher considered Schuermann's action insulting. Schuermann, however, believed that Deutscher was asking for preferential treatment for Saxons and Wends.[79]

Deutscher again wrote to Pastor Meyer on July 11, 1856, and repeated the charges of the year before. Schuermann, Deutscher stated, did not have the spirit, and knowledge and piety without the spirit was insufficient. Schuermann therefore was driving people away from the church, for which he would be punished in the hereafter. Shortly after, Schneider and a person named Schmidt in the Mt. Rouse area sponsored religious cottage meetings that concluded with sermons. Some of Schuermann's members attended and then did not attend church.[80]

The controversy was by no means settled, but there was a lull just when another group of settlers came over from South Australia. Instead of saying nothing, Deutscher asked the newcomers what they thought of the pastor. Some did not like the liturgy and the fact that Schuermann used "amen" only once instead of three times. Schuermann recognized the growing discontent and was on the verge of resigning when he called a meeting for discussion of all complaints. After all points of view had been heard, Deutscher expressed the view that more meetings should be held to examine Schuermann's sermons. In this instance the congregation disagreed and sided with Schuermann. Deutscher and eight other families then withdrew in mid-1857 and formed a separate body. Five of the families were German and three Wendish—the families of Andreas Deutscher, Peter Zieschang, and Wilhelm Petschel. Until their church was completed in 1860, they worshiped in the home of Petschel and were served by a minister from Geelong.[81]

The matter did not end, however, and on February 20, 1860, Schuermann asked Deutscher and his members if they would be interested in going to the synodical meeting in an attempt to settle their controversy. Deutscher preferred a meeting in Hamilton, and the arrangements were made. In the two meetings that followed, nothing was accomplished, so the congregation voted to ask the synodical leaders to send two pastors as commissioners. Carl A. Hensel and Phillip J. Oster conducted the hearings for four days and reported to the officials. They found no error with Schuermann's teachings and notified Deutscher that his separation from Schuermann's congregation was improper and irresponsible. Deutscher was not convinced, however, and the split was not healed. In order to restore peace Schuermann then offered his resignation, but withdrew it when fifty-nine members drafted a statement asking him to remain.[82]

Deutscher then wrote to Ludwig Harms, director of the Hermannsburg Mission Society, requesting a pious and earnest pastor. In the meantime six families who cared for neither Deutscher nor Schuermann formed yet another congregation. The pastor Deutscher's church finally received at Easter, 1862, was Dr. Carl H. C. Loessel, a fifty-year-old widower with four children. Unfortunately, he was not well accepted either, and after additional controversy with Deutscher on the charge that Loessel had not been born again, Deutscher locked him out of the church. The third splinter group asked Loessel to be its pastor and hoped that he would draw some of Schuermann's members away. But Loessel could not work harmoniously with the new congregation either; he left for South Australia and the third congregation dissolved. Finally a new pastor, C. G. Hiller, was sent from Basel, and he continued to serve in Victoria for many years. He eventually married Christiane Petschel, the Wendish girl who had migrated to Australia in 1848 and had left a detailed account of her life.

Deutscher died on August 9, 1864, at the age of 53, two days after the death of his nineteen-year-old daughter, Christiane. Both he and his daughter had contracted a severe form of influenza that lasted three weeks. He was recovering but she became delirious and then died. Amidst all the anxiety and physical exertion he then weakened and died the day of his daughter's burial.[83]

The controversy between Schuermann and Deutscher illustrates how well the Wends had been integrated into German society. Communication was in German, and the alignment of members into the congregation was not along ethnic lines at all. Of the fifty-five persons asking Schuermann to remain as their pastor, 45 percent were Wends. Half of Deutscher's congregation, on the other hand, was German.[84]

The entire episode fits closely into the pattern of conflict of an authoritarian church in a democratic society. Schuermann objected to the growing pride and confidence of the members, especially some later migrants from South Australia. The parishioners, on the other hand, were making decisions in the political and economic sectors of their lives and tried to extend their power into the religious sphere as well. From this point of view there was a similarity to the controversy at Peter's Hill.

Schuermann soon adjusted his thinking from the earlier days of the controversy and compromised. He changed the liturgy to satisfy the people, he called meetings where members could raise objections, and he even offered to resign if they desired it. His developing skill in dealing with the new type of active layperson was reflected in his actions with the migrants to the Wimmera. He was convinced that a pastor was badly needed to hold the settlers in the new region together, but the people rejected his suggestions. He then notified the synodical administration to prepare a minister to move to the Wimmera the moment the people called, and they soon did.

The other side of the argument was similar to the problems of Ebenezer, but with pietism Schuermann would not compromise. Although Deutscher's church did not unite with Schuermann's until the twentieth century, it remained Lutheran, and even the Krummnow people eventually returned to the church.

Another aspect of Wendish-German relations can be demonstrated by examining land purchases.[85] The Wends did not settle in one block with the Germans in another. Rather, land purchases were made primarily on the basis of economic factors; even Lutherans did not buy in contiguous plots. Land was purchased in such a way that Wends and Germans lived side-by-side with the English. In church they separated, but in making a living ethnic or religious factors were unimportant.

The settlement of Hamilton and Tarrington served as the nucleus for several satellite communities. Some of the early migrants moved directly to those areas because of the price of land at Hamilton. Andreas Urban,[86] a bootmaker, lived on a corner of the Mirtschin property and opened his house to the first reading services in the Penshurst (Gnadenthal) area. Penshurst, twenty-one miles east of Tarrington, had sixty-three members in 1876, including the Albert and Burger families. Johann Rentsch, Jr., left Hamilton for Byaduk (Neukirch) twenty miles to the south in 1853 to build a wattle and daub house. It lacked a woman's touch until 1856, when he married Magdalena Burger. In 1863 he was joined by Gude and Handreck to form a church. The membership at one time included Kilo, Pumpa, Towk, Kotzur, Jeitz, Bramke, Kosch, and Salzke, but because many migrated to New South Wales, only 36 members remained in 1874. The largest congregation was Tabor, which also started with the Mt. Rouse settlements. In 1874 there were 102 members including Matuschka, Rentsch, Mudra, Lehrack, Gardi, and Zschech. All of these families grew, and in searching for more land generally expanded into the Wimmera or the Riverina.

The Australian Colonies Government Act of 1850 had authorized each colony to write its own constitution and an 1853 amendment permitted each state to assume the administration of its own public lands. Victoria passed several selection acts that permitted the farmer to lease a tract of land and eventually purchase it for one pound per acre. All rents paid prior to purchase would be deducted from the original price. The Grant Land Acts of 1865 and 1869, which enabled the selector to take up 640 acres and 320 acres respectively, coincided with the settlement of the plains of the Wimmera, ninety miles north of Hamilton.[87]

The Wimmera, with a rainfall of fifteen to twenty inches and a deep gray calcareous soil, was ideal for raising wheat. The savannah woodland was comparatively easy to clear, and soon the farmers were producing twenty bushels of wheat per acre, twenty-five of oats, and thirty of barley.[88] The first settlements made by the Wends were southeast and east of the present town of Horsham at Drung Drung, Green Lake, and Murtoa, as well as due east of Horsham and Natimuk.

In spite of his own commitments at Tarrington and the ninety-mile distance, the fifty-four-year-old Schuermann assumed responsibility for these settlers and periodically traveled northward to preach and perform the sacraments. There was no one else to do it, and he reported that they lived as heathens, without divine services and without schools. In 1872 when he went north again he reported that more than eighty communicants lived in the area but that only half took Holy Communion. A full-time pastor was needed, but when Schuermann made this proposal, the settlers hesitated for fear that they could not

Andreas Kleinig home, South Australia, 1929. Galvanized metal was used for roofing, siding, and the tank holding rain water. Eucalyptus trees show behind the house. *Courtesy Thea Fenner*

maintain him. Schuermann wisely let the matter drop. But, aware that the migration would continue and that an unattended flock would fall victim to "*die Unierten*" (unionist pastors) and "heathen clergymen," Schuermann urged Pastor Hensel to make ready a preacher who possessed tact and energy. Finally in 1873 the Rev. C. Schoknecht was asked to preach some trial sermons and in 1874 he was called to the parish at Natimuk. As late as the 1890s the Wends at Natimuk met in various homes and read Scripture and devotional material in Wendish.[89]

The other Lutheran pastor of Hamilton, Pastor Hiller, also went north because his congregation, small to begin with, was decimated by migration. He visited the area in April, 1872, and then moved north himself, serving nineteen families at Murtoa, ten at Drung Drung, eleven at Natimuk, eight at Dimboola, and four at Hamilton. In February, 1873, a church of slab and pug was dedicated at Drung Drung and later that same year a church of the same construction was built at Murtoa.[90]

The stream of settlers moving northward from Hamilton converged with a smaller eastward flow from South Australia. The communities in the Wimmera that included Wends from both Victoria and South Australia were Green Lake and Drung Drung (Lehrack, Petschel, Matuschka, Scheetz, and Duschka), Murtoa (Deutscher, Gardi, Gulbin, and Starick), Natimuk (Starick, Klowss, and Lewitzka), Vectis (Noack, Harnath, Maroske), Horsham (Dushke, Proposch, Starick, and Modra), and Dimboola or Kornheim (Klowss, Salmann, Dalitz, Gersch, Lehmann, and Pumpa).

Finally the Mallee was opened for settlement in the later 1880s and the Wends followed the farming frontier northward. The Mallee was also suited to wheat, but not as well as the Wimmera. Rainfall was below fifteen inches a year and the hot summers with their drying winds produced an evaporation rate of fifty inches. The soil was sandier and more saline, but especially troublesome was the clearing of the land. The mallee tree, a member of the eucalyptus family, possesses a hard stump that sends up several thin trunks. The cost of clearing an acre was 17s. 6d. and included rolling the bushes with large rollers, burning the dead and dry plants, and then grubbing the roots with back-breaking toil.[91] Wends, including Domaschenz, Nossack, Behla, Mudra, Towk, Gniel, Deutscher, Pumpa, Geitz, and Zschech, migrated on to Mallee land around Winiam, Kiata, Nhill, Katyil, Ni Ni, Jeparit, Rainbow, and Hopetown.

ON INTO NEW SOUTH WALES

The scarcity of farm land in South Australia and its declining fertility also stimulated migrations to the neighboring state of New South Wales. The Sir John Robertson Land Act of 1861 permitted selection of 320 acres for a down payment of five shillings per acre, with three years to pay the remaining fifteen shillings. It was only a matter of time before the South Australians heard of such a liberal land act and went east to investigate. A portion of the Riverina, between the Murray and Darling rivers, had been settled by Germans from the Rhineland as early as 1851, but much of the productive land with moderate rainfall was still open for settlement.

The earliest migrants from South Australia, leaving in 1866, came from Mt. Torrens, Blumberg, Light Pass, and Neukirch. Along with the Germans were the Wends, S. C. Greschke, I. M. Greschke, Christian and Johann Salzke, and Adam Bartsch. By June, 1876, forty German and Wendish families were at Jindera (Dight's Forest) clearing land and building brick homesteads.[92]

The best-documented migration to New South Wales was one in which fifty-six people left the area of Ebenezer, South Australia, under the leadership of Johann G. Klemke. Of the eight families, four were Wends—those of Michael Wenke, Andreas Mickan, Andreas Lieschke, and Peter Hennersdorf. All four families were Saxon and had been founding members of Ebenezer. Wenke, Mickan, and Lieschke were young men with growing families, while Hennersdorf was fifty.[93]

The earlier immigrants had broken a trail, but preparations were carefully made because the trip would be undertaken after harvest during the dry months. To compensate for inadequate grazing en route, fodder was sent ahead by Murray River steamer to designated points. Heavy and bulky machinery also was sent by steamer so that the wagons could be covered and set up as sleeping and living accommodations. In contrast to the Hamilton migrants, the fourteen wagons of the Riverina settlers were pulled by teams of only two horses each. Additional horses and cattle were herded along with the train.

The wagon train left Ebenezer on October 13, 1868, following an address by the Rev. J. P. Niquet. Many friends and Pastor Niquet traveled with the group for two days as far as Blanchetown, where that evening the pastor and several others, including Johann Zwar, spoke to the group. The next morning the two groups parted and the immigrants concentrated on the trek ahead. En route they occasionally encountered Aborigines and more frequently kangaroo and emu. Sunday, typically, was a day of rest with services held by Klemke, while daily devotions were conducted by the other laymen, including Wenke and Mickan.

Five and a half weeks later they arrived at Albury and then continued on eleven miles to Jindera. For the next ten weeks they remained in the camp at Four Mile Creek near Jindera and examined the land. In January they broke camp and moved fifteen miles to the place where they established a new settlement, which they called Ebenezer. Later the name was changed to Walla Walla.

Wenke's home served as the chruch from February, 1860, until 1872, when a church of slabs and clay with a roof of straw was erected. More settlers came overland from South Australia in the following years and the congregation continued to grow.[94]

The South Australian immigrants possessed a common bond in their search for land, but in religion they belonged to different Lutheran synods. Some belonged to the Evangelical Lutheran Synod of

Australia with which Pastor Schuermann was aligned, while others identified with the Tanunda–Light Pass Synod that was in fellowship with Pastor Hiller and the Lutheran Synod of Victoria. One group of settlers in the Jindera and Gerogery area appealed to the Victoria Synod for ministerial support and dispatched a delegate to Melbourne in 1868 to attend the Victoria Synodical Convention. The convention welcomed the overtures and its newly elected president, Herman Herlitz, promised a visit to the Riverina. The majority of the Lutherans in the Riverina, however, chose the Evangelical Lutheran Synod of Australia, and on February 16, 1868, they sent a letter to the Reverend Hensel requesting a pastor. They needed a pastor to pull the people together and to preach and teach school for the first year. After one year they would be able to support a teacher as well.[95]

Finally, on June 17, 1868, the church administration of the Evangelical Lutheran Synod sent J. F. Goessling as a temporary pastor. He was actually on leave from the Hermannsburg Mission (Aboriginal) for reasons of health, and only Director Harms could make the decision for longer service. Goessling preached his first service on June 19, 1868, in a small church in the middle of the bush. In his report Goessling expressed optimism about the future of the area and also relief that he had reached the area before a pastor from the other synod, whose presence could have led to a division in the congregation.

Pastor Goessling remained in the Riverina until 1876, when Harms sent him to work among the Maoris of New Zealand. At that time the statistics of his three congregations were as follows: Gerogery had 150 souls and a school of twenty children; Jindera had 139 souls and 28 children in school; and Wodonga, Victoria, had 40 souls and 9 children in school. The next pastor was the Rev. H. Wiese, who served in the area until 1900.[96]

The Ebenezer immigrants strengthened the Tanunda–Light Pass supporters, and Elder Klemke ministered to that minority in the Jindera-Gerogery area. In 1872, four years after their arrival, the Ebenezer people and others called for a pastor from the Basel Mission Seminary. The Rev. Theo. I. Egen arrived at Walla Walla on November 18, 1872, and served the congregation at Walla Walla, Bethel, Jindera, and Gerogery. The division of the Lutherans in the Riverina into two synods therefore occurred in spite of Pastor Goessling's hopes. Wends belonged to both synods and lived in the following parishes: Jindera (Matuschka, Kilo, Kotzur, Klowss, Pumpa, Salzke, and Geitz); Walla Walla (Bartsch, Wenke, Lieschke, Mickan, Groch, Urban, Scheetz, and Hennersdorf); Bethel (Mickan, Jarick, and Urban); and Gerogery (Greschke, Kotzur, and Salzke).

Before long the original Riverina settlements were sending their people to new lands. When the price of land bought initially for a pound an acre rose as high as twelve pounds per acre, many were willing to take their profit and move north. Whatever the motive, some families including Kotzur, Pumpa, Ruschen, Lieschke, and Deutscher did take up lands and settled at such places as Pleasant Hills, Henty, Duck Creek, and Temora.[97]

The internal migration patterns of the Wends in South Australia, Victoria, and New South Wales were not related to ethnic factors but to the land legislation passed by Australian governments. The search for land had been a major consideration in going to Australia in the first place and the pursuit of good inexpensive land kept them going. They were never the first speculators who purchased large acreages for later sale, because they did not have the resources, but they did take the cheapest, least developed land, usually on the frontier, to try to improve its value as they made a living from it.

From Wend to Australian

From the moment the Wends left Lusatia, the erosion of their culture began. Only in the isolated, concentrated settlements of Europe could it be maintained, and even there it was not completely safe. The Australian experience led them further out of the Wendish tradition and into both the German and British frameworks. In economic activity, for example, the context would be English, but in religion and personal identification it was a continuation of the Wendish-German context. In some social events it was mixed: Wendish, German, and English. As time passed, the Wendish culture of Lusatia gave way.

Those who lived in the cities or moved beyond the Wendish-German settlements made a more immediate and direct change to English, but in the rural areas or small towns they generally adopted German first. The key to the association with Germans in both city and country was the church. The Lutheran church in Australia was largely a German church, and the few Scandinavian and Slavic Lutherans had to learn German or join another church. Many of the Wends already knew German and their loyalties to the Lutheran church were strong.

Absorption by the German community is demonstrated by statistics on intermarriage of the Wendish second generation children belonging to the couples that migrated. For those married in Lutheran churches: of the Lower Wends, 52 percent married Germans, 36 percent married Wends, and 11 percent married Australians of English

Gus Dreckow's home at Yadnarie, on the Eyre Peninsula, circa 1914. The metal tank at the rear was used to hold rainwater from the roof. *Courtesy Don J. Wells and the Dreckow-Stubing Committee*

descent. Of the Upper Wends, 65 percent married Germans, 27 percent Wends, and 8 percent Australians of English descent. The choice of marriage partner was probably based more upon the composition of social group than the ethnic identification of the parents. A Wend who grew up in a comparatively large, solidly Wendish community would tend to marry a Wend, but not if the community was largely German.

We can therefore assume that marriage to a German was not undesirable, even if it meant the sacrifice of the Wendish way of life. The small number marrying English Australians is understandable because they would not be in the same church or social group and would not be able to communicate as easily. In fact, more Wends than indicated here married English Australians, because these statistics are based on Lutheran records, and in most instances when a Wend married an English Australian, the couple joined an English-speaking church.

Another observation from the intermarriage statistics is that the Upper Wends more frequently married Germans than did the Lower Wends. One reason may be that the settlements of Hope Valley and Peter's Hill were more exclusively Wendish than Ebenezer and Tarrington. Another possible reason is that Upper Lusatia may have had more German residents in the villages from which the migrants originated than did Lower Lusatia, so that Wends from Upper Lusatia would have felt more comfortable with the German people and language.

Thus in a short time the Wends were listening to German sermons, attending German marriages, and witnessing the disappearance of their language and culture. The chances for a third-generation Wend to know the language would be small. One could expect it only if both parents were Wends, and less than one Wend out of three married another Wend. The chances were further reduced since there was no formal teaching of Wendish in the schools and many parents who knew Wendish themselves thought German and English acceptable for their children. As a result Wendish disappeared for all practical purposes with the second generation, and today those who remember it at all are limited to counting from one to ten and repeating some phrases and greetings. While the language remained as an identifying trait for the second generation, the Wends generally had become members of the Germany community within the lifetime of the first generation.

Already as early as 1851 the *South Australian Register* carried a letter about the necessity of Germans giving up their nationality and becoming Australians. Quite fairly the writer partly blamed English readers for excluding Germans from society, certain institutions, and some positions of employment. No matter who was blamed for failure to assimilate, the burden of change rested on the Germans and their Wendish retinue.[98]

But the Germans held fast to their traditions, and in 1871, when Germany was unified, Germans in the Ebenezer-Stockwell area celebrated the event and dressed up a princess of peace in blue and white. Several years later in 1888, when floods struck Germany, the Germans and Wends in Victoria, including those at Winiam and Warraquil, where the rainfall was less than fifteen inches a year, collected money for food relief. Although loyal to Australia, the Germans and the Wends looked upon Germany as their home.[99]

World War I destroyed that attitude and forced them into reality. Australia suffered heavy losses in the campaigns of World War I and was not tolerant of German sympathizers. Because of public pressure the two synods of the Lutheran church dropped German as the official language, and sermons, even by German-born pastors, were delivered in English, no matter how heavy the accent. The government closed the Lutheran schools where German had been taught, and the Australianization of the Germans was under way.[100]

Ironically, just as the Lutherans began speaking English, so that Australians could have understood, there was a sizable exodus from the church. What better way was there to prove loyalty to Australia than by joining the Anglican church? Also some Wends, who realized that being associated with Germans was not an advantage, were hard put to explain their actual ethnic heritage to their Australian neighbors. They solved their problem by identifying themselves as Poles, the Slavic group nearest Lusatia that the Australian would recognize. Even today there are Wendish descendants who, though Protestants, consider their ancestors to have been Poles.

The antagonisms of World War I turned into a blessing for the Australian Lutherans by forcing them to give up the idea that a specific denomination was the property of an ethnic group, and the view that the church served only as a cultural security blanket in times of drastic change. To survive, it had to become a Lutheran church for Australians and its language had to be English. Evangelizing all people was the purpose of all denominations and the lesson, though painful, was valuable.

The Wends, therefore, followed their church into the German culture, and as it became Australian, so did they. The descendants of the Wends now live in all the states of Australia, although they are most numerous in South Australia and in the areas of the early settlements.

The Wends in Australia were not visionaries laying the foundations for a greater society. They had no mission to transplant democracy or religious freedom to a foreign soil. They were simple, conservative peasants looking for a place where they could sink their roots and be left alone. They did not strive for political power or for positions of leadership or influence, but worked to get another acre of land and battled nature to keep the family fed. Their contribution to Australia (and they never intended to make one) was not dramatic, but consisted simply of developing a small portion of the Australian frontier.

3

The Texas Wends

EARLY WENDISH MIGRATION TO TEXAS

The initial stages of Wendish migration to Texas followed the same pattern as the migration to Australia. The very earliest Wendish emigrants to Texas mingled with the Germans, and then several years later, after exchanges of letters, the larger Wendish migration took place.

The first Wends who can be identified belonged to the Seydler family from Bautzen. The group of eight, consisting of Friedrich Gustave, his family of five, and his two younger brothers, migrated in 1849 on the *Hamburg*. During the following year they joined the German settlement at New Ulm in Austin County and in December of 1850 Friedrich Seydler purchased 490 acres of land for eleven hundred dollars.[1]

Other early Wendish emigrants from Bautzen were George Helas who purchased land in May, 1851, also in Austin County, and Robert Wagner. There may have been Wends who preceded the Seydler, Helas, and Wagner families, but no reference to any others is made by later Wendish immigrants. The Seydlers eventually moved to High Hill, near Schulenburg, in Fayette County. Little is known about the later history of the Helas and Wagner families except that they lived at New Ulm, a German settlement, for a period of time. They did not establish a Wendish community, nor did they give up their holdings to join the Kilian settlement, but instead identified themselves with the Germans.[2] The later Wendish migrants knew about these early pioneers, traveled directly to them when they arrived in Texas, and benefited from their advice and assistance.

The first Wends to migrate as a group left Bremen on September 4,

1853. Most of them lived along the border of Prussia and Saxony in the villages of Weigersdorf, Mucka, Kolpen, and Kosel. The ship carrying the party of thirty-five traveled smoothly for most of her voyage, but struck a shoal near Cuba on the night of October 26. Although the ship was destroyed, it did not sink immediately, and the occupants anxiously held on for four hours before the Cubans saw their emergency lantern and sailed out to the rescue. No lives were lost, but all possessions were abandoned.

A steamer took the passengers to Havana, where the German consul and a German society provided them with shelter and money for the journey. Later, another steamer took them to New Orleans where another German association furnished them with new clothing and sent them on to Galveston. Maria Michalk Krause took advantage of her unexpected visit to Cuba by learning to roll cigars.[3] In Houston they met one of the Seydlers, who worked there as a mason, and he gave them directions to New Ulm. At New Ulm the newcomers either purchased land or found agricultural employment. The male members of the Kasper family, for example, worked for Helas for a dollar a day in addition to meat and coffee, while each of the women of the family received about four dollars per month. In contrast to the Seydler and Helas families, these Wends, including Christoph Krause, Johann Noack, Johann Kasper, Mathias Mattiez, Mathias Mitschke, August Polnick, and Johann Domaschk-Janak would eventually join Kilian's congregation in Serbin.

In a letter published in *Serbske Nowiny* just one week before Kilian received the call from the independent Lutheran congregation, Johann Kasper commented favorably on the absence of state regulations in Texas, on the opportunity of obtaining firearms for hunting, and on the availability of jobs. Assuming that more Wends would follow, he criticized the Bremen ships and suggested that future immigrants embark from Hamburg. Nothing in any letters home said anything about religious freedom, although Kilian, in a letter written in 1855, reported that these 1853 migrants had left the Prussian church. Whatever their reasons for migration might have been, their letters praising their new home were on their way to Lusatia and inspired others with the desire to go to Texas.[4]

Motives for Migration

The largest single Wendish group to migrate either to Australia or to North America was the group connected with Pastor Jan Kilian. Because the religious motive is so frequently mentioned in connection with the "Kilian migration,"[5] it must be given primary consideration. People may migrate even though they are satisfied with their religious condition, or, at the opposite extreme, they may leave solely because of dissatisfaction with their church when everything else is all right. Much depends on the priority religion holds in each person's life and the extent to which religious discontent reinforces other dissatisfactions. For the Kilian group the church not only occupied an important position, but was also the source of discontent.

Religious dissatisfaction among Lutherans was especially visible and vocal in Prussia, the state that provided most of Kilian's following and in which Kilian resided from 1848 to 1854. The people most upset with the church were those of strong Lutheran traditions who objected to meddling in their faith by a Calvinist ruler. In an attempt to form a single Protestant church, Frederick William III, on October 31, 1817—the tercentenary of Luther's Ninety-Five Theses—called for a voluntary union of the Lutheran and Calvinist bodies. In 1822 he issued the *Agende* containing new and neutral liturgies, or forms of church worship, that were nebulous enough not to conflict with either Lutheran or Calvinist doctrine. He hoped that these liturgies would be adopted voluntarily and would provide a vehicle for the union of the two bodies.

The ruler nevertheless required ministers to subscribe to the symbolic books of the two bodies and ordered that those who conformed to his program be given preference in the assignment of pastors to congregations. In 1830, the tercentenary of the *Augsburg Confession*, the king decreed that the union be implemented in all evangelical churches and that the names Lutheran and Reformed no longer be used. Kilian and his followers began their chronicle of complaint in the decade of the 1830s with the intensification of enforcement and not in 1817 when the program originated.[6]

Frederick William IV acceded to the throne in 1840. Hoping to regain some of the loyalty of his subjects, in 1841 he ended the restraints on opposition groups by permitting the formation of independent churches. Two years later in 1843, some Wends, especially in Weigersdorf, began worshipping quarterly in Andreas Urban's home under the leadership of Pastor Gessner from Freistadt in Silesia. Membership of the group increased, and in 1845 the one hundred people involved at Klitten and Weigersdorf built their own little church buildings, although the state prohibited the addition of steeples. Kilian accepted their call in 1848 and resided first in Dauban, approximately midway between the two congregations, until 1852 when he occupied the parsonage at Weigersdorf. There he remained until 1854 when he left for Texas.[7]

There was dissatisfaction with the Saxon church as well, and that unhappiness may have influenced the Saxon Wends to join the Prussian Wends in migration. Because the king of Saxony was a Catholic, the Lutheran church was governed by an ecclesiastical council, and much to the chagrin of the staunch Lutherans, this council was lax and permitted the clergy and members of the church to hold a wide diversity of religious opinions. Especially objectionable was the tolerance and even sympathy of religious leaders and administrators toward religious views and attitudes associated with rationalism.

Rationalism, a philosophy that had been influential during the eighteenth century, encouraged people to approach all aspects of their lives, including theology, with reason. Those aspects of religion that subscribed to miracles or biblical inspiration were rejected because they were not reasonable. During the nineteenth century rationalism lost some influence, but the attitudes it had created remained with many in the Saxon church. Orthodox Lutherans like Kilian objected to such tolerance of religious diversity and called for the church of Saxony to live up to its Lutheran name. The staunch Lutherans were aware of the movement to remove restraints, including deletion of the oath to the Lutheran Confessions from the ordination ceremony, and dreaded the results of such acts. To Kilian and others, the oath was one of the last barriers that would keep false teachers and freethinkers out of the church.[8]

Even though Kilian criticized the church administration, he did not leave the state church until 1848, when he accepted a call to serve the independents in Prussia. Kilian was therefore well acquainted with the religious policies of the two German states and was not pleased with either. Certainly members of his congregation in Saxony and Prussia felt the same way, but whether or not conditions were sufficiently extreme to drive people to Texas is open to question.

A problem with ascribing religious motives to the Prussian Wends is that they did not leave in the days when state pressures were most restrictive, but when the religious climate was improving and the state permitted dissenters to form their own congregations. Moreover, why would some migrate and others who held the same religious views and belonged to the same congregations not migrate? The battle for religious tolerance, if that were the sole issue, would best be won through conflict within Prussia and not through a migration that would only decimate the Lutheran forces. Some of the Wends who remained did indeed criticize the Kilian migration for weakening the movement against the state church. The religious motive is further called into question by the fact that many of the migrants were members of the Prussian state church and not members of Kilian's congregation.[9]

Exclusion of religious motives would be unthinkable, however, because religion was pivotal in the lives of these faithful believers. The fact that it was a major concern can be seen by the care and precision they devoted to taking their church with them. Once they decided to migrate, they formed a new organization at Dauban on March 25, 1854, and announced that they planned to build a pure evangelical Lutheran congregation in America. Two months later they called Kilian to accompany them. So strong was their religious concern that they made their religious plans while still in Europe. They did not say that they planned to migrate in order to formulate a pure church, but they planned to migrate and there build a pure church. The church was already part of their life in Europe, it was a pure church, and when they arrived in Texas they hoped to transplant their church there. Religious motivation gives us insight into the Wends' way of life, but it does not provide us with the simple explanation for migration.

In addition to religious irritations there were also social and economic problems in Europe. These social and economic problems, so important for the Australian Wends, are mentioned by the Texas group only before the 1854 migration and never after Kilian's group was in Texas. Yet there obviously were people who were suffering hardship, because Kilian in 1845, while pastor in Kotitz, organized the society for the poor (*Armenverein*). In diagnosing the problem Kilian did not blame the changing economic conditions resulting from the end of the feudal system, but instead identified such personal shortcomings as drunkenness, irresponsibility, and lack of thrift. The purpose of the organization was to raise money for the poor, so that parish funds would be supplemented and those who asked for welfare could be provided with advice and counsel. Members of the society also hoped to increase family income by meeting on Friday evenings to teach children the arts of weaving straw and spinning thread. It soon became evident that no social improvement would result, and in his failure, Kilian considered emigration to Australia as an economic solution.[10]

Possibly the economic and religious motives blended when the independents discovered that paying a pastor's salary and financing a congregation taxed the limited resources of the scattered members; they may have hoped that by migrating to Texas in order to improve their economic status they could more easily cover the costs of maintaining a congregation. There was little difference between belonging to a free church in Prussia and to a church in Texas. In neither place was there heavy oppression and in neither was there financial support. Both churches had power over their own activities and both paid their own bills. As the single motive for migration, the search for religious freedom does not stand up. It could have served as the catalyst, however, drawing together the discontented and providing them with the blueprint of a society they desired but could not sustain in Europe.

Kilian and the Question of Leadership

Jan Kilian was born on March 22, 1811, in Döhlen, Saxony, to Peter and Maria Kilian, who died early in his life. His education, made possible partially because he was the only heir, included the *Gymnasium* (secondary school) at Bautzen and the University of Leipzig. During his years of attendance at Leipzig he became the friend of C. F. W. Walther, who migrated to America in 1839, eventually becoming the president of the Lutheran Church–Missouri Synod and the editor of *Der Lutheraner*.

After graduation from Leipzig in 1834 with high honors, Kilian, unable to obtain a pastorate, became the assistant pastor at Hochkirch, Saxony, a few miles east of Döhlen. Not satisfied with this type of service, he decided to become a missionary to East India and traveled to Basel for training with the Evangelical Missionary Society. At that time his uncle Michael Kilian, pastor at Kotitz, died, and when Kilian attended the funeral, the congregation asked him to take the position.

During his eleven-year term with that congregation he not only preached in Sorbian and German while ministering to his parish, but he composed music and wrote and translated religious material into Sorbian. His compositions were deeply religious and one of his songs, *"Serbja, zachowajće swěru, swojich wótcow rěč a wěru"* ("Sorbs, maintain faithfully the language and religion of your forefathers") was a favorite of the Texas Wends. In 1846 he published a book called *Spěwarske wjesel* (Songs of Joy) that contained twenty-eight of his hymns. His publications included translations of lengthy works such as the *Augsburg Confession* and Luther's *Large Catechism* as well as original prayer books, sermons, and tracts. His sermons especially were powerful and he attracted listeners not only from his own parish, but as far away as an eight-hour walk. Many worshipers crossed the border from Prussia where they objected to the Prussian religious policy. His views on the state churches were not disguised, so when the two independent parishes of Weigersdorf and Klitten were large enough to support a pastor, they sent the call to Kilian. Kilian moved from Kotitz to Dauban, near Weigersdorf in 1848 and shortly thereafter married Maria Groeschel of Särka.[11]

Kilian's new position was outside the state church and because of economic necessity as well as religious dedication he ministered to a widely scattered flock. He alternated services between Weigersdorf and Klitten, but once every quarter he went on a three-week tour that took him to eighteen preaching places in Prussia. Because these small clusters of Lutherans could not finance the construction of churches, Kilian conducted services in private homes and funeral chapels. Although state officials were not pleased with Kilian's energetic work, they did not harass him as long as he announced his worship services in the local papers. During his twenty-year ministry Kilian became well known in Lusatia as a devout pastor dedicated to the traditional Lutheran position.[12]

Among the Wends who migrated in 1854 Kilian was without question the spiritual leader. He was consulted on many other matters as well, but the temporal leadership of the Wendish community came from laymen. The first indication of this lay leadership was in the 1854 call to Kilian. Kilian did not gather the members of the Weigersdorf and Klitten congregation to lead them to Texas; laymen from scattered villages in Saxony and Prussia first formed an association and then asked Kilian to be their pastor. The laymen assumed the responsibility of gathering the migrants and of financing the venture. The call they sent Kilian was for one year only, an indication that the laymen could release themselves of the expenses of a pastor if they did not succeed financially.[13]

Kilian's limited leadership role was evident during the migration. Arrested on the charge of inciting to emigrate, he did not even accompany the people to Liverpool. The laymen provided the leadership and took the main body of migrants to Hamburg and from there to Hull, England, where they boarded a train for Liverpool. Kilian was not acquitted and freed until September 14, two days after the ship left Hamburg. Kilian, with his wife and child, therefore, rode to Cologne and crossed Belgium and the English channel.

Instead of gaining time, Kilian lost several days. En route through Belgium, he discovered that he had left his pass and a parcel at the border station, so he sent his wife and son Gerhard on toward Ghent while he returned to the border. Mrs. Kilian, not understanding French, by mistake traveled to Antwerp. When Kilian arrived in Ghent he could not find his family and told his problem to the dumbfounded police. Luckily a Flemish man found the two lost ones and returned them to Ghent. Kilian arrived at Liverpool on September 20, one week after the others had arrived. They were living in three houses provided by shipping agent called Meyer, waiting not for Kilian but for the readying of the ship.[14]

The power of the lay leadership was also evident during a cholera crisis in Ireland. While the *Ben Nevis* was being cleansed and the Wends were on board the *Inconstant,* Kilian received an anonymous letter criticizing him for not teaching the children during the idle hours on board ship. The leaders rebuked the complainers for their unchristian manner and defended Kilian's inactivity because no formal document or constitution had been adopted specifying when school would be in session. The secular leaders of the community were in charge and they would call for the establishment of a church council that in turn would write a constitution.

Kilian did assume leadership outside the spiritual realm on one occasion during the voyage. On board ship Kilian lived not with the other migrants, which would have cost 100 *Taler,* but in a private cabin for which he paid 254 *Taler.* At the same time that cholera was raging among the passengers, the blustery winds of the North Atlantic caused widespread seasickness. Nausea sent people to their crowded quarters, in close contact with the cholera victims. The captain, realizing that the cholera would spread further, threatened to drag the healthy out on the deck. Kilian intervened and used persuasion to achieve the desired goal, but he sensed resentment from some Wends, and years later when he encountered opposition from a segment in the congregation, he looked back at this event as the first step in the growth of hostility toward him. He was exerting leadership outside his sphere of responsibility.

Lay leadership continued in the new colony on such matters as the selection of land and the financial management of the church. Kilian's responsibility was the religious life of the people and particularly Christian education through church and school. In 1861 when a property holder in Bastrop County attempted to engage Kilian as a real estate agent, Kilian rejected the five hundred dollars because the congregation did not desire the pastor's involvement in politics, real estate, or "worldly business." "When I at any time trespassed this rule, I was always severely censured." Even Kilian's private affairs were not secret. In 1855 when he bought a cow for fifty dollars, various members of the congregation were unhappy that he did not buy the cow from them for that price. Kilian could graze cattle or farm the church acres to supplement his income, but his domain was circumscribed.

Kilian was no more satisfied with the democracy of the congregational meetings that placed him under lay control than he had been with the centralized direction of the church in Germany. At least in Europe there was peace among the parishioners, but in Serbin there was debate and one after another voting member would rise in the business meeting to "preach" in an attempt to get his views accepted.[15]

Kilian certainly exerted a great deal of influence outside the religious sphere, but that was testimony to his ability rather than the organization's policy. He was able to do this because of his strength of character and because he was the only professional man in the community. In addition, his linguistic ability enabled him to master the language of the new land so that he could readily communicate with everyone in the region. But the authority for the migration and the power of the congregation rested with the adult males and Kilian was their servant.

The 1854 Migration

Those Wends intent on emigration met at Dauban on March 25, 1854, and formed an organization to carry out their plan. The president, Carl Lehmann, owned a mill at Dauban, and Carl Teinert, another officer, had served as driver and song-leader for Kilian on quarterly journeys to the dissident Lutheran groups. On May 23, 1854, two months after incorporation, the officers of the group sent Kilian the call to be their pastor in North America. In addition to the signatures of Lehmann and Teinert, the letter bore those of Ernst Adolph Moerbe of Klix, Johann Hohle of Jahmen, Christopher Kokel of Reichwalde, and Johann Urban of Rackel.

Kilian, as the pastor, was expected to preach and to manage his position in keeping with the Lutheran tradition, to administer the sacraments, and to teach the children of the congregation for the first year in Texas. The congregation, in turn, promised to pay him an annual salary of one thousand *Taler*, in addition to specified perquisites for such services as weddings, burials, and confirmations. Kilian was also promised a plot of land in Texas and support for his family in the event of his death.[16]

Many of the migrants came from the same Saxon villages that sent out the Australian settlers, but the majority lived northward in the villages of Prussian Lusatia (see Map 5). The Saxon villages with the

Texas Wends

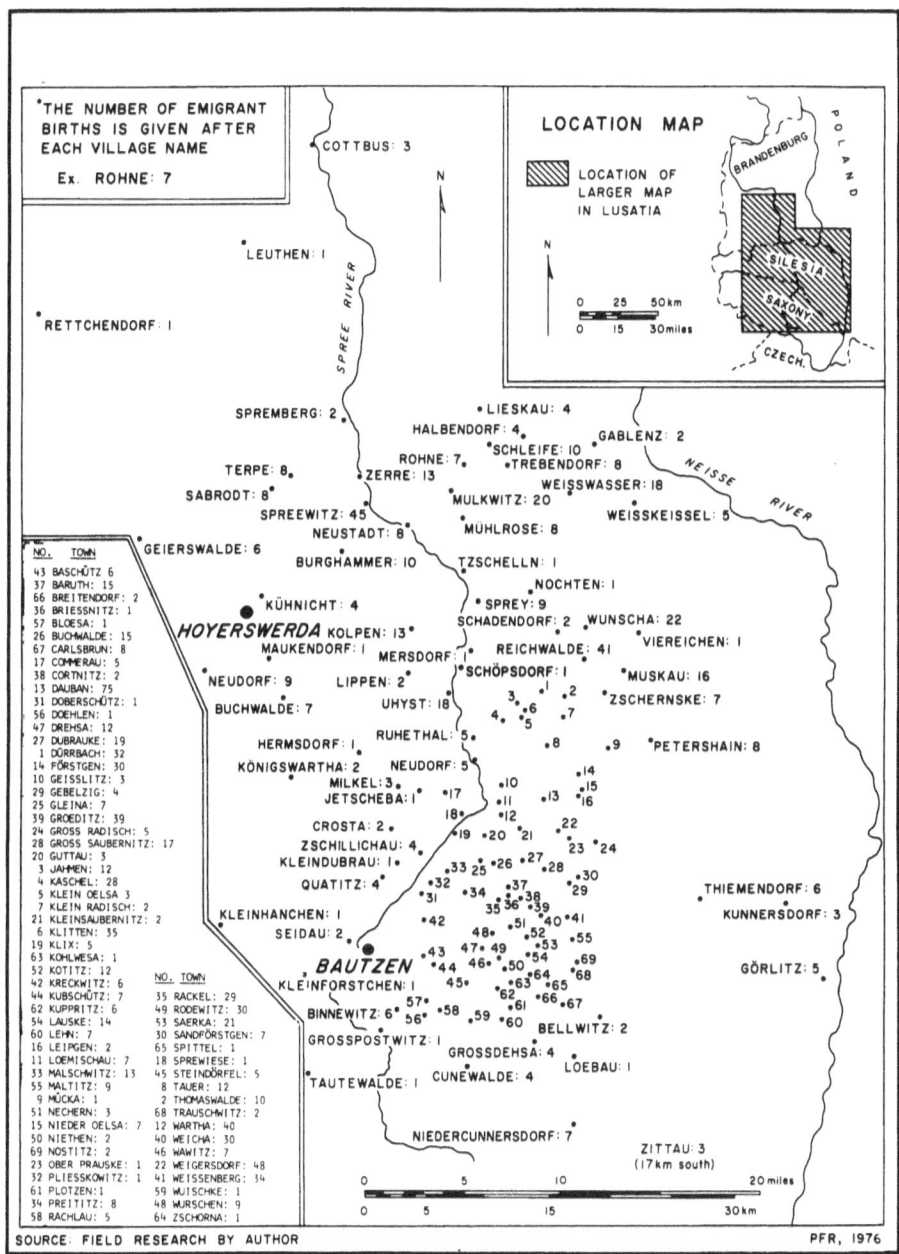

MAP 5 Lusatian Birthplaces of Texas Wends

greatest representation were Wartha, Weissenberg, Särka, and Dubrauke, while the Prussian villages were Reichwalde, Klitten, Weigersdorf, and Dürrbach. Most of the settlers came from agricultural positions or from agriculture-related occupations. Forty-four were *Häusler* and twenty were *Gärtner*.[17] But there were also cabinetmakers, masons, weavers, watchmakers, tailors, and bakers among them. Some gave up their trade in Texas to become farmers while others relinquished their membership in the Wendish settlement and practised their calling in the larger Texas towns and cities.

The average age of the parents was thirty-eight years, four years older than that of the emigrants to Australia. The entire Texas group was older than the Australian arrivals; several—Maria Bartsch, Johann Mertink, and Hanna Schubert—were over seventy years old. The age difference probably reflects the cohesion of the group that first assembled in Germany for religious reasons. The older persons were less interested in economic advantage and would not have emigrated for that reason, but they were intent on staying with their religious associates, on whom they could rely for assistance. The average number of children per family was between two and three, as for the Australian migrants.

The leaders of the Wends signed a contract with the Hamburg company of Valentin Lorenz Meyer, probably because the 1853 migrants believed that the food and accommodations of the Hamburg ships were superior to those of Bremen's. Meyer planned to send them along the usual route to America which at that time was via Liverpool, where they could obtain inexpensive passage on the cotton ships returning empty to America for more fiber for the English mills. The disadvantages, on the other hand, were those of comfort and safety. The Hamburg regulations governing direct voyages did not apply to steamships sailing to Hull, and they were not equipped for carrying passengers. Furthermore the space for steerage passengers on the Liverpool ships was considerably less than on the ships leaving Hamburg.[18]

The laymen's thorough plans even provided for an interpreter. Somewhere along the route the Wends were joined by Friedrich Matuschka, a Wend barely sixteen years old. Some years earlier his parents had left Lower Lusatia and migrated to Berlin where Friedrich was born. There he attended school and evidently learned enough English to qualify him for the position. He remained with the Wends until they obtained land at Serbin and then returned to Berlin. Later he migrated to America and became a Lutheran pastor in Missouri.[19]

Most of the Wends traveled by chartered train to Hamburg where they waited for almost a week, while others like the Groeschel and Miertschin families arrived on September 11, one day before departure.[20] The first fatality was forty-seven-year-old Mattheus Schulze who died on September 10, but his widow with their five children, nonetheless sailed with the group two days later. A steamship carried the Wends to Hull, England, a port on the eastern coast, where they boarded a train for a trip due west to Liverpool. Liverpool, however, was plagued with cholera, and while they waited for two weeks for the *Ben Nevis*, an English sailing ship of 1,347 tons, to be unloaded and readied, some Wends contracted the disease.

Hanna Schatte, a twenty-four-year-old daughter of Matthias Schatte, died on September 16, the first of fourteen to die at Liverpool, and the first of fifty-five to die of cholera. Finally, on September 26 the ship cleared the port, but almost immediately cholera broke out on board. The captain therefore stopped at Queenstown, Ireland, where the *Inconstant* brought the healthy to shore while the sick people were placed on the *Elsa*, which became a hospital ship. In the following three weeks thirty-one more Wends were buried in Ireland. At a cost of one thousand pounds the owners destroyed the bedding of the sick and cleaned and fumigated the entire ship. During this time the Wends on the *Inconstant* elected the following five men to the church council: Johann Urban and Ernst Adolph Moerbe from Saxony, and John Greulich, Matthias Schoelnick, and Johann Knippa from Prussia. Amid all the suffering and death a new family was established, when Joseph Birnbaum married Magdalena Pilak.[21]

On October 23, 1854, the *Ben Nevis* sailed into open water and arrived seven weeks later at Galveston on December 15. The remainder of the journey had been comparatively easy, although there had been one major storm and several smaller ones. At Galveston the goods were transferred to a steamship that took the containers to shore. There the customs inspectors searched for items to tax, but soon grew tired and charged fifty dollars for the entire lot. Seventy-eight Sorbs had died during the migration, including four of the five infants born en route. The survivors, approximately 500, gathered their families and sorted their belongings at Galveston and took yet another steamer to Houston, where they were given a warm welcome by Pastor Caspar Braun.[22]

Caspar Braun had begun his ministry in Houston in 1850 and in 1851 established the first Lutheran church in the young city. The Wends, in all probability, joined the congregation as it dedicated a new sanctuary on Christmas Day, 1854. Several Wendish families stayed in Houston, either because their occupations were more suited to a concentration of people or because they were too impoverished to travel farther. Johann Jannausch, a watchmaker, stayed, as well as Carl Neumann, Johann Greulich, Johann Richter, and Andreas Vogel. Those who delayed their journey westward attended Braun's communion services and in February, 1855, Braun baptized the infant Andreas Urban. Braun also sent three Wendish orphans under the care of widow Richter to the Lutheran children's home in Pittsburgh, Pennsylvania. Kilian and Braun remained friends and on at least one occasion Braun visited the Wendish settlement.[23]

The land journey from Houston to New Ulm, home of the 1853 migrants, was not made in a single mass, but in small parties which departed some time around early January. Kilian, Groeschel, Teinert, Arldt, and Kubitz, for example, formed one train of two wagons. The total amount of freight for the five families was 8,300 pounds. Twelve oxen were needed to pull one of the wagons along the muddy roads and ten for the other. The primitive roads and slow pace of the oxen extended this eighty-five-mile distance into a fifteen-day trip. Everyone walked, except Kilian's pregnant wife and the little children, and the cold January weather with occasional rain made the journey uncomfortable. On January 3, 1855, when the wagons crossed the Brazos, Kilian went to a hotel to find a dry bed for a rest, but all were occupied. The land of hope offered few comforts.

Arriving at New Ulm, Kilian found the farms of the 1853 Sorbs already full of immigrants. Anticipating the birth of another child, Kilian therefore took his family forty miles farther to Rabbs Creek, where he found shelter in the home of August Polnick, another 1853 migrant. There on February 13, Maria Theresia was born, but one month later, on March 14, she died. The leaders at this time had arranged the purchase of the Delaplain League, not far from Rabbs Creek, so the infant daughter was the first to be buried in the cemetery that has become the final resting place for many Wendish people.[24]

In that brief time when Kilian had gone through New Ulm and met the Wends who had migrated earlier, he detected hostility and heard that critical letters would be sent to Bautzen. The letters that were eventually sent to the newspaper there were signed by three Wends—F. G. Seydler, Sr., Robert Wagner, and George Helas—and two Germans. They first attacked the basic idea that a Wendish colony could be started in Texas. The days of free land were gone, they argued, and only on the frontier, next to the Indians, could one find inexpensive, productive soil. Because the Wends were so impoverished they could purchase only one league of land, an inadequate base for a colony, and the land they purchased, although reasonable in price, was overgrown with trees that had to be cleared at great effort and expense. The five authors believed that the Wends had been misled into an impossible project and that the settlers would soon be scattered.

Not only was Kilian blamed for the suffering and hunger of the colonists, but he was charged with cheating them out of what little wealth they had. The Wendish congregation lost a total of two thousand *Taler* when Kilian supposedly permitted the shipping company to charge fifty-five *Taler* for each person instead of the usual charge of forty-five. In addition, each person was required to pay three *Taler* into the congregational treasury, for an additional loss of fifteen hundred *Taler*. Finally, when the German money was exchanged for American, a quarter of it was skimmed off by the leaders to help pay the costs of the poor. The critics even blamed Kilian for taking the Wends through England where they were exposed to cholera.[25]

Kilian, in one of his letters back to Europe, cautioned about the possibility of a hostile letter and asked the editor to permit him to give a proper response. The critical letters were printed and the editor sent copies to Kilian, but no defense was ever printed. Either Kilian did not consider it necessary to reply or the editor decided against publication. The evaluation of the charges is therefore greatly complicated, if not impossible. The motivation for the hostile action could have been a sympathetic response to the suffering of fellow countrymen, or it could have been a rationalization for the decision of the three Wends not to join the main settlement. They had joined the German community, and by forecasting a bleak future for the Wendish colony defended their decision to stay where they were. Although their observations may have been accurate on the land selection and the fare, they should have blamed the lay leaders and not Kilian. Possibly the decision to sign the contract with Meyer was based on the desire to travel on the same ship, and all these secular decisions were made by the laymen and not Kilian.

It seems appropriate to commend rather than censure the congregational aid for the poor, and that again was a congregational decision. The poor received assistance for their fare, and although initially many stayed in Houston and New Ulm in order to earn money, in 1857 any faithful member of the congregation who could not obtain other farming lands was given the use of church acres. The statements on support are sketchy, and nothing other than helping to maintain church property was recorded about repayment.[26]

Purchase of the Delaplain League

When Kilian's Wends set sail, they knew only that they would purchase land somewhere in Texas. Undoubtedly the earlier Bautzen settlers—Seydler, Helas, and Wagner—as well as the members of the 1853 migration, led them to the New Ulm region. The land around New Ulm, however, was occupied, and if the congregation hoped to maintain its unity, a large tract of contiguous land was needed.

Many reasons have been advanced for the selection of the Delaplain League. Some say that the settlers needed timber to build, and they were too poor to purchase lumber. Others suggest that the price for better prairie or floodplain land was too great for the poor to afford. Another explanation could be that the Wends were familiar with the light sandy soil of Lusatia and as a result purchased the same type of land in Texas. Whatever the primary reason may have been, the Wends were limited in their selection because locating a large tract of land with a clear title near New Ulm was a problem.[27]

Kilian, writing to Andreas Dutschmann in Weigersdorf, emphasized the confusion of land titles in Texas and the problem of locating a person with clear title to land. Much of the land had been granted by the Republic of Texas in the 1830s and the recipients often had died or disappeared. Carl Lehmann, for example, found a suitable tract, but when he went to the Land Office in Austin, he learned that the owner had lived in Galveston and had died leaving no evidence of descendants. In order to avoid future litigation, Lehmann carried on his search until he was able to find land with an owner who was willing to sell. Lehmann was successful on February 11, and the twenty-five families who had spent six weeks in camp near the present site of Warda looked forward to occupying their own land. Unfortunately the final phase of migration with the transfer of title was delayed until mid-March and the planting of crops was too late for good yields.[28]

The transfer of title from A. C. Delaplain to Carl Lehmann and John Dube was made on March 21, 1855, for a "league and a labor of land" that totaled 4,254⅔ acres at the price of one dollar per acre. Dube then conveyed title to others from 1860 to 1867 for the farming land and Lehmann sold the lots in the village of Serbin.[29]

The nature of the financial arrangements that Dube and others made between 1855 and the time when the title was legally transferred is not clear, but we can assume that Dube received money from the others at the time of purchase and that each person took a portion of the land. The price that Dube received in nearly every instance was one dollar per acre, no matter when the transfer was recorded. Part of

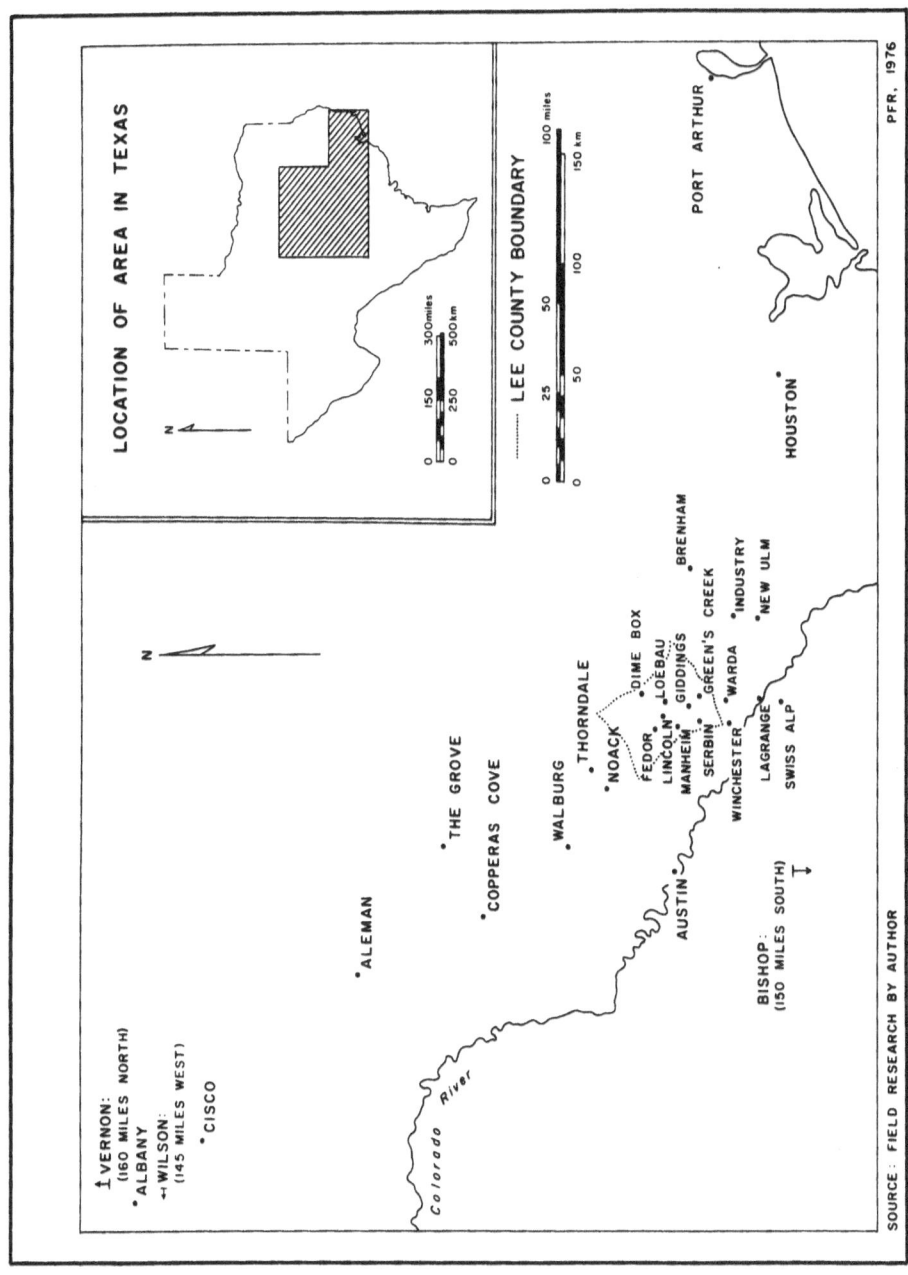

Map 6 Texas Locations of Wendish Settlers

the delay in issuing titles to the various members of the settlement resulted from the fact that the thousand-dollar note that Delaplain accepted was not paid until December 8, 1859, and that the final title to Dube was not conveyed until that time.

In chronological order of purchase the individuals below received the portions of the league indicated; the figures refer to acres of land and names are as they appear in the deeds. The remainder was evidently kept by John Dube.

Mathes Wukash: 171 3/5	Johann Zischang: 257 2/3
Lutheran Church: 95	Michael Dube: 166 2/3
August Groeschel: 85 1/4	George Bamsch: 47 1/2
Johann Domaschk: 74	Math. Schuster: 20
Johann Noack: 50	Jacob Paulick: 114 1/2
Johann Kubitz: 30	Andreas Lowke: 202
Mathias Wagner: 95	F. A. Engelke: 15
Christoph Kokel: 76	George Iselt: 47 1/2
Christoph Schatte: 95	Johann Merting: 95
Peter Fritsche: 95 1/2	George Schelnick: 97 1/2
Matheas Schilling: 110 1/2	Math. Domasch: 101
Math. Mroske: 50	Johann Urban: 84 3/5
Mathias Schmidt: 180	George Lorentschk: 73
George Haken [Hocker]: 47 1/2	Charles Lehmann: 247
George Mertink: 67	Andreas Kieschnick: 117 1/2
John Hohle: 95	Magdalena Jurak: 95
Carl Wenke: 85 1/2	Christoph Schellnick: 46
Anna Zwahr: 55	Johann Pillack: 29 4/5
Johann Handrick: 85 4/5	Johann Mickan: 43 3/5
Matthias Wukasch: 85 1/4	Johann Malke: 85 4/5

SERBIN LOTS

Andreas Kappler	Andreas Mathiez
John Sucky	Peter Pampell
M. Matthiez	Carl Graf
Mary Kubitz	Johann Neumann
Charles Simank	John Jannasch

The difficulties of acquisition of land and the lateness of subdivision had delayed clearing and planting of the first crops. Unfortunately, the next two years were years of severe drought and although enough food was produced to maintain life, the profits needed to pay expenses and creditors were insufficient. Essential food and supplies were brought in by ox-cart from Brenham, seventy miles distant. Basic commodities such as flour cost twenty-four dollars per hundred pounds and corn sold for three dollars per bushel.[30] Nevertheless, the time not spent in cultivation and harvesting was applied to clearing land and building shelters.

Adequate housing was extremely important, especially during the first year as the Europeans became acclimatized to their new homeland. Yellow fever, malaria, and dysentery took a heavy toll of those individuals whose diets were not balanced and whose shelter was inadequate. So widespread was ill health that construction of the cabin for church, school, and parsonage was postponed until the fall, and the pastor continued living with the parishioners.

Although some settlers lived in dugouts along the creek bank, most erected small cabins of logs. The typical cabin was patterned after the southern-style dwelling called the dog-trot or dog-run cabin. Two cabins were erected about ten feet apart and the breezeway was covered by extending the roof of the two buildings. One cabin was used for cooking and eating while the other was reserved for sleeping. The passage helped cool the cabins and was used as a living area, especially in summer. Advantages of such construction lay in adaptation to the climate, and easy utilization of the logs of Texas trees—smaller than those in Europe. The pioneers could build a single room first, add the other cabin and breezeway as time permitted, and eventually attach a veranda for additional cooling. There were no wooden floors in the cabins; the structures were built directly on the ground. Placement of cabins was also different from what the migrants had known in Europe in that, instead of living in a village, each farmer built on his own acreage. Serbin, which became the village, was only for those people whose occupation was merchandising or processing farm goods.[31]

The purchase of the Delaplain League did not bring instant stability to Kilian either. While the other settlers were building their homes, Kilian was forced to continue living with members of the congregation. Drought placed pressure on the financial resources of the Wends, and little money was left for the church. Kilian waited until he believed most people had solved their immediate problems and then on October 14, 1855, aired his complaints to the congregation. He first reviewed the promises made in his call and pointed out where they had not been honored. He had not, for example, received the financial support they had promised, so he was forced to live as the very poorest. Kilian then notified the meeting that the Australian brethren desired him as their pastor and if the Texas congregation could not support him in keeping with pastoral office and status, he would leave.

Kilian preferred to stay in Texas and asked for a new call, signed by every member, that specified a salary and perquisites. Like the first arrangement the new call was to be terminated after one year, so that there could be renewed negotiations if Kilian discovered that living on the proposed amount was not possible. He also requested that the members construct a smokehouse for the parsonage and a pen for his pigs and cows and that they assist in preparation of his field and garden.[32]

Kilian stayed in Texas, having evidently arrived at an agreement. Three days after his address, Kilian moved into a cabin that was his home until his death in 1884. One of the two rooms served as the school and church until 1859, when the first church was erected. After that a kitchen and veranda were added to provide more comforts for the family. The following excerpts from Kilian's notes show the large amount of work involved in construction of Kilian's farmyard and the generous contribution of donated labor.[33]

> On September 7–8, 1855, George Merting and Johann Domaschk-Jurz hauled boards from Rabbsmill (400 feet of good boards; 300 feet of scrap).
>
> On September 20–21, Andreas Lowke and Johann Zieschank hauled 2,000 roof shingles from Mr. Cord at Rabbs Creek.
>
> On October 3, Ernst Adolph Moerbe hauled 300 feet of scrap lumber from Rabbsmill.
>
> On October 17, the pastor moved from Groeschel's home where he had lived since July, to the newly constructed house. Before then he had lived with the Polnik family. During the change of dwellings the pastor's possessions were moved by George Merting and Carl Lehmann.
>
> On October 26 blacksmith Schatte was paid for door hardware.
>
> On October 27 Kurijo received payment for whiskey and nails purchased for building of the parsonage. It was used by people from Rabbs Creek.
>
> On October 27, August Polnik and Johann Biar began the construction of the pastor's corncrib.
>
> On November 2–3, Matthaus Schmidt from Reichwalde worked alone on the construction. Because he had no assistance, he also split fence rails.
>
> On November 5, Christoph Kokel and Matthaus Schulze from Forstgen finished the pastor's corncrib.
>
> On November 21, George Merting and Matthaus Schmidt plowed the post oak sod near the pastor's home. Merting plowed and Schmidt drove the two yoke of oxen.
>
> On December 4 John Zieschank plowed the pastor's land using two yoke of oxen.

On December 6, Andreas Lowke plowed the pastor's land using his own and Domaschke-Jurz's oxen.

In October 1855 August Dube and Jacob Moerbe had cut the logs for the smokehouse;

so on February 4, 1856 Matthaus, George, and Christoph Schellnick and Matthaus Mroske split and peeled the logs; and

On February 5, Johann Domaschk and George Lorentsk split and peeled the remaining logs that were needed.

On February 6, Johann Urban, George Bamsch and George Iselt prepared the elevation for the smokehouse. Urban and Bamsch both provided a yoke of oxen and hauled logs in the afternoon.

On February 7, the smokehouse was erected. The workers were Johann Merting, blacksmith Christoph Schatte, Carl Traugott Wenke, Johann Pilak and Christoph Wuensche who worked for Michael Urban.

On February 8 the raising of the smokehouse was completed up to the rafters. The workers were Johann Domaschk, George Lorentsk, George Hocker, and Johann Hohle.

On February 9, Matth. Schuster worked for one-half day.

On February 11, Mattheus Wagner, Ernst Moerbe, and Johann Matthiez made laths and prepared beams.

On February 12, Johann Urban, working with Wagner, and Christoph Kokel cut out the doors and attached the laths.

On February 13, George Merting and Johann Hattas finished attaching the laths and began roofing.

On February 14, Michael Kurijo worked on the roof.

On February 15, Carl Lehmann, Johann Dube, and August Dube prepared boards and worked on the roof.

On February 18, August Groeschel, August Polnik, and George Iselt, working with Matth. Wukash, made shingles, worked on the roof, and made the door.

On February 19, it rained.

On February 20, Zischang and Andreas Lowke made shingles.

On February 21, Matth. Domasch-Jurz and Jacob Morebe worked on the gables.

On February 23, August Groeschel almost finished the smokehouse and made two school benches.

On February 26, Peter Fritsche finished the smokehouse.

Kilian's record continued from February 12 to April 1 with a list of the men who split logs for the fence. During this time four thousand rails were split with a quota of one hundred rails per person per day. Most of the work on Kilian's homestead, with the exception of the well, was completed prior to spring planting, and the well waited until the following fall.

The Texas Farm

During the time when the Lusatian peasants were adjusting their thinking to the Texas setting, they also were forced to modify their ways of making a living. For the sake of survival they had to learn quickly which crops were suited to the new environment and what kind of care they required. Some experimentation was carried out with familiar crops, but the Wends generally imitated experienced Texas farmers who had already decided on the most successful types of agriculture.

The climate of Texas was both warmer and wetter than that of Lusatia, but because of higher temperatures the evaporation rate was greater and summer droughts were not uncommon. The temperatures, averaging almost twenty degrees (Fahrenheit) higher than in Lusatia, meant a longer growing season of 230 days and directly influenced the Wends' agricultural decisions. The average temperature in January was 51°F, and in July 84°F. The average annual rainfall was 35 inches. Farming in Texas was still farming, and the Texas Wends continued to be agriculturalists just as in Europe, but practically everything else was different.

The Wends adopted corn (maize) almost immediately, and for each census period over 90 percent of the farmers grew some corn. Corn, relatively unknown in Lusatia, became the staple for the Wendish diet just as it had been for the Indian and the frontier American, and also served as feed for the farm animals. Almost immediately after landing, Kilian learned to grind corn by hand, and the household baked corn bread daily.[34] The total corn production for each Wendish farm was not high, and at no time did the Wends equal the production of their neighbors in Bastrop and Lee counties or the Germans in Austin County (Table 1). A small surplus may have been sold, but corn was primarily for home consumption, not for cash sale.[35]

The Wends also readily adopted cotton, another completely unfamiliar crop.[36] While corn provided nourishment, cotton was grown primarily for revenue. Since initially concern was to grow food, in 1860 only 73 percent of the Wends grew cotton, but over time their cotton production increased so that by 1880 they were producing almost as much as their neighbors. Cotton demanded hand labor, and women and children had to help in the fields to make the crop profitable because in its first ten years the Wendish settlement competed with slave labor. Cotton acreage was so heavily dependent on the availability of workers, however, that the end of slavery and the break-

Table 1. Production of Corn and Cotton by Population Groups

Item	Year	Wends	Texans	Germans
Corn	1860	34.9 (100%)	274.8 (99%)	198.0 (90%)
bushels per farm	1870	141.2 (98%)	433.8 (94%)	256.0 (98%)
and percentage of	1880	75.7 (92%)	134.9 (96%)	263.0 (100%)
farms reporting				
Cotton	1860	1.6 (73%)	15.7 (51%)	7.4 (83%)
bales per farm and	1870	5.3 (98%)	11.7 (92%)	6.4 (98%)
percentage of farms	1880	4.9 (95%)	5.2 (98%)	7.7 (99%)
reporting				

SOURCE: U.S. agricultural census for Bastrop (1860, 1870), Fayette (1870, 1880), and Lee (1880) counties.

ing up of plantations reduced production for most large farmers, while the cotton acreage of the Wends increased.

The remainder of the agricultural crops were grown on a much smaller scale, primarily to meet family needs. The Wends grew both the familiar white and the totally unknown sweet potato, but the amounts were generally small. When the census enumerator recorded potato production at all, the total yield per farm for either kind was seldom more than ten bushels. Another new crop that some Wends adopted was sorghum. Its purpose was to provide the family with an inexpensive sweetener, but seldom was production over fifteen gallons of molasses per farm. The 1870 census was the first to indicate the Wends' cultivation of sorghum; its acceptance was not as rapid as that of corn and cotton.

The other crops grown by the Wends were wheat and rye. Both were familiar from Europe, but neither grain was well suited to Bastrop County. The twenty-six Wends who planted these small grains in 1859 produced only sixty-eight bushels of rye and sixty-two bushels of wheat, and in the years that followed, production remained small.

While the climate limited options in the choice of crops, more alternatives were available with animal husbandry. During the first two decades in America, the Wends relied on oxen as much as on horses to supplement human muscle. Oxen specialized in plowing and pulling heavy freight loads, while horses were used for riding and pulling light wagons and carriages. Oxen were the main draft animals in Europe and their relatively low purchase cost and durability made them popular in Texas as well. The Wends were distinctive in their use of oxen because on the average more Wends reported oxen than did their neighbors, and they continued to work with these animals until near the close of the nineteenth century.

Table 2. Possession of Draft Animals by Population Groups

Item	Year	Wends	Texans	Germans
Oxen	1860	2.8 (85%)	5.4 (73%)	5.0 (76%)
number per farm and per-	1870	3.5 (83%)	5.6 (74%)	5.0 (66%)
centage of farms reporting	1880	2.5 (36%)	3.3 (32%)	4.0 (15%)
Horses	1860	2.0 (92%)	7.4 (94%)	4.0 (95%)
number per farm and per-	1870	3.2 (95%)	7.1 (97%)	4.0 (98%)
centage of farms reporting	1880	3.0 (96%)	3.2 (97%)	4.0 (99%)
Mules and asses	1860	1.0 (12%)	4.5 (26%)	2.0 (19%)
number per farm and per-	1870	1.7 (16%)	3.9 (48%)	2.0 (33%)
centage of farms reporting	1880	1.7 (18%)	1.8 (19%)	2.0 (46%)

SOURCE: U.S. agricultural census for Bastrop (1860, 1870), Fayette (1870, 1880), and Lee (1880) counties.

Speed, provided by horses, was desirable for transportation at all times, but this was especially true after 1870 when farm machinery began to be designed for more rapid movement. Although more Wends reported ownership of horses in 1870 than in 1860, the Wendish farmers owned proportionately more oxen than horses. A shift took place between 1870 and 1880, when average ownership of oxen dropped by one ox per farm and the farmers reporting oxen fell to 36 percent from 83 percent in 1870. Continued use of oxen can be ascribed to the Wends' resistance to change as well as shortage of capital for buying horses and new equipment. While the Wends showed their preference for oxen, they owned few mules and always reported fewer than did their neighbors.

In keeping with their custom in Europe, nearly all Wends owned milk cattle that produced milk products for the household, butter for sale, and calves for the herd. There was little dairying in Bastrop County, and the milk, after it had been separated from the cream, was fed to the swine and chickens. Butter was a widespread source of revenue, but unfortunately the whims of the census enumerator prevented complete returns. One of the enumerators in 1880 did record butter production, and from his list of thirty-nine farmers, thirty-five reported an average annual butter production of 258 pounds. While the Wends disclosed fewer milk cows in 1860 than did their neighbors, by 1880 the difference was insignificant. Without milking machines and without refrigeration there was a limit to the profitability of working with milk cows.

Although the Wends settled near the frontier where one would expect many range cattle, the census showed that they had few and always lagged behind their neighbors. Grazing required large invest-

Table 3. Possession of Cattle and Swine by Population Groups

Item	Year	Wends	Texans	Germans
Milk cows	1860	4.5 (100%)	13.4 (89%)	11.0 (97%)
number per farm and per-	1870	7.8 (100%)	10.1 (95%)	9.0 (99%)
centage of farms reporting	1880	6.6 (97%)	6.6 (92%)	7.0 (98%)
Other cattle	1860	11.7 (100%)	78.3 (87%)	45.0 (92%)
number per farm and per-	1870	24.0 (98%)	51.0 (89%)	25.0 (87%)
centage of farms reporting	1880	13.4 (95%)	20.9 (91%)	17.0 (92%)
Swine	1860	10.2 (80%)	35.9 (79%)	12.0 (85%)
number per farm and per-	1870	13.7 (92%)	28.9 (93%)	11.0 (84%)
centage of farms reporting	1880	9.5 (94%)	16.0 (75%)	9.0 (91%)

SOURCE: U.S. agricultural census for Bastrop (1860, 1870), Fayette (1870, 1880), and Lee (1880) counties.

ments in land and cattle but few workers, whereas the Wends had the laborers and not the investment capital. They turned to farming immediately, while their neighbors carried on both grazing and farming and then slowly sold off portions of grazing land or began cultivating it themselves. Grazing was important to the Wends, nevertheless, and cattle numbers on their farms for the ten-year period from 1860 to 1870 reflect the growth of small herds in an environment supporting grazing. The decline of grazing stock for the next ten years, from 1870 to 1880, illustrates increased clearing of grazing land for cultivation.

The Wends raised hogs in Europe and continued the practice in Texas. The animals had a high rate of reproduction and in Texas required as little care as did cattle. Hogs roamed the woods foraging for acorns and roots, and survived without shelter. As the land became more densely occupied, the number of hogs per family declined and was limited to what a farmer could retain within a fence and feed with corn. Although hogs were at times sold for cash, the relatively small size of their carcass made them ideal for farmyard butchering and household meat.

Few Wends in Texas kept sheep, but neither did their German and other neighbors. The census forms also show very few barnyard fowl, but that reflects failure of the census enumerator rather than absence of the fowl. Chickens, ducks, and geese provided eggs and down, and their meat was important in summer when the entire bird could be eaten and there was no need to preserve the remainder.

In both raising crops and caring for animals, the Wends showed a dramatic adjustment to the ways of the new land. Like their neighbors, they specialized in cotton and corn, giving up wheat and rye. In those instances where the Wends showed some distinctiveness, there was either no pressing need for change, or, as in the use of oxen, financial limitations or traditions prevented rapid adjustment.

A significant difference existed, nevertheless, between the Wends' agricultural wealth and that of their neighbors. The expenses of migration had depleted the Wends' limited resources and therefore their land purchases and holdings were small. By the 1860 census the Wends had worked the land for only five years while others who had preceded them to Texas had had the advantage of time to accumulate more land and wealth. The fact that Wend farmers had improved an average of over sixteen acres of land in five years shows that they equalled the land-clearing skill of other frontiersmen. Even though they increased their improved lands to twenty-eight acres over the next twenty years and by 1880 had narrowed the gap between their holdings and those of their neighbors, they still farmed the smallest acreages in the area.

A superficial examination of the statistics on unimproved land leads to the conclusion that the Wends made economic strides surpassing those of other farmers. While Wends owned an average of 80 unimproved acres in 1860 and other Bastrop County residents held 288 acres, by 1880 Wend farmers owned 168 and their Lee County neighbor only 140 acres. This looks impressive for the Wends, but not all unimproved land was worth improving and this category in the census information is not a good indicator of economic growth. Unimproved land was generally associated with livestock, but, although typically the Wends had more unimproved land than non-Wendish neighbors, the Wends owned less livestock. Either the neighbors overstocked their grazing land, or the Wends' lands could not support as many cattle. The Wends never were large-scale graziers, and the dense timber cover as well as the low fertility of the soil prevented heavy grazing.

More important indicators of agricultural wealth are the value of farm production and the value of the farm itself. No statistics were collected for the value of farm production in 1860. The 1870 census reported that the Wends produced only half as many farm goods as their neighbors. By 1880 the difference had narrowed, but the Wends still produced much less. Their farms also were consistently worth less than those of their neighbors, and even though the Wends again narrowed the differences over the period from 1860 to 1880, the typical Wend's farm was worth $233 less in 1880 than the neighbor's.

Throughout those twenty years the Wends held the lowest position in land value, value of livestock, and agricultural productivity. Even

Table 4. Farm Acreages and Agricultural Values by Population Groups

Item	Year	Wends	Texans	Germans
Improved acres per farm	1860	16.3	63.1	26.0
	1870	23.8	64.1	33.0
	1880	28.2	35.6	43.0
Unimproved acres per farm	1860	80.0	287.5	143.0
	1870	147.1	349.3	150.0
	1880	167.6	140.4	141.0
Value of livestock per farm	1860	$257	$1,160	$626
	1870	$231	$551	$398
	1880	$193	$250	$283
Average value of total farm production	1860	—	—	—
	1870	$406	$897	$894
	1880	$308	$331	$547
Average cash value of farm	1860	$194	$2,239	$1,162
	1870	$763	$1,883	$1,405
	1880	$795	$1,028	$1,664
Average value of farm production per acre	1860	—	—	—
	1870	$1.91	$2.46	$4.89
	1880	$1.48	$2.34	$2.99
Average cash value of farm per acre	1860	$2.07	$7.90	$6.88
	1870	$4.83	$4.71	$7.67
	1880	$4.12	$7.44	$9.09

SOURCE: U.S. agricultural census for Bastrop (1860, 1870), Fayette (1870, 1880), and Lee (1880) counties.

when the smaller size of their farms is considered, their land did not command the price per acre of their neighbor's acre, and the production per acre was lower. Germans, for example, produced twice as much agricultural material per acre, and native-born Texans approximately 30 percent more. Was this testimony to the nature of the Wends, or was it the result of starting out with less desirable land in smaller amounts and then being restricted by this handicap?

There is some evidence that the Wends were satisfied with less, did not make improvements as readily, and delayed in adopting advanced methods. Wendish homes were unpainted and contained fewer furnishings and comforts than those of the Germans. Even thirty years after the colony had been established, many still lived in small log houses. They continued to use inefficient wooden sleds for hauling because wagons were too expensive, and their orchards were not carefully tended. It could well be that their position in Europe had led

Wendish wedding party, Texas, circa 1880–90. *Courtesy Marie Kilian Luecke Collection, Texas Wendish Heritage Museum Archives*

them to expect little from life and that instead of spending money on comforts and improvements, they were satisfied with a basic life and some security for old age.[37]

On the other hand, the low productivity of the Serbin soil may have restricted growth. The effect of soil fertility on the Wends' livelihood can be tested by considering what happened to those Wends who farmed land away from Serbin. Already before 1870 some Wends settled across the border in Fayette County. Although the distance from Serbin was small enough for them to return to Serbin for worship, the agricultural conditions were better because the topsoil was deeper and more fertile, and the area along the creeks and the Colorado River was more easily tilled.

In 1880 the agricultural productivity of the Fayette County Wends was equal to or greater than that of the Texans and the Germans in most categories, especially in cotton production. Their total farm production per acre in 1880 was $3.25, twenty-five cents higher than that of the Germans. One could still argue that the more aggressive Wends migrated out of Serbin, but the comparison supports the proposition that soil fertility was more important than cultural disposition.[38]

A reasonable view would be that Wends were just as industrious as Germans and Texans. Exceptionally ambitious as well as indolent persons existed in all three groups, but in general the farmers were similar, especially as they adopted American attitudes. More significant was the initial 1855 selection of land that was not highly fertile and required the demanding process of clearing trees.

Another glance at the average value of the farm per acre is instructive (Table 4). In 1860 Serbin land was worth little in comparison to others lands, although the Wends had doubled the value of the land in just five years. Once the trees were cleared and the better soil placed into cultivation, the value per acre increased proportionately, but never equaled that of the Germans' or Texans' lands. This difference was related more to the soil productivity than the improvements on the farm. It is easier to make a productive farm out of good soil than out of barren soil, and purchase of the Delaplain League proved to be a poor investment. Economic disparity existed throughout the period with the Wends on the bottom, although they did narrow the gap over the decades.

Women and children worked in the fields with the men and provided the extra effort needed to make a living from the unyielding soil. They improved their position not only through hard work but through frugality and self-denial. Thrift was a trait the Wends knew well in Europe, and it enabled them to exist in Texas. The agricultural response was more a matter of agricultural environment than a reflection of ethnic distinctiveness, and the Wends' adjustments in the economic sphere were rapid.

The low productivity of the soil prevented the dense settlement of a Wendish colony, and just as in Australia, the Wends scattered in search of more farm lands or city jobs. Only fertile land could have supported intensive agriculture, and only then could the Wendish settlement have maintained a compact, cohesive existence.

THE FIRST SCHISM, 1858–67

The first internal controversy to threaten the unity of the congregation was that provoked by the *Stundenchristen* who sought a religious life beyond the worship service on Sunday morning, and set aside specific hours during the week for religious observance. At these little cottage meetings, often held without the benefit of clergy, the devout read sermons, discussed the Bible, and sang hymns.

The *Stundenchristen* movement emanated from a double tradition. The one root was Pietism, stressing the role of each believer being his own priest and in turn stimulating the development of lay leadership for the religious community. It also encouraged religious emotionalism in the worship service in contrast to a formal, ritualistic observance and fully expected visible results in the daily lives of the members. Many of Kilian's flock had been influenced by the pietist approach in Europe.[39]

A second root, that of separation from the state church, reflected more a course of action than a set of beliefs, and Kilian himself, during his Prussian ministry, was a separatist, as were most of the 1854 emigrants. Although Kilian did not leave the state church because of Pietism, separatism also emphasized lay participation and provided a method of handling his scattered flock.[40]

When Kilian left his home in Weigersdorf to visit his followers, he performed the role of the visiting pastor who administered the sacraments and exercised the authority of the trained clergyman, but when he continued on his circuit the initiative for religious leadership reverted to the layman. In Texas, however, the situation was changed, and Kilian became the official pastor both because there was no state church and because he had the call from the congregation. Separatism which he once fostered was undesirable in Texas because it would weaken the congregation.

Some members of Kilian's flock had been attracted to the practices of the *Stundenchristen* before their departure from Europe, and their concept of congregational practices conflicted with that of the majority. The strain between these two views surfaced at Serbin during the formulation of the congregational constitution and policies, but nothing serious took place until 1856, when a German Methodist, the Rev. E. Schneider, conducted a camp meeting several miles south of Serbin in the Pin Oak and Rabbs Creek area. In addition to Sunday services, the Methodists held weeknight sessions and prayer meetings to which they invited their Wendish neighbors. Some Wends, especially the Saxons, were impressed with the Methodist worship. At least one woman received the Spirit and, in an ecstasy, expressed the desire to be taken to heaven. Kilian attributed this "waywardness" to the absence of a struggle for a true church in Saxony. The names of the Wendish enthusiasts were not mentioned, but judging from the initials in a Kilian letter to Schuermann of Australia, Johann Urban of Rackel and Johann Noack of Gröditz were probably two leaders.[41]

The *Stundenchristen* asked Kilian to introduce similar opportunities for religious experiences into the Serbin congregation and Kilian consented. The meetings were held every Wednesday and Friday evening and many from the congregation attended. Although he permitted group discussion and the prayer of a layman at the close, Kilian adhered to a formal procedure and expounded on the less than exciting *Augsburg Confession*. No awakening spirits rose, and the inclement spring weather further chilled the enthusiasm. Attendance sagged and Kilian ended the sessions at Easter, 1858, six months after they had been started.[42]

But shortly thereafter, with further stimulation from the Methodists, the movement revived and Kilian took the matter to the congregation. Still searching for a visible sign of the Spirit's power, the emotionalists asked Kilian for more law and less Gospel in the sermon, with hellfire and brimstone so that there would be an awakening. Kilian preached, but it was against those persons who would run after awakenings from one church to another, and he especially attacked the legalism that demanded outward signs of holiness. There could be no reconciliation.

The final split took place on October 16, 1858, but instead of forming a Methodist church, the dissidents founded another Lutheran congregation. Kilian explained that these individuals could not accept the Methodist views of the sacraments, so different from what they had always believed. He was in a sense happy to see them go because it was a sifting of his congregation, and he was pleased that they formed a Lutheran, rather than a Methodist, church. He was not happy with the fact that they continued in fellowship with the Methodists and that they affiliated with the Texas Synod, which he considered too much like the church of Prussia with its Calvinist flavor.[43] Kilian also admitted to great sadness over the split because he viewed it as the result of hatred toward him. He saw a parallel between his work and that of Moses, who similarly made enemies leading people into a new land, and saw a "gang of Korah" arise and try to assume leadership.[44]

The splinter group, led by thirteen men, built a church on the outskirts of Serbin and called their congregation St. Peter's Church of Rabbsville. In 1860 St. Peter's was formally admitted into the Texas Synod and obtained the services of Pastor J. George Lieb of Round Top. The congregation did not grow, however; its membership never exceeded forty-five communicants. Only German was preached at St. Peter's, so few Wends were drawn away from Kilian's congregation. Pastor Lieb accepted a call to Austin in 1864 and after the departure of the second pastor, C. C. Rudi, St. Peter's could not find another resident pastor. On November 3, 1866, the congregation received title to 54-⅓ acres of land from Johann and Johanna Urban for $66.30, but the following year they voted to return to Kilian's church and deeded that land to the mother church for $1.00, provided that it would be used for church and school purposes.

Even though forty-five communicants had withdrawn from Kilian's congregation in 1858, others joined, and a larger church building was needed. Quite possibly competition from St. Peter's may have hastened the action. In rapid succession, yet with conservative fiscal outlook, the voters, on August 7, 1859, decided to build and collected five dollars from every member by September 29. Working assiduously with donated labor, they constructed the building and dedicated the new structure on Christmas Day. The frame building, fifty feet long and twenty-five feet wide, was dedicated by Kilian with three sermons: in English, German, and Wendish.[45]

Joining the Nation

The year 1860 was a significant one for the Wendish community, because it closed out a period of tenuous local existence and opened the community to national events. The Wends had been in Texas for five years, during which time they had located land, built homes, planted crops, raised children, and constructed a new church building. Their spiritual leader, Pastor Kilian, in 1860 traveled to St. Louis, where he attended the national convention of the Missouri Synod. Also in 1860, the United States established a post office in the community and changed its name officially from Low Pinoak Settlement to Serbin. During the summer months the census enumerator combed the woods for settlers, counting the Wends into the United States population for the first time. Then, in November, 1860, when the American people elected Abraham Lincoln to the presidency, the stage was set for a national war.

Although the Wends had not departed from Europe because of opposition to military service, they did not desire to become embroiled in a war in America. Taking their cue from the Germans, the Wends opposed secession and made no rush to the colors. This conflict was not their war; they owned no slaves and no plantations. The folklore of Serbin contains stories of how men worked in the fields on moonlit nights and hid by day to avoid the recruiting officer. When the nights were dark and the field work heavy, the men donned women's clothing and worked during the day.[46] But it was only a matter of time before the Wends were apprehended under the conscription acts and enrolled into the Confederate Army or the Texas Militia.

The majority were recruited into Waul's Legion, which was organized at Brenham in the summer of 1862. Waul's Legion served at Vicksburg, Tennessee, and in Arkansas and Louisiana. Five young Wends lost their lives in the campaign of mid-1863, and Kilian recorded their names in the congregational Death Register. They were

Ernst Bernstein and Maria Kulke, Warda, 1891. *Courtesy Texas Wendish Heritage Museum*

Johann Kasper, Christoph Lowke, Johann Noack, George Prellop, and Matthes Mitschke. Some newly enrolled young men such as Jacob Moerbe were soon discharged on the basis of a surgeon's certificate, and others deserted. A few men, including Charles Michalk, left for Mexico in the summer of 1862 and joined the First Texas Cavalry of the United States under the command of the future governor of Texas, Edmund J. Davis. Michalk was captured in the closing weeks of the war and imprisoned near Hempstead, not far from Serbin.[47]

The war, coupled with a drought, was especially disheartening to Kilian, and in the early months of 1861 he commented that the people's courage was almost gone. His communication with friends in Australia and Europe suffered from the Union blockade, and his letters had to be channeled through a German firm in Matamoros, Mexico. As a pastor in a rural community he was isolated enough from his colleagues, but the war made it worse; even the Missouri Synod leadership was located on the enemy side. Near the end of the war in 1864 Kilian requested a position in Europe that would take him away from Serbin. He expressed his unhappiness with the war as well as the controversy in the congregation.

While dislocation and emotional depression were associated with the war, so was prosperity. Cotton was in demand in both Mexico and Houston. The Wends profited not only from better prices, but also from freighting cotton bales. They returned from the long journeys with goods and gold, and even Kilian in a letter in 1865 commented on the people's prosperity.[48] Most of Texas and all of the Serbin area was spared the devastation of war, and peace was achieved in 1865. A new attitude pervaded the Wendish community after 1865, because the period changed them from Europeans living in America into Americans.

The Second Schism, 1870–1914

As Serbin became less isolated and the Wends came into contact with other ethnic groups, it was almost inevitable that there would be more conflict. Progressive Wends and Germans considered the language of the future to be German, while Kilian and his supporters preferred Wendish. The conflict would not be resolved in Serbin until Kilian's Wendish church made its way slowly into the German language track to catch up with the more progressive group so that there was no longer any reason for separation. The episode illustrates how a relatively minor matter based on speed of acculturation can jeopardize

Picking cotton on the Carl Benjamin Weise farm, Lee County. *Courtesy Texas Wendish Heritage Museum Archives*

the inherent stability of a homogeneous group. While this controversy, at the turn of the century, resulted in the adoption of German, a similar conflict, though not as serious, took place later in the twentieth century, between the use of German and English.

The Kilian congregation had never been purely Wendish, because a few of the *Ben Nevis* migrants were married to Germans. More Germans migrated into the Serbin area in 1861, and by 1869 88 of the 581 congregation members were from all-German households or from mixed German-Wend families. This was not a large portion; obviously there were many purely Wendish families who preferred German to Wendish.[49] While most of the Germans could not speak Wendish, most of the Wends knew German, and Kilian could meet the religious needs of both groups just as he had in Europe. Kilian's training had been in German; he preached in German and kept the church records in German.

At first, beginning around 1862, German was preached every six weeks; then in 1867 German services were held every month and on the third feast-day of Christmas and Easter and soon thereafter on every Sunday. Congregational meetings were conducted in Wendish until 1866, when separate meetings for the Wends and Germans were held, but in August, 1867, the decision was made to conduct joint meetings in German.[50] The language problem was being solved, and there was no reason why the practices could not have been continued in harmony. Language, however, became the focal point for several old and new tensions and the split would not be healed until the old irritations as well as the conflict over language could be settled.

Several writers have argued that the Wends migrated to Texas in order to establish a colony where their language and culture could be practised without opposition. Much of this claim is based on hindsight, and nowhere in the documents is this reason stated.[51] The problem the 1854 migrants faced was the difficulty of maintaining an independent church in Europe, and their solution was to relocate their

Johann Kilian family, circa 1865. *Courtesy Texas Wendish Heritage Museum Archives*

Teacher Gerhard Kilian with his family at home, 1899. *Courtesy Texas Wendish Heritage Museum Archives*

church to Texas with Kilian as their pastor. Would they have decided against migration if Kilian had rejected the call? The 1853 group went on its own. Possibly the 1854 settlers would have accepted a German-speaking pastor whose theology was suitable, as migrants did in Australia; the fact that they were able to obtain a Wend was simply that much better. Because Kilian was a Wend and the people were too, it was logical to maintain the language and practices just as they had been in Europe, but to migrate in order to establish a haven for these things was not the purpose.

Wendish language and culture had always been under pressure; how would migration have solved that problem? Those Wends who were most conscious of their heritage did not migrate, but remained and fought for their program in their homeland, whereas many of the Wends in the Kilian congregation preferred the change to German. The language controversy was not one that undermined the unity and purpose of the settlement, because maintenance of the

Butchering for the beef club, Vernon. Christian Schoppa is holding the knife.
Courtesy Clara Schulz Bernstein

Wendish way of life was not the reason for migration. The unifying force was the Lutheran church, and disagreement was over the way Lutheran teachings and practices should be expressed. Kilian and the majority believed that no change was necessary, while the Germans and some Wends believed the use of German was better. Kilian compared the situation to that of Abraham and Lot. They parted ways because of practice, but did not separate in philosophy or fundamentals.[52] The second split within the Serbin congregation belongs to the history of the Wends because it illustrates what was happening to them and what they all would become by the time of World War I.

The earlier attacks of the New Ulm Wends, the *Stundenchristen* episode, and the language controversy all built up the tension, but the second split began in 1866 when the Rev. Gottfried Lehnigk, a Wend from Lower Lusatia and a graduate from the seminary in St. Louis, came to Texas. Pastor Lehnigk, who had restricted his ministerial activities because of poor health, left Missouri for Serbin to become the teacher. Kilian, who had conducted school for the children since landing in Texas, had not been called as the teacher and was willing to relinquish the position. If Lehnigk's health improved he could become the Serbin pastor, and Kilian could return to Europe or accept a different parish. As a teacher Lehnigk was a success, but his support for the St. Peter's group actually retarded the dissolution of the congregation. He attended the Chicago convention of the Western District in 1867 to present testimony regarding what he considered to be Kilian's laxity in church matters, but instead of returning he remained in the north and sent back a letter of apology.

Kilian had enjoyed his retirement from the classroom, and upon Lehnigk's departure he wrote to request a teacher from the Teachers' Seminary in Addison, Illinois. There were not enough candidates, however, and Kilian resumed teaching duties. Having experienced the benefits of a full-time teacher, members now charged that Kilian was not a capable teacher. Kilian responded by stating that he never had been called to be the teacher and did not claim to be one. There was no alternative, however, and Kilian continued as pedagogue.[53]

The next year the Serbin church again requested a teacher, and this time the assignment was made. On August 31, 1868, Ernst Leubner was installed as teacher and organist. As a German he was required to teach only German and English in school, but he was expected to learn Wendish hymns and versicles to accompany the congregational singing. The initial call also had included the position of cantor, but because of the language problem he was not appointed to his office, possibly pending his learning more Wendish.

While Kilian was happy to be relieved of teaching, the lay organist and cantor, Carl Teinert, did not care to relinquish his position. He had held it in Germany and was thoroughly acquainted with the Wendish language and music. Instead of permitting Teinert to remain as cantor, Leubner expected to occupy the position because of his call. In addition he reflected an anti-Wendish bias, in that instead of learning Wendish, he hoped to teach the Wends how to sing in German. The pro-Wendish element stood behind Teinert and the pro-German behind Luebner, with neither side willing to yield.

The language problem in the school was a clear victory for the Germans because instruction was to be in German and English. All Wendish children would learn German, therefore, although until they knew German well, Kilian would instruct them twice a week in Wendish. In the church it was another matter, and the older Wends were not about

St. Peter's School, Serbin, circa 1900. Teacher Ernst August Weise is in the light coat. The building was constructed largely of wood on cedar posts. *Courtesy Texas Wendish Heritage Museum Archives*

to give up their mother tongue, just as the pro-German people did not care to learn Wendish.

There was an attempt to resolve the problem in the voters' assembly of June 27, 1869, but more hard feelings resulted. Kilian accepted advice not to attend the next meeting, but on August 8 he prepared a statement for the voters and told them this was a problem of both the spirit and the body. The spirit evidently was the ill will that had gone before, and the problem of the body was the conflict between Wendish and German ways (*Wendentum und Deutschtum*). Kilian supported the *Wendentum*.

Nothing was settled in the months that followed, so on May 22, 1870, Kilian resigned. The Wendish majority sent Kilian a new call in June and then, in September, asked for Leubner's resignation. Kilian accepted the call and also took over Leubner's position in the classroom. The Germans, therefore, organized themselves into a congregation and called the Rev. John Pallmer, a Missouri Synod pastor from Baden, Missouri. Pallmer was a Wend, who, after working for an orphanage near Hamburg, had migrated on his own to America. On his arrival he attended the seminary at St. Louis and graduated in 1869.

The formal separation from Kilian's congregation took place on September 23, 1870, and in October the new congregation, also named St. Peter's, received the land given earlier for $1.00 by the first St. Peter's, in addition to $623.53, and the old church organ. They agreed to share the cemetery, and any work the secessionists had contributed to Kilian's new stone church would be paid back. The fact that the church was named St. Peter's and that they could expect a return of the land indicated that many of the people who broke away were those who had left earlier. Pastor Pallmer was installed by Kilian and served in both German and Wendish languages until his death in 1873.[54]

It was during this controversy that Kilian's church changed its name from "The First Sorbian Lutheran Church in Texas" to "The First Wendish and German St. Paul's Evangelical Lutheran Church, Unaltered Augsburg Confession, in Serbin, Lee County." In the early years of the division his congregation built the finest monument to the Wends of Texas. The new church building had been started in 1866 before the schism, but the language controversy had delayed its completion. The building was opened finally in 1871 and is still in use.

Simple Gothic in design and similar to the Kotitz church, it is seventy feet long and forty feet wide with seating for six hundred people. With the exception of four tall Gothic windows on the north and south walls, the outside of the building is plain, although the stone walls, two and a half feet thick at the base, impart a feeling of strength and stability. The distinctive interior of the church has a balcony that completely circles the building. The pulpit is part of the balcony and stands above the altar, while the organ is opposite the pulpit, above the entrance. In the days of segregated worship men sat on the balcony and women on the main floor.

The two Serbin churches, St. Paul's and St. Peter's, both serving Germans and Wends, remained separate until 1914, when members closed St. Peter's church and returned to St. Paul's. Teinert, one of the participants, had left in 1873 to organize a new church in his neighborhood of Warda; Kilian had died in 1884; and by 1914 German had become the common language for most of the people of Serbin.[55] Good will had existed between the congregations before 1914, so that joint mission festivals were held from 1883 to 1889, and in 1886 they served as co-hosts for the Southern District Convention of the Missouri Synod. The peak membership for St. Peter's was approximately 212 communicant members in the period from 1890 to 1900. After that, migration to other areas led to a decline in the population.

Pastor Herman T. Kilian, who facilitated the reunion, served from the time of his father's death in 1884 until his own in 1920. Wendish services died with him, and his successor, the Rev. Herman Schmidt, although a Wend, used the language only in private devotions and conversation.[56] The church was an institution of ethnic stability if it could be maintained as a Wendish church, but it could become an agency for change if it lost its ethnic identity.

Further Migration from Europe

The migration to Texas, in contrast to that to Australia, flourished after 1865 and continued until the end of the century. Nearness to America, inexpensive fares, and the large number of Wends in Texas all helped to sustain the flow of immigrants. Because the post-1865 migrants traveled as individuals or in small groups and because Texas had become more of a "civilized" region, their migration was not as dramatic as that of 1854. The contribution of this wave of settlers cannot be ignored, however, and the number of migrants after 1865 totaled well over 600 and equaled the number of Wends who had migrated before 1860. The later migrants came from the same towns in Upper Lusatia that had witnessed the earlier exodus, but there was a distinct shift in proportions northward to the villages of the Schleife and Spreewitz parishes. Tracing the movement of these later migrants is actually more difficult than for the earlier groups, because many of the passenger lists are missing. However, Wends migrated each year from 1866 to 1886, with peak years in 1869, when more than 105 left Lusatia, and 1881, when at least 51 left.

After landing at either Galveston or New York, migrants made their way to Serbin, where they generally became laborers or leaseholders with an established family. Many of them joined Kilian's church, and he recorded their presence at the Lord's Supper, their home town in Lusatia, and the place of residence in the Texas community. While many stayed at Serbin for the remainder of their lives, most settled in satellite communities such as Manheim and Warda and then followed other Wends as they migrated to various places in the state.[57]

The migration is significant because in the first place it shows the communication chain between the Texas Wends and their homeland; risk and anxiety were greatly reduced for these new migrants and their adjustment less difficult than that of the earlier settlers. It is also significant because it helped perpetuate the Wendish language and traditions in Texas and reinforced the association of the older community with Germany. The new Wends married the children of the earlier settlers and retarded Americanization by infusing the older society with European ways. So cohesive was the community that 75 percent of the children of the 1850s immigrants married Wends and, with a few exceptions who married Anglo-Americans, the remainder married Germans. Wendish culture in Texas was considerably more durable than in Australia for several reasons, but especially important was the influence of the new immigrants.

Expansion of the Wends

As a result of reproduction, continued immigration from Germany, and the limited productive capacity of the soil, the Wends left the Serbin area for better lands. A few settlers at Fedor (West Yegua Creek), such as Andreas Melde, never did own land near Serbin but purchased property about fifteen miles away in what was then Burleson County.[58] Later some families from Serbin and others directly from Europe joined the settlement. Not until 1870 did they decide to leave Kilian's congregation to form their own.

Kilian at first objected to the new congregation because he considered that part of his parish, but the distance was too great for convenient travel. George Boback, who had settled in Australia and then returned to Europe, had migrated to the Fedor area in 1869 and purchased more than three thousand acres of land. He donated fifty acres to the church and the congregation began construction of a building. The first pastor was Pallmer from St. Peter's and the first teacher was J. A. Proft, a Wend from Bautzen. Proft had been trained as a cabinetmaker but then studied at Hermannsburg, Hanover, and at the Practical Seminary in St. Louis. He happened to be living with his sister, Mrs. Johann Gruetzner, in the Fedor area when he was hired as the teacher. In 1871 he was installed as the resident pastor on condition that he conduct twelve Wendish services a year, of which four would be with the Lord's Supper.[59]

At first Proft and his family lived in some rooms attached to the church, but after the death of his wife and child, he built a home on a lot on the San Antonio Prairie, three miles away. Proft's own health was not sound and he was temporarily excused from teaching school. Because some dissatisfaction lingered over Proft's change of residence and the haphazard education of their children, the congregation eventually asked for Proft's resignation. Some Wends objected, realizing that they would be unable to obtain another Wendish pastor.

Frame home in Lee County. *Courtesy Maria Kilian Luecke Collection, Texas Wendish Heritage Museum Archives*

However they soon saw that their arguments supporting Proft, especially if he could not teach school, were not persuasive, so several Wends, including August Lehmann, joined Proft on the San Antonio Prairie and called him as their pastor. The new church, founded in 1876, was named Eben Ezer.[60]

The loss of membership from Fedor was small, and additional migrants joined, so that by 1884 the Fedor congregation had a membership of fifty families. Many of the Wends did not join Proft, being satisfied with German services. Fedor members included Melde, Doman, Domaschk, Lehmann, Jakob, Kunze, Noack, Pillack, Symank, Dube, Handrick, Polnick, Moerbe, Patschke, Wuensche, Winkler, Falke, Zschech, Urban, Michalk, and Krautschick.

Ebenezer at Manheim, five miles south of Fedor, was founded in 1888 and included such families as Teinert, Schkade, Kieschnick, Birnbaum, Proske, and Noack. In 1890 they sold the first church building, but kept the cemetery, and re-established the congregation four miles toward the southwest. Manheim was a particularly popular area for the new Wends who came to Texas, even though German was the language of the congregation after Proft's departure for Sherman, Texas, in 1877.

As the land around Fedor became more densely occupied, a migration began to Thorndale, twenty-five miles north. August Polnick was the first to move, in 1882, and Carl Michalk followed in 1883. Eventually thirty families followed, and in 1890 a church was founded by families with such names as Moerbe, Urban, Simank, Weiser, and Wuensche. Other members of these same families left in 1911 for Bishop, 180 miles to the south.

Another stream of settlers left Fedor and Manheim for Lincoln, Loebau, and Dime Box. Lincoln was only three miles east of the original Eben Ezer congregation and was founded in 1886 with such families as Medack, Schkade, Proske, Niemtschk, Leitko, and Symank. Loebau, seven miles north of Giddings, was founded in 1896 and in-

The Kurio log cabin. This cabin has been relocated to the grounds of the Texas Wendish Heritage Museum. *Courtesy Daphne Dalton Garrett*

cluded such families as Beisert, Matthiez, and Iselt. Finally, Dime Box, seven miles farther north, was settled in the last years of the nineteenth century by Fedor families including Zschech, Dube, and Jatzlau.

The origin of the Warda congregation was surrounded by extended controversy. Several Wend families had settled in the Rabbs Creek area in the early days of the migration, but the distance of five to ten miles did not prevent them from participating in the Serbin religious community. They even sent their children to the Serbin school, some boarding with families near Serbin. One of the settlers, Karl Teinert, who was sympathetic to the problem of sending children to Serbin, supported the establishment of a branch school. Finding a suitable teacher, however, was impossible so Teinert and the others sent their children back to Serbin where they studied under a new teacher, Gerhard Kilian, son of the pastor. Even though Kilian and Teinert had worked together for many years and had stood together on the language issue, hard feelings grew when Gerhard Kilian was also in-

St. Paul Lutheran Church, Serbin, 1988. Descendants of the Wends walk from their school to waiting buses and automobiles in front of the sanctuary, which was constructed in 1871.

Texas Wendish Heritage Museum, Serbin, 1988. The newly completed central structure unifies a complex that includes two display and exhibit buildings and two restored log cabins.

stalled as organist. In 1873 Teinert and seven others asked for a peaceful release from the two Serbin congregations, so they could begin another congregation. Kilian opposed the formation of still another body and rejected distance from Serbin as a reasonable argument. Undaunted, Teinert's group formed a congregation at New Start, five miles from Serbin, without anyone's approval, and applied for membership in the Missouri Synod. The synod refused to admit the congregation, however, and the Rev. Andrew Schmidt, a Wend who had been called as pastor, refused the position.[61] Teinert then went to the Texas Synod, obtained the services of the Rev. Eduard Zapf, and learned how to worship in German.

With the death of Pastor Zapf, the congregation apologized to the entire Missouri Synod with a letter to *Der Lutheraner,* and in 1878 it was admitted into the synod. The Reverend A. L. Y. Stiemke had become the pastor in 1874 and endeared himself to members by learning Wendish well enough to administer the Lord's Supper in that language. In 1881 the congregation relocated farther away at Warda, seven miles southeast of Serbin, and built a new church building.[62] Members, including some of the 1854 settlers, as well as many of the more recent migrants, were Schneider, Domaschk, Krakosky, Stephan, Kasper, Schiwart, Kasperick, Falke, Bernstein, Kunze, and Herbrig.

From the Warda base, settlers moved on toward the Colorado River, forming a congregation at Winchester in 1876, and then to the area of Green's Creek, eight miles southeast, where they founded a congregation in 1895.[63] One other extension of settlement made in the early 1880s from Warda and Serbin was that of Walburg. Families such as Neitsch, Schulze, Andres, and Schneider moved northward to the prairie soil of Williamson County. Then in the early 1900s, members from Warda including Schoppa, Lowke, Graf, and Zoch journeyed all the way to north Texas, where they settled at Vernon.

Another settlement had already been started in the mid-1860s at Swiss Alp in Fayette County by the Ritter, Knippa, Kiesling, and Kolba families.[64] The destinations in later migrations from Lee and Fayette counties to the north and west included The Grove (the Winkler family), Noack or Hochkirch (Zieschang and Noack families), Copperas Cove (Jakob, Falke, Weiser, and Nerettig), Cisco (Weise, Weiser, and Hilscher), Albany (Jentho, Bernstein, Kulke, and Dutschmann), and Wilson (Noack and Wuensche). Some Wends migrated to the cities such as nearby Austin (Knippa, Zoch) for employment and to the coastal Port Arthur (Domaschk, Jurischk, Mitschke) when its oil fields opened. The largest migration came early in the twentieth century, when many people moved to Houston.

From Wend to American

While Texas Wends may have made rapid changes in the economic sector, they held on to their cultural past. They read the Bible and religious books in Wendish. They subscribed to *Serbske Nowiny* and *Předźenak*. They spoke Wendish, sang Wendish hymns and songs, and exchanged letters in Wendish. Their children studied Wendish in school, and until 1881 used it as the language in confirmation instruction.[65]

Most of the Wends, at the time of migration, were bilingual in German and Wendish. Those who knew only Wendish soon became more versed in German, after they arrived in their new homeland.[66] In Texas as in Australia, Wendish generally continued to be the language of the home, but only in Texas was it the language of the church. Some Wendish families in Texas, the more "progressive," spoke German at home and, until St. Peter's was founded, listened to Wendish in church.

As in Australia, the Wends traded their language for German before they adopted English. The majority of Wends in Serbin and all Wends outside Serbin had made the shift to German well before World War I, and German was the more popular language. The *Giddings Deutsches Volksblatt*, begun at the turn of the century, illustrated the transition of the Wend. Most of the newspaper, including letters from Lusatia correspondents, was in German, but some of the articles continued to be in Wendish.

In 1934, fourteen years after Wendish sermons ceased, George Engerrand prepared a questionnaire asking respondents to provide Wendish words important in daily usage. Only two could complete the entire word list and Engerrand concluded that Wendish was very little used. Many of those interviewed filled in the spaces with German.[67] A few individuals continued to use Wendish, however, and even now, fifty years after Engerrand's study, there are several people who can still speak the language. Engerrand's conclusion, nevertheless, was valid; the Wends had become Germans.

American entry into World War I came later than Australian involvement and the hostility toward Germans in Texas was not as intense. Practically all German Americans were bilingual, and many Wends were trilingual. As early as 1855 the Wends introduced into their vocabulary such English words as postoak, "smokehaus," logs, box, fence, and whiskey.[68] Some Lutheran congregations in Texas introduced English into their services before World War II, and opposition to the use of German came as frequently from the younger Lutherans, who felt more comfortable with English, as from the Anglo-American neighbors. Nevertheless, in rural Wendish settlements, German services continued through World War II. The Serbin congregation continued to use German in its congregational meetings into the 1950s.[69]

Of all the Wend migrants, it was among those who went to Texas that Wendish awareness was strongest and interest in their heritage greatest. Serbin served as the base and no matter where Wends settled, they kept in touch with Lee County. The two agencies to assist in this were the Missouri Synod, which stimulated a feeling of community among its Texas following, and the *Giddings Deutsches Volksblatt*. This newspaper sold subscriptions all over the state and printed letters and reports from subscribers. Its frequent attention to Lutheran affairs in Texas and in the United States at large made it an unofficial church journal. The Missouri Synod Lutherans in Texas formed a subculture, and within that group was a strong identification with the Wendish heritage.

4

The Wends in Canada, Nebraska, and South Africa

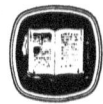

Canada

In addition to the migrations to Australia and Texas, many Wends migrated to other corners of the world. Three areas that deserve some attention are Ontario, Nebraska, and South Africa. The settlements of these regions occurred in conjunction with German migrations and because of the small number of Wends, attracted little public attention.

The Canadian migration began in the late 1850s, peaked in the 1860s, and tapered off in the 1890s. Most of the migrants came from Lower Lusatia, especially from the area north of Cottbus. The village of Tauer led with thirty-three, Drachhausen followed with twenty-two, Schönhöhe had seventeen, Maust fifteen, and Drehnow ten. Other villages represented were Sachsendorf, Jänschwalde, Schmogrow, Heinersbrück, Drewitz, Preilack, Strobitz, and Sielow. These villagers had originally sent their people to Australia, and as the Canadian migration rose, the Australian migration declined.

Many Wend family names of Australia also occur in Canada, including Budarick, Noack, Koal, Kossatz, Schmienz, Miatke, Woito, Buder, Kielow, Nagora, and Teschner. These families undoubtedly knew about Australia and made a conscious choice to try Canada rather than joining their relatives in Australia. Possibly the shorter, cheaper voyage to Canada—thirty-one *taler* as opposed to a hundred *taler* to Australia—may have been responsible, or complaints from Australia may have been discouraging. The Canadian government did distribute pamphlets in Europe publicizing the country, and when Germans began migrating to Canada, so did Wends.[1]

The Wends who settled in Canada did not form a colony, but they established themselves within a district along the Ottowa River in Renfrew County. This loose concentration was more the result of their migration coinciding with the opening of the frontier in that region than with their desire to retain their Wendish connections. One of the first to notice the Wendish presence was Ludwig Hermann Gerndt, a Lutheran missionary to the Ottowa Valley. He sensed a problem in his ministry because the Wends were Lutheran and part of his flock, yet they understood only a small amount of German.[2] Although the Wends Germanized rapidly, the ethnic distinction has continued to the present and individuals of both German and Wendish extraction refer to certain families as being "Vendish."

Pastor Gerndt kept precise records on the background of his parishioners. His education in Berlin and Bonn included the importance of records for both religious and civil purposes and the information he included on the member's village of origin in Prussia was most valuable in identifying Wends. Not all Wends remained Lutheran, however. Many of them were won over by the Evangelical United Brethren (now part of the United Church of Canada), known as the German Methodists. Possibly the less formal church service appealed to them, and in contrast to Kilian's Wends, they did not find the doctrinal difference as objectionable. Other reasons, expressed in oral tradition, may have been the distance to the church or dissatisfaction with Lutheran church discipline. The German Methodist pastors were generally from the German community in the United States and their interest in German villages was not keen, nor did their training ingrain the value of extensive church registers. As a result, their records contain little about the background of their members and identification of Wends from that source is difficult.[3]

Another source for identifying Canadian Wends is the work of Gerhard Krüger. Although not all the migrants in the study were Wends, most had been residents of villages where Wends predominated, while only a few originated from the German-dominated cities such as Cottbus. Many of the immigrants who identified their destination as Canada to the German authorities may have changed their destination when they arrived in Hamburg, and many migrants of the Cottbus region did not regiser at all and were not part of Krüger's study. In spite of these qualifications, Krüger's study is a valuable source. He lists 96 people bound for Canada, including 24 adult males, while my own research there revealed 134 people, including 47 males. Many of the Wends located in Canada were not on Krüger's list

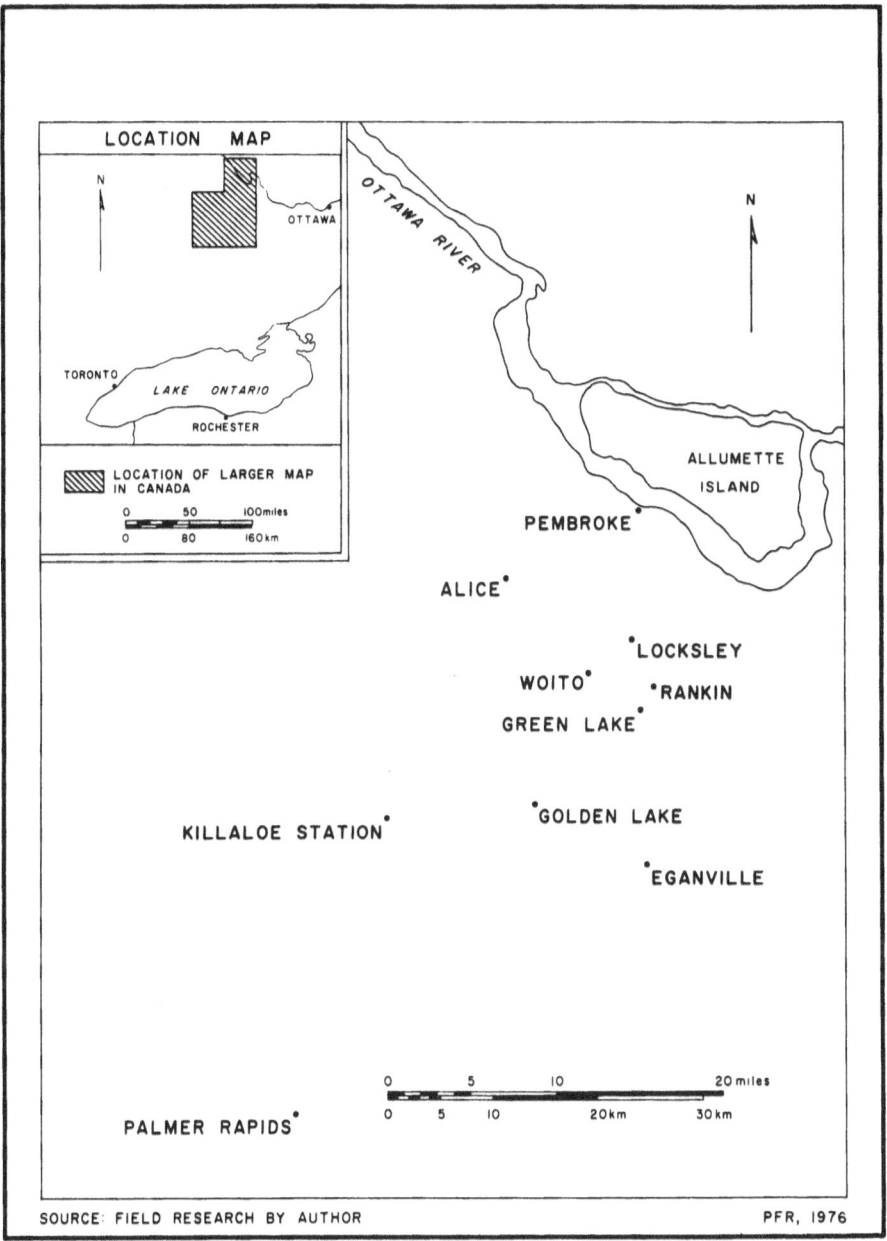

MAP 7 Canadian Location of Wendish Settlers

and numerous Wends on Krüger's list were not found in Canada. Taking into consideration the overlap as a result of missing or inadequate records, the total Wendish migration to Canada was well over 150 people. The picture drawn from those Wends who could be identified is thus the most accurate one possible.[4]

The Wendish settlements in Canada were established in the thirty years after 1860 in Ontario, in an area between Locksley and Palmer Rapids, with the greatest concentration around Green Lake. As a result of glacial action, the soil was shallow and rocky and the drainage poor. A heavy growth of pine and cedar covered the land. Not only were the settlers forced to clear the land of stones and stumps through back-breaking labor, but they also faced the prohibitive cost of constructing a transportation system for the shipment of goods.

The initial sources of money for the immigrant came from labor in lumber mills or from sale of timber. Agriculture practised on the rocky soil consisted of mixed farming with cultivation of wheat, rye, hay, garden vegetables, and fruit. Because of poverty, oxen and horses were scarce, and trudging miles to market and mill with a sack of grain on the shoulder was common. In her study of the material culture of the Germans in Renfrew County, Brenda Lee-Whiting observed a disproportionately large percentage of Wends among the craftsmen in the community. Individuals such as Boehme, Noack, Markus, Liebeck, Schimmens, and Kelo crafted furniture, spinning wheels, bobbin-winders, and baskets.[5]

While there was some marriage between Wendish families, the Wends generally attended German church, married Germans, and fitted into the German tradition. Wendish was spoken at home for a while, and if Wend married Wend, the language continued a bit longer in their family. There were neither Wendish pastors nor teachers of the Wendish language. Even so, the Wendish tradition has continued up to the present, and there are still several Wendish speakers around Green Lake in the Melcher and Jonas families.[6]

The Nebraska Wends

Although individual Wends migrated to other locations in the United States in the late nineteenth century, little evidence can be found to trace their movements. The only location outside Texas to have a Wendish concentration was at Sterling, Nebraska. There the few Wendish families scattered throughout the community, but most belonged to the Lutheran church south of town that was affiliated with the German-speaking Nebraska Synod.[7]

The settlers originated from the villages of Proschim, Gosda, Muckwar, and Stradow in Lower Lusatia, south of Cottbus between Spremberg and Senftenberg. The first Wend to settle at Sterling evidently was Matthias Panko, who migrated in 1869. Others followed, including Gottlieb Wusk in 1878 and Matthäus Wusk in 1880. There was considerable intermarriage between the children of these families, especially from the family of Matthäus Wusk; four of his five children married Wends. Identification of Wends is hampered by inadequate records, but probably no more than ten Wendish families settled at Sterling.[8]

Although not part of the Sterling community, Mato Kosyk, the most prominent Lower Sorbian poet, migrated from Werben to the United States and eventually visited the Sterling Wends. After his migration in 1883 Kosyk had studied for the ministry in Lutheran seminaries in Springfield and Chicago, Illinois, and then had served parishes in Iowa, Oklahoma, and Nebraska. As a Nebraska pastor he attended a church convention at Sterling in 1890 and conversed in Wendish with the older residents.

Kosyk was aware of the Wendish community in Texas and became acquainted with a Texas Wend while he was at the Springfield, Illinois, seminary. Yet Kosyk rejected the Missouri Synod, the synod of Kilian; he affiliated with the more liberal German Nebraska Synod and never expressed any thought of serving as pastor to the Texas Wends. He came from Lower Lusatia while most of the Texas Wends originated from Upper Lusatia. Kosyk resigned from the ministry in 1913 and retired to a farm at Albion, Oklahoma, far from either Wends or Germans. Most of his major poetic works had been written prior to his departure for America although he continued to write in America. He died in 1940 at the age of 87.[9]

Migration to South Africa

The Wendish migration to Cape Town in South Africa took place almost exclusively in 1858 and 1859 and was closely tied to German migration. Two scholars have examined the German migration, and from their publications certain facts affecting Wendish migrants may be gleaned.[10]

Most of the ships that transported the settlers belonged to J. C.

Godeffroy and Son, the same company that carried the Australian migrants. The *Peter Godeffroy* in 1859, for example, sailed from Rio de Janiero to Cape Town where some Wends disembarked while others continued on to Adelaide where they planned to settle. Schmidt-Pretoria includes an appendix of passenger lists with home villages of the migrants.[11] From this source, together with details provided by Krüger, one may deduce that approximately 150 immigrants to Cape Town were Wends and half of those came from Werben. The remainder came primarily from Preilack, Jänschwalde, and Turnow.

In size the migration was slightly smaller than that to Canada, but while the Wends continued to migrate to Canada, the African migration ceased and the African Wends never benefited from a continuing infusion of their countrymen. In typical fashion the Wends of Africa turned to agriculture for their livelihood and also settled in German communities. Evidently there was no attempt to form a Wendish community, and assimilation with the Germans proceeded at such a rapid pace that by 1900 little other than artifacts and tradition was left of the Wendish culture and language.[12]

5

Wendish Folkways

Religious Festivals and Practices

One of the most noticeable characteristics of the Wends, both in Lusatia and in emigration, is their devotion to the church. While this loyalty was strong in Europe, the migration experience, which destroyed so many of the old certainties, drew people even closer to the one institution that provided stability. Not only did the church furnish them with the church calendar to identify their festivals, such as Christmas and Easter, but it helped highlight the milestones of each life with ceremonies associated with birth, marriage, and death. The church, whether Lutheran or German Methodist, was at the center of community activity and religion was a vital part of individual lives.

Easter, so highly regarded by peasant people after a long, cold winter, was celebrated both with strictly religious activities and also with old secular customs. In Europe it was a common practice for the young maidens to sing in front of the village homes after midnight on Easter morning and in turn receive refreshments or coins. Toward dawn the singing was interrupted and the maidens, with as much silence as they could muster, went to the nearest brook to fetch "Easter Water." The water supposedly stimulated health and beauty, and some was saved for a newborn baby's first bath. Once this task was completed, the young maidens returned to singing and walked slowly through the fields as they sang their hymns.[1]

No reference has been found in Texas to Easter singing, but at Peter's Hill, South Australia, the young people formerly gathered at the cemetery to sing from sunset on Easter Saturday until midnight. "Easter Water," on the other hand, was used in Texas, and at least one grandmother, early in the morning, would walk to Rabbs Creek for water, and on her return, go from bed to bed sprinkling the sleepers' faces with it. Well into the 1940s one Texas Wend, early on Easter morning filled a bucket and encircled the house with a trail of water in the belief that it would reduce the spider and insect population of the house for the remainder of the year.[2]

The coloring of eggs is common practice among Slavic Christians, and references are found in Australia, Texas, and Canada to the practice among Wends of using the color from vegetables, especially onions and beets. Coloring eggs was a family activity, and the materials were readily available on a farm, but the other practices of group singing and going from house to house would be much more difficult, because the Wends of Texas and Australia did not live in villages, but in scattered farm houses. The practices that remained were those associated either with the family or with church services.[3]

Observances of the other festivals are even harder to tie to European practices. Christmas, for example, was the primary event of the church year, but more of the activity centered around food and drink than around community functions. The Texas Wends decorated a cedar tree in church and presented gifts to the children, but these practices were universal, at least among Germans. In Texas the term widely used for Santa Claus or one of his helpers was *Rumplich*, and Mrs. Blasig reported that eight *Rumpliche* visited her home prior to Christmas, giving candy and nuts. The term is very much like *Rumprich*, which is common in Lusatia, and *Umprich*, the name used in Canada. The Wends in Texas, Australia, and Canada also conducted church services on three consecutive days for the major church festivals well into the twentieth century, as they had in Europe, and Kosyk reported that in the 1880s the Texans on the third feast day visited their neighbors for a sausage meal.[4]

The observance of the Birds' Wedding (Vogelhochzeit) was not widely practised in the early years of the Texas settlement, but enjoyed a resurgence in the 1960s. During the morning of January 25 children placed empty plates on window sills or on fence posts. They were told that the birds were celebrating a wedding on that day and would bring gifts to the plates as part of the celebration. The mother generally baked a cake and, using a three-pronged fork, made marks on the cake resembling birds' feet. Secretly she placed the cake on the plates in time for the children's snack.[5]

Of all the personal religious celebrations, the marriage ceremony was the most elaborate and festive. While the preliminary arrangements between the two families were not precisely prescribed, the celebration of the wedding was. In Upper Lusatia all the arrangements, personal invitations, food, and the ceremony itself were made by a professional wedding manager called a *braška*. On the day of the wedding the *braška* called at the home of the bride. He was treated discourteously and gruffly, and when he was finally granted admission he was presented with a girl other than the one he sought. Eventually the bride was produced in her splendid dress, and the wedding party set off for the church with much fanfare and singing. After the ceremony, the wedding was celebrated at the bride's home for three days and sometimes even longer. Neighbors and relatives helped in supplying and preparing the food.[6]

In Australia the services of the *braška* could not be obtained and Carl Hempel complained that he was forced to make all the preparations himself. The extensive celebrations were maintained, however, and Hempel's Wendish friends came to visit and celebrate the wedding. In Peter's Hill, the people also kept the tradition of extensive celebrations, undoubtedly because the great distance of travel prevented frequent visits.[7]

The Texas Wends, at least until the 1920s, maintained not only the extensive celebration but the utilization of the *braška* as well. Although the Texas bride and groom sent out the invitations, the *braška* arrived at the bride's home, led the wedding party in prayers and songs, and then led the procession to the church. After participation in the ceremony, the Texas *braška* accompanied the people to the home of the bride and assumed responsibility for the refreshments for the three-day celebration.[8]

While many Sorbs in Lusatia wore the traditional, ornate, wedding costume, those of the Bautzen area where the Texas settlers originated, had already dropped the practice in Lusatia. In Texas the traditional wedding dress was black and tight-fitting to remind the bride of the hardship of married life. At the turn of the century Texas brides made the transition to gray, and soon adopted the white gown.[9]

The observances of death and birth were not as intricate or distinctive, and it is next to impossible to separate the Wendish traditions from the German. The tolling of the church bell announcing a death and the burial service in the church were common practices. One practice that was reported in both Lusatia and Texas was associated with the return of the mother to church after the birth of a child. The pastor met the mother at the door of the church with the greeting, "The Lord blessed your departure and is now blessing your return."

Both then proceeded to the altar for a prayer before she went to her place in the congregation.[10]

The church was the pivot for Wendish life in both Lusatia and the New World, although in Europe the parishioners lived in the village near the church or in a village within walking distance. In the New World people lived on isolated farms at varying distances from the church. In spite of the distance, the church provided at one and the same time the path to eternity, the center for social activities, and the educational agency for the children. The church, therefore, was a significant aspect of Wendish life and played a major role in maintenance of Wendish culture.

The primary differences between Texas and Australia was that Kilian went to Texas as the Wendish pastor. The church in Australia actually became an institution for Germanization of the Wends while in Texas it served to preserve Wendish traditions. The only manner in which the Wendish tradition was maintained in Australia or Canada was through reading services such as those at Peter's Hill or through inter-family devotions. Here they could repeat their Wendish liturgy, sing their hymns, and hear their language spoken. At the church gatherings for social purposes people could converse in Wendish and refresh their memory of the homeland. The young, however, were not taught Wendish formally, and as they learned German and English in school and associated with few others who knew Wendish, they soon forgot their tradition.

In Texas, however, Wendish was taught by the Kilians, who loved the language and knew it well. Not only was the language studied in school until 1916, listened to in church until 1920, and spoken in the homes, but the Texas settlement was constantly stimulated by an infusion of new settlers from Lusatia.[11] Even though they may not have settled in Serbin, they did appear there from time to time. While the Wendish migration to Australia had ended, for all practical purposes, by 1866, the migration to Texas continued until 1891. No single reason explains the remarkable longevity of Wendish traditions in Texas, but the religious context accounts for much of it.

Daily Life

Spinning evenings were an important aspect of Sorbian social life in Europe. Between October 11 and Maundy Thursday in Lusatia the girls met in one of the homes to spin, and in addition to work and conversation, they also learned songs and practiced singing. But the practice was not carried over to Texas or Australia.[12] Cotton in Texas and wool in Australia became the preferred fibers instead of flax, and in both places the Wends produced the material as a cash crop. Industrialization probably made spinning unnecessary.

The memory of spinning, however, remained with some Australian Wends. According to a story told by an Australian, conversation at spinning evenings often turned to the subject of ghosts. One of the girls whose home was a long distance away said she was not afraid of any ghosts. On the way home that night a white figure stopped her and she asked him his name. When he failed to reply, she hit him with her spinning wheel and ran. The next day a man from the village was found dead.[13]

Another practice, feather stripping, was carried to Texas, Australia, and Canada. Soft goose down plucked from the breast was used for stuffing pillows and feather beds, but the more rigid feathers could also be used if their shafts were removed. Taking one feather at a time, each woman removed the barbs from the shafts and when a cup was filled, she had met her quota. At these events there were always light refreshments and generally dancing and singing. In Texas and Canada quilting soon replaced feather stripping as the focus for social meetings.[14]

In Europe the diet of the Sorbs included meats such as pork, fish, and fowl; garden vegetables, especially cucumbers and potatoes; cereals such as rye; and dairy products. In Australia wheat became the major cereal and in Texas it was corn (maize). Hogs continued to be a primary source of meat, but in Texas the animals were fed corn rather than small grains as in Europe and Australia. Fowl continued to be common, as was beef.

Pigs were butchered during the winter, after the first frost, each family handling the operation themselves. Beef was slaughtered in Texas and Australia through the "beef club" and the animal was shared among the various members. Inadequate refrigeration dictated this form of cooperation; as families took turns providing the animal and took only a portion of each carcass, the butchering could take place more frequently with less effort at preserving the meat.[15]

The traditions of the Wends also include medicine and cures. In Texas and Australia home remedies were widespread and in Texas there was occasional reference to the use of magic for curing purposes. Much of this can be found in any peasant society and is not exclusively Wendish. For the most part patent medicines were used, and they were of German manufacture. The use of *Lebenswecker* and *Alpenkräuter* was reported in both Australia and Texas, and Germany was the source of supply. Johann Zwar, well known for his skill at homeopathy, ordered all his medicine from William Schwabe in Leipzig.[16]

Closely associated with medicine and folk cures is the topic of folklore. Kosyk in 1884 reported that many of the old legends about the Woman of Midday (*Připolnica* or *Mittagsfrau*), of dwarfs, dragons, and of the Waterman (*Wódny muž*) were repeated in Texas. In Australia children were frightened with tales of this creature, which inhabited streams and ponds waiting for people to approach the water so that it could grasp the victim into its watery world. These stories were not perpetuated for long, however, and disappeared with the first generation of Wends.[17]

Only one set of stories shows some continuity between the various Wendish settlements, and they are associated with the Seventh Book of Moses, a book of magic. This book evidently gave secrets of magic to those who studied it, although it was crucial to pass the book on before death, or the owner would not rest in peace. One Wend in Australia obtained a copy so that he could gain wealth without work, but instead, it brought him misfortune and loss of property. A story in Texas tells of a master blacksmith in Europe who went to church and left the apprentices alone in the shop. In their idleness they explored the building, found a book, and began to read. As they read, a crow flew in through the open window and alighted on a beam. The reading continued and more crows flew in. At that point the blacksmith returned, saw the birds, took the book, and read it backwards. The crows left in the order in which they had come.[18]

In Australia a similar story is told that some people paid an unannounced call on the neighbors, but there was no one at home. Expecting the owners to return soon, the visitors entered the house to wait. There they found the Seventh Book of Moses and began reading it. Crows arrived and settled on the roof of the house. When the owner returned, he took the book and read it backwards, and the crows left in the order in which they had arrived.[19]

Wendish practices and folkways were under little pressure to change. Exposure to the customs of other people, marriage into other ethnic groups, scattered settlement patterns, and even technology led to modifications. But change in this aspect of life was made without duress, and the decision to preserve practices or to modify them was left to individuals.

6

The Wends, Comparative Frontiers, and Turner

Almost one hundred years ago, in 1893, Frederick Jackson Turner addressed the American Historical Association and presented his views on the influence of the frontier on American institutions and society. According to his interpretation, or thesis, Turner maintained that the frontier, as it moved constantly westward, created not only a new, distinctive American, but also new American institutions. To an extent his interpretation of American history was a reaction to the historical orientation of that era, which looked across the Atlantic for European antecedents, and to an extent it was a conclusion based on his own observations and study of the American frontier. His speech touched off extensive investigations of the frontier and the American West, and these generally took one of two routes. One approach focused on the impact of the frontier in creating and modifying American institutions and looked at the *process* of change. The other described the frontier itself as a *place* and examined such topics as the fur trade, mining, Indian relations, and the grazing economies.

Forty years later, in 1932, Turner broadened his horizons even further and encouraged scholars to examine the frontier in other areas such as Canada, Australia, and Africa in order to compare their experiences with those in America. During those forty years Turner's ideas went unchallenged and he exerted an influence on the discipline of American frontier history that has not been matched by any single individual. However, beginning in the 1930s and continuing into the 1940s, Turner's findings were questioned on every side. Since that time there has been intermittent debate between Turner's defenders and his critics.[1]

In his presidential address to the Western Historical Association, a contemporary scholar of the American West, W. Turrentine Jackson, pointed out that most of the criticism was directed to that part of frontier studies called *process*, where the major goal was to articulate a theory of the frontier's influence on the country. The possibility of arriving at such an overarching theory, in Jackson's mind, was not realistic, even though the search for such a statement, and the ensuing debate, had been stimulating and beneficial. Nevertheless, Jackson argued, there had been no resolution to the debate, and efforts had reached the level of diminishing returns.

Jackson proposed instead that historians should focus on the frontier as *place*, especially within the context of comparative frontier studies as Turner himself had suggested in 1932. Jackson admitted that the theoretical grandeur would be absent, but he pointed to many solid comparative studies that had been made in recent years.

But at the most recent meeting of Western historians, in another presidential address, Martin Ridge, a self-proclaimed "neo-Turnerian" argued for the need of a theoretical framework. He maintained that to remove Turner's thesis [process] from "the study of the nineteenth-century West" would make the study nothing more than "a parochial exercise." Jackson's advice is well-taken, and his evidence that comparative work has produced valuable results is convincing. But Ridge reminds us of what most Western historians know: the inescapable presence of Turner's ideas. Valid or invalid, the Turner thesis still exists as a point of reference.[2]

Such is the case with the Wends. Even though this study is intended to be an ethnic study, some elements are present that show an affinity with comparative frontier studies, and those elements should be sorted out. Possibly the Wends' experiences on the various frontiers can cast light on Turner's thesis.

Paul Sharp, yet another scholar of comparative frontiers, attempted to bring some precision to the study of frontiers and proposed several prerequisites. First of all he suggested that "the cultural heritage of the pioneers must possess basic similarities and corresponding technology."[3] The Wends meet this requirement because they possessed cultural unity, a common religion, minority status, and an agricultural orientation concentrating on rye, flax, hay, and small farm animals.

Sharp's second requirement specified that the settlement must occur during the same historical period. The Wendish migration began in 1848 and continued until the end of the century. Texas received the largest number, with Australia a close second and Canada a distant third.

The final requirement was that the physical environments must possess a general likeness. Within the general similarity of the environments there were variations in rainfall, temperature, growing seasons, and soils, but in all three areas, the Wends found it possible to establish an agricultural economy. And in addition there was the added similarity of the English cultural environment. In all three locations the Wends did not move to a remote frontier where there might have been conflict with the aboriginal population, but purchased small parcels of undeveloped land from earlier pioneers.

In contrast to the Lusatian homeland, Australia possessed a Mediterranean climate with hot, dry summers and cool, moist winters. The Wends immediately adjusted their agricultural practices to the new seasons by plowing and planting in May and June as the winter rains began and harvesting in November and December during the spring. The primary products included wheat and oats (but no rye), along with vegetables and fruit. The animals were the same as in Europe: fowl, hogs, and cattle, and oxen as draft animals.

In Texas, the climate was warmer and wetter than in Lusatia, but evaporation was greater, and summer drought common. The warmer temperatures and longer growing season directly influenced the Wends' agricultural decisions: they adopted corn (maize) almost immediately, and it rapidly became a staple in their diet as well as feed for farm animals. Instead of fattening hogs with small grains as in Germany and Australia, the Texas Wends used corn. They also planted cotton, another completely new crop. Cotton was the cash crop, and although the Wends held no slaves, they found cotton profitable. Rye and wheat not being suited to the Lee County setting, very few bushels were grown. As in Australia, the farm animals were those familiar from the homeland. In contrast to other Texas farmers, the Wends did not readily accept mules for pulling wagons and plows, but preferred their accustomed oxen.

In Canada the climate was more like that of Europe, with even colder winters. Canadian Wends, therefore, made few changes, most of which were related to the soil. Agriculture practiced on the poorly drained, shallow, and rocky soil consisted of mixed farming with cultivation of wheat, rye, hay, garden vegetables, and fruit. Initial sources of income here were labor in lumber mills or sale of timber.

On all three frontiers, the first and most rapid adaptation was made to meet the demands of climate or soil. The immigrants had to accept crops suited to the environment and use new implements and new agricultural methods. The physical environment also discouraged concentrated settlements, resulting in considerable dispersion and loss of cultural vitality.

Rapid adjustment to climate was also visible in housing design. In Australia the Wends utilized local resources the same way earlier settlers had done. Early homes had straw roofs just as in Lusatia, but the walls were either pug or wattle and daub. The prime ingredients of clay, straw, and mud were mixed and plastered on the wooden slats making pug, or on a mesh of wattle branches for wattle and daub. Tall, straight trees suitable for European-style construction were not readily available.

Homes built by the Texas Wends similarly resembled Texas homes rather than European ones. Tall, straight trees were not available in Lee County either, so they used the smaller Texas trees. The design was the southern style log cabin called the dog-trot or dog-run: two cabins about ten feet apart, joined by a covered breezeway. One cabin was for cooking and eating, the other for sleeping, and the passage helped cool the dwelling—a dwelling thus well adapted to the climate and building materials.

The Canadian homes differed because large trees were available and the builders had to consider the winter cold. The log cabin made of huge, hewn logs in the Canadian pattern became the home of the Wends there.

Clothing changes are difficult to document, but there are several examples of adaptations. Garments or cloth were generally purchased and not produced at home, so the change to clothes suitable to the environment was quickly made. Folk costumes displaying beautiful needlework were not worn on the new frontiers, in all probability because of the expense and investment of time. The Canadian Wends continued spinning wool and flax, but the heat of Texas and Australia made that unrealistic. On all three frontiers the Wends continued, for a time, the tradition of making feather bedding, but in Texas the cotton quilt became more common.

There were also changes in foods. Rye, the staple in Europe, was replaced by wheat in Canada and Australia, while in Texas people turned to corn. In Lusatia fish had been popular but in Australia there were few ponds. In Texas people entertained with fish fries, but those were special occasions. For sweetening food the Texan Wends gradually began to use molasses, which they produced themselves from sorghum. But in all regions they ate pork and fowl and, in general, the same vegetables they had in Europe.

The cultural context was less demanding than the physical and permitted more options. Because of this greater tolerance, change in social, linguistic, and religious activity was more deliberate, and many Wendish ways were retained. The extent and degree of pressure to change depended on several factors. Wends who settled in the cities were brought into proximity with other cultures, and there was a need for greater conformity, so they made a relatively rapid transition to the English and American systems.

Those Wends who settled in the country or were in a community with a large Wendish population accepted elements of the English way of life only where that was necessary, and at a slower pace. But time and distance also played a role and weakened memory of the homeland. Gone were the hills, brooks, and land associated with the old culture, and in its place grew attachment to a new and increasingly familiar nation. Stories and customs were maintained as long as they remained meaningful, but they soon became blurred and faded from the folk memory. In Texas the large size and cohesion of the settlement and the late and continuing migration kept Wendish cultural traits alive longer than in other areas, but there too they eventually died of disuse.

The adjustment in language serves as a good example of slow change. Relatively few of the first generation were interested in learning English, and those on isolated farms did not see the need to do so. When necessary they appointed as their spokesman a Wend who more readily grasped the new ways. Except for some minimal English, most Wends continued to converse in their native language or in German. Most had been bilingual in Lusatia, so as German was spoken in the community and in church, they became more familiar with that language.

The second generation in Australia did not learn Wendish in school, but studied in German and English. The common language for the second generation therefore was German, and the Wendish community was assimilated into the German community. The adjustment was ironic in the sense that the Wends had suffered from the Germanization policy for so many years in Europe. It was also not the best decision because with the outbreak of World War I, Australia joined the fight against Germany. The Wends were again subjected to state pressure to change cultures, but in this instance they were expected to sublimate the German culture and adopt the English.

In Texas, because of the large Wendish core and the work of Jan Kilian, Wendish enjoyed a longer existence, but there also, German became the replacement language. As in Australia they eventually made the shift to English, but because public opposition was not as strong, the Wends did not make the final break with German until World War II.

The slowest change was in religious life. There was little pressure to change and religious life was the one constant in a context of change. Some Wends in the city left the church soon, and others who married a spouse who spoke only English found it easiest to join an English-speaking denomination. The majority, however, remained within the Lutheran church. Because of their Lutheran faith and their familiarity with German culture, they usually settled in the German community. Thus religious assimilation was not dramatic, and the adaptation reflected sympathy with the German culture rather than that of the host country.

Where the Wend could keep the language of the pulpit, the order of service, hymns, and procedures in Wendish, the church helped to preserve the Wendish way and provided a bond with the past. In some instances, however, when Wendish could not be maintained, the church became an instrument of assimilation. First it taught the Wends German and then English. The church, therefore, was at times an institution of preservation and at other times a vehicle of change. The church mirrored the level of the Wends' cultural change. Of all the Wendish contributions, the church remains as the only living artifact, even if it is not purely authentic.

The frontier, in summary, exerted pressure on different aspects of the settler's life with varying degrees of intensity. Its influence was strongest as regards the physical environment limiting alternatives. There the Wends' modifications were rapid and appropriate. Their experience underscores Turner's view on the powerful influence of the environment: "at the frontier the environment is at first too strong for the man. He must accept the conditions which it furnishes, or perish. . . ."[4]

The frontier, however, played the smallest role in the Wends' religious life and dictated few adjustments. The church was where the Wends first learned and practised democracy, and this was not on the American frontier, but in Europe. There many left the state church and eventually brought their church to the new frontiers where they could continue to make religious decisions. Both in Europe and on the frontier they wrote constitutions, elected officers, taxed themselves, and voted on questions of communal concern. In that democratic context there was conflict and schism, and on at least one occasion Kilian grew weary of democracy, where it seemed as if everyone felt constrained to expound a view.

While the experience of the Wends harmonizes with many of Turner's ideas, it does not support the heart of his thesis. Turner argued that "the most important effect of the frontier has been in the promotion of democracy here and in Europe."[5] In the Wendish community democracy did not originate on the frontier, but in Germany. Nevertheless, the questions raised by Turner's thesis and by comparative frontier studies help explain the nature of the Wends' experience in their new homelands.

Appendix

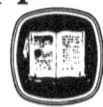

The following list gives the names and other details of migrants identified by the author as Wendish. The name of the husband and the wife's maiden name are shown together as one entry. In some cases only partial information is available as to date and place of birth and death, but all persons shown are considered to be Wends except those whose names are given in square brackets. Entries consisting of more than two names show parties to second and third marriages. The names in parentheses are either alternative spellings or *Hofnamen*—the name a person used if he obtained a piece of property through marriage or purchase and assumed the surname of the previous owner. The names of the Texan Wends who emigrated on the *Ben Nevis* are marked with an asterisk.

The list was begun in the early days of the research, and as each Wendish family was identified a record sheet was started, details of the migrant parents and children being gradually added. Publication constraints would not permit the inclusion of all the information so collected.

The primary purpose of appending the names of selected couples to this volume is to provide information to those people of Wendish ancestry who may be interested in their family history. Another reason is to provide a checklist of Wendish families so that families omitted in this research may be added in some future study along with the details of their experiences. A number of inconsistencies, varying spellings, and date variations remain; any relevant information would be welcomed by the author.

Australian Wends

Name	Date and Place of Birth		Date and Place of Death	
Andreas Albert	6 Dec. 1821	Rachlau	25 Nov. 1905	Penshurst
Agneta Heinze	9 Nov. 1826	Wartha	5 Sept. 1901	Penshurst
Michael Albinus	9 Nov. 1826	Nechern	28 Feb. 1864	Bethel
Agneta Kaiser [Johann H. Koenig]	18 Mar. 1820	Gröditz		
Agneta Pillack Altus	1799	Rodewitz	13 May 1864	Ebenezer
Johann Altus	4 Sept. 1820	Rodewitz	26 Apr. 1860	Bethel
Anna Schneider (Krautz)	Sept. 1822	Nechern		Peterborough
Adam Bartsch	28 Nov. 1808	Särka	2 Dec. 1887	Jindera
Maria Dorothea Meinart	18 Jan. 1811	Nechern	15 May 1880	Jindera
J. Friedrich Bartusch	6 June 1851	Turnow		
Maria Schwartz				
Matthes Behla (Borlock)	1828	Zahsow	21 May 1897	Kiata
Christiane Domaschenz	15 Sept. 1832	Werben	13 Mar. 1913	Kiata
Andreas Biar	6 Jan. 1827	Gröditz	2 Nov. 1896	St. Kitts
Magdelena Lehmann	19 Dec. 1834	Jerchwitz	18 June 1916	St. Kitts
Johann Biele	20 Nov. 1832	Wurschen	19 Dec. 1899	St. Kitts
Magdelena Altus	1 Aug. 1826	Rodewitz	4 Oct. 1907	St. Kitts

Name	Date and Place of Birth		Date and Place of Death	
George Bisse	30 Apr. 1807	Jänschwalde	1 Dec. 1883	Edithburg
Eva Petow	15 Dec. 1803	Turnow		
George Boback	1825	Dauban	[See Texas List]	
Magdalena Stephan (Schippan)	1828	Rascha		
Matthes Borrack	3 Feb. 1808	Werben		
Elizabeth Baschzisch	5 Oct. 1807			
Christian Bramke	8 Nov. 1827	Ruben		
Anna Kschammer				
Christiane Jeitz, n. Roschk				
Johann Britza	6 May 1839	Jänschwalde	20 June 1907	Quorn
Maria Schuppan	19 Jan. 1849	Tauer	21 Aug. 1930	Quorn
Johann Bubner		Drehnow		
Anna Hansel Peschick			1853	
Christian Budarick		Burg Kauper		
[Maria Wichert]				
Friedrich Buder		Turnow		
Anna Tannebring (Ziesche)				
Peter Burger	1 Oct. 1795	Meschwitz	30 Oct. 1878	Penshurst
Agnes Schmidt	19 May 1808	Hochkirch	19 July 1892	Tabor
Christian Dahlitz	3 Dec. 1825	Werben	20 Aug. 1905	Gawler
[Christiane Menzel]	23 Sept. 1839		21 July 1925	Gawler

Matthes Dalitz (Hansko) Maria Habner	8 Dec. 1834 6 Apr. 1834	Werben Werben	1921 12 Jan.	Ngapala Robertstown
Johann Dallwitz Maria Hanschke	16 Sept. 1816 1821	Cortnitz	30 Oct. 1863 13 Apr. 1891	Ebenezer Ebenezer
Andreas Deutscher Agneta Albert [Marie Ernstine Hartwich]	27 Aug. 1816 14 July 1819	Sollschwitz Rachlau	25 Feb. 1897 18 Mar. 1879	Hamilton Hamilton
Michael Deutscher Christiane Schwarz	1 May 1811 15 Oct. 1816	Doberschütz Seitschen	9 Aug. 1864 13 Aug. 1880	Hamilton Murtoa
Andreas Doecke Amalie Diesner	2 July 1811 24 July 1818	Nechern Cortnitz	4 Nov. 1893 2 Sept. 1906	St. Kitts St. Kitts
George Doecke Magdalena Wuensche	16 July 1818 13 Jan. 1821	Nechern Spittel	16 Mar. 1894 23 May 1891	Steinthal Steinthal
Michael Doecke Agneta Falland [Ernestine Auricht]	24 Sept. 1827 31 Oct. 1833	Nechern Buchwalde	8 Jan. 1892 10 Aug. 1882	Bethany Ebenezer
Peter Doecke Maria Felfe	6 Feb. 1824 17 July 1829	Nechern Prauske	29 Nov. 1906 31 May 1901	Bethel Bethel
Christian Domaschenz Maria Grabia, n. Paulenz Maria Lehmann	14 Apr. 1846 18 Feb. 1832	Werben	18 July 1913	Yorketown
Christian Domaschenz Elisa Albin (Salman)	10 Jan. 1814 30 Dec. 1808	Werben Werben	13 June 1892 24 Oct. 1893	Yorketown Yorketown

Name	Date and Place of Birth		Date and Place of Death	
George Domaschenz	25 Nov. 1834		11 Nov. 1899	Kenmore
Elisabeth Schielka	1833		3 Apr. 1875	Peter's Hill
Matthias Domaschenz	27 Sept. 1821	Werben	11 Nov. 1899	Kenmore
Christiane Gardi	6 Feb. 1829	Werben	3 Apr. 1875	Peter's Hill
Anna Borrack	5 Nov. 1831	Werben	10 Nov. 1899	Rainbow
George Domsch	1804		13 Dec. 1861	Sandy Water Hole
Elisabeth Rocha	8 July 1804		23 Jan. 1896	Emu Downs
Martin Dreckow	26 Dec. 1810	Sielow	12 Sept. 1864	Birdwood
Marie Anna Gardi	28 Oct. 1820		17 May 1910	Eudunada
J. G. Ernst Dreckow	23 Dec. 1824	Sielow	16 Aug. 1876	
Johann Noack	21 Apr. 1815	Schönhöhe	24 Dec. 1890	Peter's Hill
Gottlieb Dubrau	1828	Kolkwitz		
Elizabeth	1830	Kolkwitz		
Johann Duldig	11 Nov. 1825	Tauer	23 Apr. 1912	Peter's Hill
Anna Nogora	30 Aug. 1831	Tauer	11 July 1922	Peter's Hill
Christian Duschke		Werben		
Anna Wendo		Brahmow		
J. Karl Dutschke	23 Apr. 1817	Walddorf	2 Nov. 1885	South Kilkerran
Marie Simmank	8 Sept. 1820	Gröditz	22 Nov. 1882	South Kilkerran
George Eckert	25 Oct. 1831	Tauer	21 May 1884	Emu Downs
Maria Thok (Towk)	1831	Jänschwalde	10 Apr. 1922	Springton
Friedrich Wilhelm Starick	26 Aug. 1829	Jänschwalde	Aug. 1922	

Martin Eckert	10 Mar. 1824	Tauer	13 July 1895	Emu Downs
Elisabeth Jurban	9 Mar. 1822	Tauer	23 May 1915	Emu Downs
Andreas Falland	29 July 1820	Rackel	12 July 1892	Ebenezer
Johanne Dachwitz	11 Sept. 1820	Weicha	28 Nov. 1903	Ebenezer
Christian Fladrich	26 Mar. 1824	Papitz	14 May 1900	Cambrai
Maria Lehmann	1 May 1832	Milkersdorf	17 Sept. 1903	Rhine Villa
Johann Fleisher	8 Feb. 1815	Gröditz	19 Aug. 1860	Rosenthal
Maria Gude	8 Dec. 1812	Hochkirch		
Andreas Freund (Brindt)	Dec. 1805	Rackel		1890	Ebenezer
Magdalena Hennersdorf	July 1815	Rackel		1894	Ebenezer
Johann Freund (Brindt)	29 Apr. 1833	Rackel	10 Feb. 1919	Mt. Mary
Anna Jenke (Miersch)	12 Dec. 1842	Cortnitz	26 Jan. 1905	St. Kitts
Mathias Gardi	24 Sept. 1822	Werben		
Marie Werban	25 Dec. 1819	Babow	18 Aug. 1861	Tabor
George Gassan	9 May 1819	Turnow	16 Apr. 1901	Odgen, Iowa
Hanna Jaschan	7 Sept. 1819		11 Nov. 1898	Odgen, Iowa
Christian Geitz	5 Oct. 1818	Brahmow	20 Jan. 1907	Yorketown
Anna Roschk	3 Dec. 1817	Werben		Yorketown
George Genzer	13 Feb. 1837	Tauer		
Johann Gersch	1 Jan. 1817	Buchwalde	4 Mar. 1890	Moonta
Hertha Kubitz	1 May 1816	Buchwalde	19 Apr. 1872	Moonta
Christian Gniel (Muschwitz)	1 Jan. 1812	Papitz		
Christiane Kowal	May 1820	Dissen		

Name	Date and Place of Birth		Date and Place of Death	
Ferd. Gollnisch	1828	Kolkwitz		
Christiane Piska	1829		14 Feb. 1911	Greenock
George Gomala		Guhrow		
Anna Noack		Ruben		
Johann Gormann	13 Dec. 1824	Turnow	17 Aug. 1858	Lyndoch
Anne Gassan	4 Jan. 1825			
George Proposch	5 Feb. 1836	Babow		
Mathes Grabia		Werben		
Johann Graff	1799	Mauschwitz	9 June 1886	Thomastown
Johanna Hobrack	1803		19 Aug. 1887	
J. Christian Greschke	29 June 1846	Heinersbrück	19 Oct. 1902	Gerogery
Friedrich Groch	9 Jan. 1823	Preilack	12 Mar. 1900	Walla Walla
Anna Bela	28 Feb. 1828		17 Nov. 1920	Walla Walla
Martin Groch	25 Sept. 1820	Preilack		
Elizabeth Lewitzka, n. Marschall	13 Jan. 1835	Babow	10 Oct. 1862	Peter's Hill
[Maria Brezinsky, n. Wuttke]				
Jakob Grutzner	1823	Wartha	1912	Westgarthtown
[Luise Grundel]				
Gustav Herrmann Gruhl	11 Aug. 1817	Kleinwelka		
[Anna Maria Purrmann]				

Johann Gude	9 Feb. 1820	Baschütz	15 May 1879	Byaduk
Marianne Handreck	22 Feb. 1854	Werben	13 Feb. 1896	
[Charles Gerdts]				
Christian Gulbin	5 Nov. 1824	Werben	29 Aug. 1903	Murtoa
Anna Lieska (Honich)	1826	Werben	24 June 1896	Murtoa
Matthies Habner	2 Aug. 1828	Werben		
Maria Reichart	1836	Kolkwitz		North Adelaide
Matthes Handreck	5 June 1818	Werben	26 Nov. 1902	Byaduk
Anna Dalitz (Metk)	2 Jan. 1825	Werben	21 Aug. 1907	Byaduk
Christian Harnath	28 Feb. 1819	Jänschwalde	29 Dec. 1897	Hamilton
Maria Groch	16 Mar. 1825	Radewiese	27 May 1894	Hamilton
Johann Christian Hempel	8 Mar. 1794	Kohlwesa	15 Nov. 1881	Penshurst
Fridericke Pauli	Mar. 1814		15 Apr. 1890	Penshurst
Peter Henersdorf	10 Sept. 1819	Rackel	29 Oct. 1883	Walla Walla
[Juliana Weiss]	9 Mar. 1839		26 May 1922	Walla Walla
Johann Hona	1813	Sielow	28 June 1895	Hamilton
Maria	1813			
Martin Hondow	1834	Tauer	9 May 1914	Peter's Hill
Anna Kollosche, n. Miatke	30 Nov. 1831	Schönhöhe	6 June 1919	Peter's Hill
Johann Hundrack	25 July 1803	Baschütz	31 July 1887	Hamilton
Anna Rentsch	18 Jan. 1806	Kuppritz	28 Dec. 1873	Hamilton
Johann Huppatz	1816	Tauer	27 Feb. 1903	Peter's Hill
Maria Sonke	26 Mar. 1816	Preilack	5 July 1875	Peter's Hill

Name	Date and Place of Birth		Date and Place of Death	
Christian Hussock	18 Dec. 1819	Brahmow		
Anna Scholder		Werben		
Christian Jarick	7 Apr. 1808	Werben	10 June 1891	Bethel, N.S.W.
Maria Baschzisch	9 June 1817	Werben	28 Jan. 1858	Peter's Hill
[Friedrika Pluckhahn]				
Mathes Jeitz	14 Dec. 1834	Brahmow	29 Oct. 1909	Byaduk
Christiana Schaetz	24 June 1836	Papitz	6 Dec. 1912	Byaduk
Johann Jenke	19 May 1823	Rackel	26 Apr. 1875	St. Kitts
Maria Kleinig	15 May 1819	Cortnitz	20 Oct. 1911	Neale's Flat
Andreas Kaiser	20 Nov. 1827	Drehsa	15 Mar. 1901	Melbourne
[Maria Finger]				
Martin Kalauka	1 May 1797	Briesen	20 Jan. 1863	Tarrington
Maria Dachs				
Christian Kamenka	31 Jan. 1822	Werben	20 Oct. 1903	Peter's Hill
Maria Domaschenz	1834	Werben		
Wilhelm Kammenz	1821	Preilack		
Christiane Tannebring	16 Aug. 1833			
Andreas Kappler	15 Nov. 1802	Kleinhänchen	3 June 1877	Mt. Gambier
[Henriette Berger]				
Christian Kielian (Kielow)	2 Nov. 1817	Tauer	8 Mar. 1898	Davidston
Maria Jurban	27 Jan. 1816	Tauer		

Christian Kielow	8 Oct. 1842	Turnow	27 Mar. 1928	Emu Downs
Catharine Bartusch	14 July 1841	Preilack	18 July 1921	Emu Downs
Christian Kies	1827	Heinersbrück	22 Feb. 1887	Lyndoch
Maria Kuhlmann, n. Jaschen	1821	Guben	2 June 1892	Lyndoch
Johann Kihlo	24 July 1824	Preilack		
Christiane Schilka	24 Apr. 1833	Werben		
Andreas Kleinig	15 Oct. 1820	Cortnitz	26 Feb. 1904	Neukirch
Agnes Steffan	22 May 1830	Baschütz	26 Oct. 1871	Neukirch
George Kleinig	15 Jan. 1808	Cortnitz	14 Nov. 1878	St. Kitts
Magdalena Huebner	1831		25 Nov. 1909	Ebenezer
Johann Kleinig	21 Apr. 1812	Cortnitz	15 Feb. 1886	Ebenezer
Magdalene Wenke	22 Feb. 1821		20 Jan. 1902	Ebenezer
Martin Klows	1 Jan. 1827	Drewitz		
Ana Zech	7 May 1833			
Johann Klowss	1829	Drewitz	14 July 1919	Dimboola
Elisabeth Gross (Baltzke)	3 Aug. 1828	Drewitz	4 Apr. 1900	
Matthes Koalick	4 Mar. 1811	Werben		
Christiane Melcher (Melchrick)	26 Aug. 1821	Werben		
George Kolosche [Auguste Henel]	14 Oct. 1830	Werben	9 Apr. 1891	Birdwood
Friedrich August Konzag	1827	Werben	30 Oct. 1895	Wasleys
Christiane Jurtz		Werben		

Name	Date and Place of Birth		Date and Place of Death	
Martin Korreng [Fredricke Jannacke]	3 Jan. 1858	Kolkwitz	16 July 1940	Adelaide
Martin Kosch	16 Apr. 1818	Dissen	9 Apr. 1897	Tarrington
Catherine Pumpa	20 Aug. 1822	Drewitz	13 Feb. 1904	Tarrington
George Kossatz				
Anna Friederika Lehmann		Drehnow	14 Apr. 1903	Edithburg
Martin Kotzur	12 Mar. 1833	Jänschwalde	21 Sept. 1916	Alma Park
Elisabeth Towk	17 Sept. 1834	Jänschwalde	13 Nov. 1900	Henty
Johann Krause				
Maria Kies	1824	Heinersbrück	18 Sept. 1911	
Johann Carl August Krueger	11 Jan. 1802	Cottbus	4 Oct. 1871	Tabor
Maria Duch	6 Apr. 1805	Cottbus	23 July 1878	Tabor
George Kschammer (Nechilla)	28 June 1833	Werben		
Christiane Koalick		Werben		
Matthes Kschenka	19 Apr. 1836	Kolkwitz		
Louisa Pumpa	14 June 1832		10 Aug. 1876	Peter's Hill
Marie Kschiwan				
Martin Tilka		Papitz		
Carl Kubasch	22 July 1818	Prauske	3 July 1897	Bethel
Anna Doecke	11 May 1816	Nechern	14 Apr. 1874	Bethel

Martin Lange (Hanschk)	24 Oct. 1819	Drewitz	1899	Nhill
Anna Schlauk	20 Apr. 1819	Tauer	1905	Nhill
C. T. Andreas Lehmann	29 April 1821	Pommritz		
Maria Elisabeth Graff			10 June 1886	Peter's Hill
Friedrich Lehmann	24 Jan. 1819	Milkersdorf		
Christiane Noka	24 Nov. 1844	Milkersdorf	13 Sept. 1880	Peter's Hill
Anna Domaschenz	1821	Werben		
Johann Lehmann	27 Feb. 1817	Heinersbrück	9 Aug. 1880	Hamilton
Anna Kies	3 May 1821	Heinersbrück		Hamilton
Johan Lehmann	1827	Laubsdorf	3 Nov. 1891	
Elisabeth Krueger	1839	Laubsdorf	3 June 1894	
			4 Feb. 1893	
Martin Lehmann	19 Nov. 1811	Turnow	28 Oct. 1876	Sedan
Elizabeth Krautz	24 Aug. 1812	Heinersbrück	19 Jan. 1903	Sedan
Christian Lehrack	1 Jan. 1812	Glinzig	7 Dec. 1890	Drung Drung
Elisabeth Scheetz	15 July 1811		17 May 1883	Drung Drung
Christian Lewitzka (Baschzisch)	10 Nov. 1837	Guhrow		
Christiane Habner	11 Oct. 1836	Werben		
Matthis Lewitzka (Baschzisch)	6 Apr. 1833	Werben	30 Oct. 1914	Norwood
Anna Drekow	26 May 1846		1940	
Martin Lewitzka	1829	Briesen		
Elisabeth Marscha	13 Jan. 1835	Babow	10 Oct. 1862	Peter's Hill
Martin Groch				

Name	Date and Place of Birth		Date and Place of Death	
Andreas Lieschke	28 Oct. 1831	Rascha	14 May 1892	Walla Walla
Maria Altus	7 May 1835	Rodewitz	24 July 1912	Walla Walla
Johann Lischka	28 Jan. 1821	Kolkwitz	19 Sept. 1911	Peter's Hill
Christiane Borrack	11 Oct. 1811	Werben	27 Sept. 1901	Peter's Hill
Matthes Lokan	1822	Turnow	12 Aug. 1868	Hope Valley
Elisabeth Jurk	1816	Drehnow	12 Feb. 1895	Hope Valley
Peter Lowke	1819	Kotitz	11 Mar. 1895	Ebenezer
Magdalena Simmank	1 Dec. 1815		22 July 1904	Ebenezer
Matthes Lucas	28 Jan. 1814	Werben		
Elizabeth Duschka	25 Feb. 1812	Werben	3 Nov. 1905	Gawler
George Maroske	1845	Turnow	1918	
[Emilie Kroehn]				
Christian Marschall	22 June 1809	Babow	9 Mar. 1896	Peter's Hill
Elise Russchen		Babow		
Martin Materna	2 Dec. 1827	Werben		
Johanna Henrietta Hammerman				
Matthes Matschke	2 Aug. 1825	Werben	26 Aug. 1879	Natimuk
[Maria Schubert]				
Christian Matuschka	21 Feb. 1810	Dissen	7 Mar. 1874	Tabor
Anna Recho (Kossech)				
[Henriette Mueller]				

Christian Matuschka	24 Sept. 1811	Drewitz	28 Sept. 1894	Walla Walla
Maria Petatz	1 Jan. 1814	Drewitz	30 Oct. 1889	Jindera
George Miatke	18 Sept. 1812	Tauer		
Maria Lehmann	23 May 1811	Preilack		
George Miatke	1831	Preilack		
Elizabeth Noack	3 May 1828	Ruben	3 Mar. 1893	Peter's Hill
Andreas Mickan	31 Jan. 1821	Cortnitz	8 Nov. 1889	Walla Walla
Johann Hänschke	5 June 1826	Rackel	20 Aug. 1894	Walla Walla
Johann Mickan	10 Feb. 1818	Gröditz	25 Dec. 1904	Ebenezer
Christine Triede	2 Mar. 1821		14 Nov. 1898	Ebenezer
Peter Mickan	26 Aug. 1828	Cortnitz	18 Mar. 1907	Ebenezer
Johanna Preusker	6 Apr. 1826	Blösa	8 Dec. 1903	Ebenezer
Johann Mirtschin	14 Mar. 1809	Döhlen	26 Mar. 1884	Penshurst
Maria Gude	1 Aug. 1814	Döhlen	14 May 1878	Tabor
Matthes Modra	28 Oct. 1810	Werben	4 Mar. 1896	Kangaroo Flat
Christiana Kukawa	10 Mar. 1818		2 Jan. 1913	Kangaroo Flat
Friedrich Moeschke		Brahmow		
Elisabeth Domaschenz, n. Bischoff		Milkersdorf		
Martin Mudra (Nossack)	9 Dec. 1815	Papitz		
Anna Konzag (Koinzach)				
Christian Nagorka	31 Dec. 1826	Radewiese	19 May 1908	Hamilton
Emilie Zbierske	18 May 1847	Grabo	23 June 1890	Hamilton

Name	Date and Place of Birth		Date and Place of Death	
Johann Niemz	3 May 1847	Cortnitz		
Johanna Karoline Lange	19 Sept. 1852	Gebelzig		
Gottlieb Noack	2 July 1818	Schönhöhe	29 Dec. 1896	Peter's Hill
Anna Noack	10 Mar. 1825	Ruben	14 Apr. 1904	Peter's Hill
Johann Noack	21 Mar. 1815	Schönhöhe	24 Dec. 1890	Peter's Hill
Anna Hondow	22 Dec. 1809	Tauer	16 Nov. 1877	Peter's Hill
Maria Dreckow, n. Gardi	28 Oct. 1820		17 May 1910	Eudunda
Johann Noack	25 Nov. 1818	Reichwalde	9 Oct. 1902	St. Kitts
Agnes Bartsch	11 Dec. 1827	Särka	19 Feb. 1898	St. Kitts
Christian Nossack (Mudra)	31 Oct. 1849	Babow		
Anna	1843		5 July 1941	Nhill
Martin Nowotna	22 Oct. 1828	Brahmow	16 Jan. 1888	Murtoa
Elisabeth Jeitz	1827	Brahmow	23 Dec. 1900	Murtoa
Andreas Pannach	9 Oct. 1818	Rachlau	14 Oct. 1891	Ebenezer
Maria Schneider	1821		19 Sept. 1890	Ebenezer
Johann Pannach	1826	Rachlau		
Anna Gude	8 July 1829	Hochkirch	1865	Ebenezer
Johann Carl Pech	4 June 1810	Eulowitz	19 Oct. 1892	Vine Vale
Maria Stephan	4 Nov. 1823	Ebendörfel	7 May 1911	Vine Vale
Martin Petatz (Warnack)	13 Aug. 1821	Schönhöhe	12 Dec. 1888	Peter's Hill
Anna Groch	23 June 1818	Preilack	2 Aug. 1901	Peter's Hill

C. G. Wilhelm Petschel	4 May 1831	Neukirch	10 May 1914	Hamilton
Anna Magdalena Rentsch	27 Jan. 1831	Wohla	7 Feb. 1924	Hamilton
Christian Gotthelf Petschel	28 Jan. 1816	Neukirch	26 Nov. 1897	Murtoa
Anna Rosina Rösler	31 Dec. 1818	Neukirch	2 Dec. 1889	Dimboola
Christian Pösch	3 Jan. 1825	Kolkwitz		
Anna Noack				
Martin Posch	15 Mar. 1819	Kolkwitz		
Christiane Kschiwan	1810			
Johann Traugott Pötschke	28 Apr. 1831	Kuppritz		
Traugott Preusker	26 Jan. 1823	Blösa		Robertstown
[Anna Rosina Wende]				
Jacob Prochno	25 March 1811	Rackel	6 Apr. 1879	Gröditz
Agnes Preusker				
George Proposch	8 Apr. 1799	Dissen	11 Nov. 1877	Robertstown
Anna Koal	1809	Babow		
Christian Pumpa	24 Dec. 1815	Tauer	10 Dec. 1870	Jindera
Anna Jurban	25 Feb. 1818	Tauer	14 Aug. 1875	Jindera
Johann Pumpa	5 Jan. 1834	Drewitz	1893	Hawker
Catherine Groch	1834		20 June 1892	
Johann Georg Pumpa	9 Nov. 1820	Drewitz	14 Feb. 1878	Eden Valley
Elisabeth Klohs	2 Dec. 1821	Drewitz	18 July 1905	Eden Valley

Name	Date and Place of Birth		Date and Place of Death	
Martin Pumpa	11 Apr. 1820	Tauer	11 Apr. 1896	Henty
Marie Hondow	21 Oct. 1825		31 Oct. 1869	Jindera
Johann Carl Raedel	10 June 1823	Bautzen		Walla Walla
Marie Rosine	24 Aug. 1815	Bautzen	11 Feb. 1904	Chown Creek
Johann Urban	1789			
Christian Rapko (Marcula)	7 Jan. 1831	Werben		Dublin, S.A.
Christiane Klauk	1831	Burg		
Christian Reichert	1812	Kolkwitz		
Elisabeth	1816	Kolkwitz		
Johann Rentsch	30 Sept. 1801	Kuppritz	11 Sept. 1877	Hamilton
Maria Nettig	31 Mar. 1807	Trauschwitz	27 Aug. 1876	Hamilton
Johann Friedrich Rethus	24 Sept. 1855	Peter's Hill	20 Oct. 1936	Netherby
Maria Hondow	16 Apr. 1858		23 Oct. 1941	Nhill
Johann Rosel (Rusla)	1803	Pillnitz	1897	Gippsland
Johanna Zimmer	1804		1874	Doncaster
Christian Russchen	22 Mar. 1825	Babow		
Anna Schularick	1831	Drachhausen		
Maria Sapiatzer	31 Aug. 1828	Ruben		
Martin Russchen	1 Jan. 1822	Babow		
Anna Gurka	1 Dec. 1831	Babow		
Anna Salmann		Werben		

Christian Salzke Elisabeth Kasparik	14 Apr. 1809	Schmellwitz	20 May 1862	Hamilton
George Sapiatzer Anna Maroske	1823 16 Jan. 1822	Ruben Turnow	1883 20 June 1876	Millicent, S.A. Millicent, S.A.
Johann Traugott Schaefer Maria Klinger Anna Schultz	1821 24 May 1823 27 July 1847	Preilack Preilack	1 Sept. 1907 5 June 1867 28 May 1943	Armidale, N.S.W. Aberfoil, N.S.W. Armidale, N.S.W.
Matthias Schautschick Agnes	1820 1814	Kläfen	16 July 1913 14 June 1888	Ebenezer Ebenezer
Martin Scheetz Maria Konzack Anna Hussock, n. Schiack	14 July 1825 24 May 1827 1826	Werben Papitz Werben	22 Jan. 1908 10 Jan. 1865 24 Jan. 1912	Brocklesby Tabor Walla Walla
Friedrich Schiemenz Maria Drekow	14 Oct. 1827 24 Aug. 1833	Werben		
Johann Schlemmer Magdalena Gude	1815 23 Apr. 1827	Rodewitz Baschütz	19 Dec. 1902	Byaduk
Matthew Schlodder [Anna Margaret Cordes]	1852		9 July 1936	Gawler
Andreas Schmidt Maria Nowsck (Noack)	1817 1838	Gordanitz		
Andreas Schneider Maria Pannach	15 Jan. 1815 28 Oct. 1821	Kumschütz	23 Sept. 1892 5 Jan. 1908	Ebenezer

Name	Date and Place of Birth		Date and Place of Death	
Friedrich Moritz Schuppan	7 Feb. 1825	Kolkwitz	27 Sept. 1875	Emu Downs
Hanna Kappa	26 Sept. 1828	Kolkwitz	30 Dec. 1904	Emu Downs
Johann Schuppan	2 Nov. 1819	Tauer		
Anna Domsch	5 Sept. 1825	Tauer		
Matheus Schüppan (Schippan)	31 May 1825	Werben	10 Mar. 1903	Birdwood
Ana Schilka	6 May 1828	Werben		
Martin Schurgott				
Maria Kschinka		Kolkwitz		
Peter Schwartze	18 Feb. 1810	Kohlwesa	21 June 1895	Bethel
Agneta Mickan [Florentine Marks]	25 Feb. 1811	Cortnitz	20 Apr. 1851	Light Pass
Matthias Schwarz	2 Oct. 1820	Krieschow	3 Sept. 1892	Peter's Hill
Maria Russche	12 Dec. 1819	Babow	28 June 1892	Peter's Hill
Michael Ernst Seiler				
Agnes Lehmann	1822	Salzenforst		
Albin Starick	13 May 1828	Werben		
Anna Schilka			1886	Green Lake
Christian Starick	1 Dec. 1817	Werben	12 Mar. 1877	Murtoa
Christiane Warmo	23 Nov. 1821	Werben	4 Feb. 1890	Murtoa
Friedrich Starick	25 Dec. 1842	Jänschwalde	1 June 1917	Cambrai
Maria Forth	15 Jan. 1837		5 Aug. 1923	Cambrai

Friedrich Wilhelm Starick	26 Aug. 1829	Jänschwalde	Aug. 1922	Springton
Anna Wendt (Wentow)	4 July 1826		1 May 1884	Springton
Maria Eckert, n. Towk	1831		10 Apr. 1922	
Martin Starick	14 Mar. 1840	Peitz	27 June 1915	Dimboola
[Friederike Schmidt]				
George Stephan	10 Aug. 1799		24 July 1868	Neukirch
Anna	1802		4 Aug. 1876	Ebenezer
Johann Stephan	14 Nov. 1810	Gr. Saubernitz	9 Jan. 1885	Tabor
Agneta Kaiser				
Martin Stojan		Schmellwitz		
Elisabeth Hondow				
George Tannebring	9 Sept. 1828	Preilack		
[Caroline Hänschel]				
Johann Tannebring (Ziesche)	2 Jan. 1825	Turnow		
Anna Richter	1830	Turnow		
Martin Teschner	2 Jan. 1816	Turnow		
Elisabeth Stapke	17 Sept.	Preilack		
Martin Tilka	9 Sept. 1842	Kolkwitz	13 Oct. 1896	Yorketown
Maria Kschiwan				
Martin Towk	1819	Jänschwalde		Kangaroo Island
Anna Pipkorn (Pipke)	16 Nov. 1825	Drehnow		
Christian Twartz (Schillo)	18 Aug. 1818	Werben	31 Dec. 1870	Hamilton
Maria Melcharik	18 Nov. 1823	Werben	26 Nov. 1890	Neales Flat
			1907	

151

Name	Date and Place of Birth		Date and Place of Death	
Andreas Urban	30 Jan. 1790	Weigersdorf	8 Feb. 1879	Tabor
Christiane Neumann	11 July 1805		2 July 1882	Tabor
Johann Urban	24 May 1817	Weissenberg		Walla Walla
Maria Jurack	Aug. 1816	Dubrauke	Dec. 1878	Walla Walla
Maria Rosine Raedel				
Martin Vogt	7 Dec. 1816	Werben		
Maria Balow				
Andrew Wenk	26 Jan. 1809	Gröditz		
	16 Nov. 1831	Rachlau	14 June 1911	Bethel
Adam Wenke			17 Mar. 1855	
Anna Lischke				
[Christiane Siegert]				
Michael Wenke	19 Mar. 1829	Rachlau	14 June 1906	Walla Walla
Agnes Pannach	30 May 1830	Rachlau	7 May 1911	Walla Walla
Friedrich Werchon		Burg		
[Anna]				
Gottfried Woite	5 Dec. 1842	Drachhausen	4 Feb. 1913	Point Pass
[Anna Louise Lindner]				
Christian Wotzko	4 May 1831	Milkersdorf	1 Dec. 1916	Adelaide
[Hanna Pain]				
Johann Wuchatsch	8 Apr. 1802	Särka	29 Sept. 1884	Melbourne
Magdalena Bartschist	2 July 1825	Särke	27 Sept. 1903	Melbourne

Matties Zerna	1814	Milkersdorf	
Anna Böttcher	6 Mar. 1815		
Peter Zieschang	13 Oct. 1827	Kreckwitz	12 Mar. 1910 Noack, Texas
Magdalena Rentsch	1827	Drehsa	12 Mar. 1857 Tarrington
Magdalena	6 Mar. 1824		10 Nov. 1898 Noack, Texas
Michael Zimmer	1823	Bautzen	
Maria Graf		Bautzen	
Mattheus Zöllner	Nov. 1825	Fehrow	Rockwall, Texas
[Elizabeth Schmidt]			
Johann Zschech	23 Dec. 1802	Rackel	27 July 1865 Tarrington
Anna Nerettig	1811		9 May 1882 Tarrington
Johann Zwar	16 Oct. 1821	Drehsa	15 July 1912 Ebenezer
Magdalena Schmole	13 June 1819	Kumschütz	22 Oct. 1859 Ebenezer
Anna Kaiser	27 Mar. 1837	Drehsa	15 June 1917 Ebenezer
Michael Zwar	24 Mar. 1829	Drehsa	27 Dec. 1900 Broadford
Agnes Zimmer			16 June 1891
Peter Zwar	15 May 1824	Drehsa	27 June 1917 Appila
Magdalena Petzold (Batz)	24 Dec. 1826	Nechern	19 May 1910 Appila

CANADIAN WENDS

Name	Date and Place of Birth		Date and Place of Death	
Friedrich Ashick	5 Sept. 1832	Striesow	17 May 1883	Green Lake
Pauline	14 Feb. 1832		11 June 1889	Green Lake
August Boehme	30 Sept. 1841	Tauer	3 May 1907	Palmer Rapids
Marie Kilow	3 Jan. 1841	Tauer	9 Feb. 1894	Palmer Rapids
Johann Friedrich Bruchartz (Bossenz)				
Christiane Hokkum		Drehnow		
Martin Budarick	23 Oct. 1837	Drachhausen	9 July 1935	Palmer Rapids
Anna Rinza (Risto)		Drachhausen		
Johann Buder		Tauer		
Maria Kilow		Tauer		
Martin Coal	1833	Drachhausen	1913	Golden Lake
Elisabeth Rinza	1840	Drachhausen	1917	Golden Lake
Martin Dobring	1821	Schmogrow		
Luise Ruben	18 Aug. 1826		20 Mar. 1856	Schmogrow
Christiane Greschwald	26 Sept. 1834	Schmogrow		
Martin Doman [Amelia Muller]	18 Dec. 1832	Drachhausen	25 Apr. 1914	Woito
Matthes Doman			1898	Golden Lake
Louise Krueger	21 June 1830	Drachhausen	30 May 1905	Green Lake

Christian Fabian		Heinersbrück		
Christiane Schneider		Heinersbrück		
Martin Goldberg	20 Aug. 1863	Tauer	10 Mar. 1930	Woito
Elizabeth Fritsch	7 Feb. 1865	Drehnow	24 Dec. 1925	
Martin Gollick		Schmogrow		
Maria Eckert				
Matthes Guttke		Maust		
Anna Suekora				
Carl August Haentschel	17 Aug. 1831	Sachsendorf	15 Feb. 1905	Pembroke
Johanna Hannusch	4 Aug. 1834	Sachsendorf	6 July 1927	Pembroke
Friedrich Hammel		Schönhöhe		
Liese Gresenz	1836	Jänschwalde	7 Dec. 1866	Atica
Johann Gottfr. Hannusch	21 Mar. 1844	Sachsendorf	19 Dec. 1906	Pembroke
[Caroline Linder]				
Haschick (see Aschick)				
Matthes Hokum (Okum)		Drachhausen		
[Anna Lobde]				
Martin Huppatz	9 Dec. 1839	Schönhöhe	26 Oct. 1893	Green Lake
Anna Jurban	June 1842		19 July 1914	Brightview
Johannes Jonas	10 Aug. 1836	Tauer	1 Jan. 1918	Green Lake
Anna Hanschke	28 Feb. 1841	Tauer	26 Jan. 1917	Green Lake
Gottfried Jordan	22 Jan. 1828	Kolkwitz	4 July 1913	Pembroke

Name	Date and Place of Birth		Date and Place of Death	
Martin Junop (Schonnop)	1844	Drachhausen		
Anna Kilow			1898	
Koal, Kowal (see Coal)				
Martin Kielow	6 Jan. 1853			Tauer
[Maria Krueger]				
Christian Kossatz (Klausch)	2 Jan. 1822	Staakow	30 Jan. 1896	Pembroke
Christiane Nicklio (Pietzner)	25 Nov. 1817	Staakow	1 Dec. 1899	Pembroke
Martin Krueger	7 July 1827	Schönhöhe	3 Nov. 1908	Green Lake
Elisabeth Hammel	7 May 1823	Schönhöhe	19 May 1892	Green Lake
Friedrich Lehmann	22 Nov. 1846	Schmellwitz	27 Aug. 1934	Pembroke
Maria Ottilie Kuester	27 Jan. 1852	Cottbus	7 Oct. 1900	Pembroke
Martin Lehmann	29 Nov. 1838	Tauer	2 June 1924	Woito
Maria Baltzke		Tauer	1919	Woito
Matthias Liebech	1822	Dissenchen	19 May 1916	Green Lake
Elisabeth Berger	1843	Drehnow	31 May 1916	Green Lake
Johann Lisk	May 1841	Drachhausen	Aug. 1918	
Anna Yurt		Drachhausen		
Martin Loback	19 Dec. 1839	Preilack	19 Sept. 1917	Locksley
Louise Urban	16 May 1851		1928	Locksley
Martin Markusch (Markus)		Drachhausen	17 Aug. 1925	
[Caroline Yandt]				

156

Martin Melcher Elisabeth Richter	30 May 1830	Tauer Turnow	28 Sept. 1896 Green Lake
Martin Miatke Anna Retus		Drewitz Schmogrow	
Christian Nagora Anna Kilow		Tauer	
Christian Noack Elisabeth Regel	11 Nov. 1841 7 Dec. 1844	Sielow Sielow	6 Oct. 1912 Locksley 24 Jan. 1935 Locksley
Johann Noack Wilhelmine Mielke	27 Mar. 1839	Strobitz	6 Jan. 1919 Locksley 11 Aug. 1919 Locksley
Mattias Noack Wilhelmine Schilka	22 June 1835 1845		15 Jan. 1900 Killaloe 1918 Killaloe
Martin Noack Anna Schettke	30 Aug. 1828 23 Apr. 1841	Strobitz	17 Nov. 1909 Locksley
Okum (see Hokum)			
Martin Riese Anna Schmelick		Drachhausen Drachhausen	
Christian Schimenz (Schimmens) Anna Schergon	12 Jan. 1835 12 Sept. 1833	Peitz Drachhausen	10 Feb. 1916 Golden Lake 5 Mar. 1912
Schonnop, Zonnop (see Junop)			
Martin Schwitzer [Marie Hamann]		Tauer	

Name	Date and Place of Birth	Date and Place of Death
Gottfried Tadt	Drachhausen	
Anna Keine	Drachhausen	
Johann Teschner		
Wilhelmine Wust		
Johann Woito	8 Oct. 1813 Tauer	8 Jan. 1892 Woito
Catherine Hanschke		
Martin Woito	Tauer	
Maria Wushiga (Baschka)	July 1842 Tauer	23 Sept. 1885 Green Lake
Gottfried Yurt	Drachhausen	
Anna Koina	Drachhausen	

Nebraska Wends

Name	Date and Place of Birth	Date and Place of Death
Matthes Kaspar	Skandow	1894 Sterling
Christiane Kubisch	Horlitz	
Mato Kosyk	18 June 1853 Werben	22 Nov. 1940 Albion, OK
[Anna Wehr]		
[Wilma Filter]		
Johann Panko	17 Apr. 1846 Proschim	20 Oct. 1925 Sterling
Christiane Boslau	4 Feb. 1863	17 May 1941 Sterling

Name	Date and Place of Birth		Date and Place of Death	
Walter Ch. Pohlenz	9 May 1823	Senftenberg	5 Sept. 1916	Sterling
Karolina Schultz			26 Nov. 1899	
Johann Adam Rulla	13 July 1836	Gosda	8 Jan. 1919	Sterling
Johanna Paulisch	15 June 1838	Gosda	3 Feb. 1919	Sterling
Gottlieb Wusk	10 May 1852	Proschim	1 July 1922	Sterling
Pauline Merting	1856	Welzow		
Matthias Wusk	21 Aug. 1840	Proschim	15 Mar. 1914	Burr
Johanna Maria Koppenz	23 Apr. 1846	Wendish-Lieske	20 July 1926	Burr

Texas Wends

Name	Date and Place of Birth		Date and Place of Death	
Christian Aug. Andres	12 Feb. 1852	Lieskau	28 Dec. 1929	Walburg
Anna Maria Kalz	6 Jan. 1850	Leuthen	15 Jan. 1933	Walburg
*Johann Arldt	17 Mar. 1810	Weigersdorf		
Agnes Stary	24 Aug. 1811	Forstgen	29 Aug. 1868	Serbin
Maria Schneider, n. Kerk	2 July 1824	Dauban	1 Sept. 1903	Serbin
Ernst Balzer	18 May 1863	Weissenberg	5 June 1943	LaGrange
Auguste Schiwart	24 Dec. 1863	Uhyst		
*George Bamsch	17 Nov. 1813	Dürrbach	17 Mar. 1885	Serbin
Rosina Schatte	9 Jan. 1825	Jahmen	5 May 1897	Serbin

Name	Date and Place of Birth		Date and Place of Death	
*Rosina Bartsch	24 Oct. 1822	Klitten	3 Feb. 1906	Fedor
Jacob Paulik				
Johann Zieschang				
*George Becker	24 Dec. 1823	Jahmen	12 June 1855	Serbin
Rosina Drosche (Hofmann)	25 July 1826		14 May 1901	Serbin
*Joh. Carl Behser [Hanna]	28 Aug. 1808	Weissenberg		
Fr. Hermann Beisert	7 Oct. 1832		3 Oct. 1888	
Agnes	1829		13 Nov. 1873	
Maria Nokonz, n. Bohot	22 Jan. 1847	Neustadt	30 Sept. 1923	Serbin
August Benofsky	6 May 1840	Breitendorf	22 June 1915	Fedor
Magdalena	2 Feb. 1842		23 Sept. 1923	
*Andreas Bensch	1840		30 April 1907	Winchester
John Ernst Berger	26 Oct. 1844	Kleinhänchen	Mar. 1927	Giddings
Hanna Wukasch	2 July 1849	Buchwalde	30 July 1915	Giddings
Johann Berk	6 Jan. 1833	Hermsdorf		
Maria Buhl	27 Mar. 1834			
Johann Carl Bernstein	8 May 1827	Lehn	27 Dec. 1869	Serbin
Magdalena Jirus (Jeremias)	1832	Trauschwitz	30 May 1920	Albany
Carl August Stephan				

*Johann Biar	16 Feb. 1823	Gröditz	9 June 1885	Serbin
Magdalena Mehle	19 Nov. 1825	Särka	18 Sept. 1867	Serbin
Andreas Bibass	26 Sept. 1852	Zschorna	2 Dec. 1933	Serbin
Maria Mag. Groeschel	14 July 1857		9 Dec. 1939	Serbin
Matthes Biegon	27 Oct. 1830	Dürrbach	16 Oct. 1888	Serbin
Maria Schellnick	2 Feb. 1830	Dürrbach	17 June 1872	Serbin
August Biehle	15 Dec. 1836	Wurschen	27 July 1894	Giddings
Christiana Regemann	4 July 1841	Wawitz	16 July 1909	Giddings
Carl Heinrich Birke	6 Mar. 1849	Buchwalde	21 Sept. 1939	Giddings
Christiane Theresia Schneider	9 Aug. 1863	Preititz	1939	Giddings
*Joseph Birnbaum	15 Aug. 1830	Oberlichtenwalde	1 Nov. 1855	Serbin
Magdalena Pilak		Rodewitz	16 July 1874	
Andreas Melde				
George Boback	1823			
Maria Dallwitz	1828	Niederkotitz	1 Oct. 1869	Fedor
Matthes Bohot	23 Jan. 1825	Neustadt	9 Sept. 1892	Serbin
Dorothea Nowak	2 Mar. 1821	Neudorf	13 June 1902	Serbin
Carl D. Boike	1821			
Johanna Doman		Terpe	2 Mar. 1870	Serbin
Johann Boriack	19 June 1838	Spreewitz	5 Sept. 1899	Lincoln
Magdalena Bolding (Baltink)	30 Mar. 1844	Neudorf	11 Apr. 1899	Lincoln

Name	Date and Place of Birth		Date and Place of Death	
*George Born	9 Jan. 1826	Crosta	1893	Serbin
Maria	4 Nov. 1823		1905	Serbin
Johann Brosk	4 Apr. 1825	Förstgen		
Maria Magdalena Synatschk				
Carl Buchhorn	17 Aug. 1859	Weigersdorf	30 Aug. 1925	Walburg
Maria Schneider	22 July 1858	Reichwalde		
Johann August Budschick	1855	Weisswasser	27 Aug. 1934	Warda
Maria Nagorka, n. Kubitz	6 Feb. 1843	Kaschel	28 Nov. 1907	Warda
*Andreas Buettner	15 Feb. 1802	Wartha		
Andreas Buettner	1834		18 May 1913	Warda
Magdalena	13 May 1838		21 Sept. 1901	Warda
Theodore Buettner	1836			
Anna Kallenbach	4 Dec. 1840	Weisswasser	25 Dec. 1910	Walburg
Fr. Gottfried Domschula	25 May 1850			
Matthes Buscha	21 Sept. 1861	Trebendorf	20 May 1953	Warda
Marie Vobuza	6 Nov. 1859	Schleife	3 Jan. 1932	Warda
Johann Buscha	30 Aug. 1864	Trebendorf	22 Dec. 1940	Green's Creek
Christiana Noack	31 Dec. 1874	Mulkwitz	17 Nov. 1952	Green's Creek
Johann Deo	31 Dec. 1819	Preititz	5 Aug. 1870	Serbin
Maria Hillsberg	20 Nov. 1822	Weicha	7 May 1883	Serbin

Matthes Doman	3 Oct. 1840	Zerre	16 Dec. 1925	Fedor
Maria Grosa (Jakob)	13 May 1841	Spreewitz	18 Mar. 1909	Fedor
Johann Domaschk (Janak)	20 Nov. 1819		12 Oct. 1857	Serbin
Hanna Sarodnik	30 Apr. 1826		12 May 1870	Serbin
Johann Hohle (Kruper)				
*Matthes Domaschk (Jurz)	8 Nov. 1818	Kaschel	25 Nov. 1875	Serbin
Hanna Jurz	19 Mar. 1824	Kaschel	9 Mar. 1875	Serbin
Matthaeus Domaschke	1858	Reichwalde	31 Dec. 1880	Warda
Maria Winzer	1854	Terpe	11 June 1928	Warda
[August Lorenz]				
August Domel	26 Feb. 1875	Spreewitz	24 Feb. 1950	Walburg
Hulda Mathilde Zoch	17 Jan. 1882		15 Dec. 1962	Walburg
Fr. Gottfried Domschula	25 May 1850		25 Nov. 1922	Walburg
Anna Buettner, n. Kallenbach	4 Dec. 1840	Weisswasser	25 Dec. 1910	Walburg
Johann Traugott Droik	1840	Weisskeissel	1874	Serbin
Anna Budschick	31 Aug. 1839	Weisswasser		
Johann Drosche	8 Apr. 1821	Forstgen	10 Apr. 1884	Fedor
Christiane	12 Sept. 1822	Forstgen	3 Apr. 1890	Fedor
*Johann Dube	24 Apr. 1826	Prauske	17 Jan. 1879	Manheim
Magdalena Gross	22 June 1829	Wuischke	19 Dec. 1860	
Maria Symny	6 Oct. 1842	Rackel		
*Michael Dube	27 Sept. 1807	Trauschwitz	29 Sept. 1854	Serbin
Johanna Rosina Tanniger	15 Dec. 1807	Bellwitz	18 Aug. 1889	Serbin

Name	Date and Place of Birth		Date and Place of Death	
Johann Duerrlich		Weicha	11 June 1855	Roeder's Mill
*Johann Carl Dunzer	3 Jan. 1824			
Christiane	6 Jan. 1826	Muskau		
Johann Dutschmann	2 Feb. 1841	Neudorf	17 Aug. 1931	Thorndale
Anna Boschk	21 Sept. 1843	Geierswalde	6 Feb. 1925	Thorndale
Matthes Fabian	15 June 1866	Mühlrose	10 Oct. 1943	Copperas Cove
Elisabeth Wobusa	16 May 1865	Schleife	3 Aug. 1946	Copperas Cove
Andreas Falke	22 Mar. 1819	Buchwalde	12 Dec. 1903	Fedor
Anna Maria Gruhl	13 Jan. 1822	Lauske	22 Aug. 1909	Fedor
*George Falke	15 Nov. 1812	Buchwalde		
Agnes Rudel	2 June 1816	Rackel	4 Aug. 1876	Warda
Johann August Farrack	9 Nov. 1866	Rackel	30 Nov. 1938	Serbin
Maria Greilich	23 Jan. 1867		5 Mar. 1946	Serbin
Traugott Faske	19 Dec. 1851		3 Mar. 1933	Giddings
Maria Auguste Geier	16 Feb. 1847	Niedercunnersdf.	29 Sept. 1885	Fedor
Ernst Traugott Felfe	19 Nov. 1858	Lauske	29 July 1941	Thorndale
Emma Schulz	5 Apr. 1867		26 Jan. 1949	Thorndale
*Carl Aug. Fiedler	9 July 1816	Görlitz	Sept. 1855	Houston
Johanna Christiana	16 Aug. 1816			

Johann Fischer		1826	Rackel	22 Nov. 1906 Manheim
Anna		1827		17 May 1906 Manheim
August Foerster	2 July 1824		Dauban	6 June 1892 Warda
Caroline Freund		1830		
*Peter Fritsche	26 Feb. 1815		Dubrauke	24 Sept. 1900 Serbin
Johanna Krischke		1816	Dubrauke	6 Dec. 1854
Hanna Kerk	4 Feb. 1823		Dauban	10 Mar. 1885 Serbin
*Johann Fritsche	18 Feb. 1807		Gröditz	
Hanna	18 Feb. 1810			
Peter Gersch	19 Dec. 1827		Buchwalde	29 Sept. 1900 Serbin
Hanna Christiane Winkler	27 Aug. 1833		Weigersdorf	10 Mar. 1912 Giddings
Ernst Graf	4 Feb. 1839		Bautzen	29 Mar. 1921 Vernon
*Johann Greulich	5 Oct. 1822		Gebelzig	27 Aug. 1855
Johanna Christiane Brauer	24 May 1828		Ober Gebelzig	
*August Groeschel	22 July 1827		Särka	4 Oct. 1905 Serbin
Agnes Malke	19 Sept. 1832		Weicha	12 Feb. 1899 Serbin
Johann Gross	5 Oct. 1800		Weicha	29 Jan. 1867 Serbin
Hertha Lowke	16 July 1800		Nechern	
Johann Gruetnzer	25 Dec. 1829		Grossdehsa	17 Aug. 1872 Fedor
[Magdalena Proft]				
[Johann Wolf]				

Name	Date and Place of Birth		Date and Place of Death	
Andreas Handrick	5 Oct. 1822	Weicha	17 Oct. 1884	Fedor
Ana Noack		Rackel	2 Apr. 1902	Lincoln
*George Handrick	2 Jan. 1818	Dubrauke	28 Jan. 1888	Serbin
Johanna Rek	1820	Dubrauke	5 Feb. 1893	Serbin
*Johann Handrick	1 Oct. 1811	Weicha	18 July 1889	Serbin
Hanna Schneider	14 June 1818		3 Nov. 1894	Serbin
Johann Handrick	17 Nov. 1832			
Maria Puebner	25 Nov. 1842		3 Jan. 1914	Winchester
Andreas Hannusch	2 Oct. 1839	Gleina	15 Sept. 1932	The Grove
Maria Noack	1848		25 Feb. 1909	The Grove
*Andreas Hantschke (Prochneschko)	6 Mar. 1794	Rackel		
Hanna Zieschang		Weicha		
Agnes Krischke		Dubrauke		
Anna Drosche	5 Dec. 1818	Oelsa	23 Sept. 1869	Serbin
Matthes Heinze	29 Sept. 1856	Rohne	1 Nov. 1940	Thorndale
Theresia Symmank	16 Nov. 1861	Rodewitz	2 Nov. 1922	Thorndale
George Helas	1806			
Caroline Mathilde	1810			
Johann Hentschel	1839	Dauban	20 Nov. 1913	Winchester
Maria	1839		21 Jan. 1915	Winchester

166

Name	Birth date	Birthplace	Death date	Death place
*Gotthilf Herbrig	16 Feb. 1809	Weissenberg	8 June 1888	Warda
Johanne Christiane Lehmann	22 Oct. 1821	Weissenberg	26 Feb. 1902	Warda
Johann Herenz	19 Jan. 1827	Klein Oelsa	1 Nov. 1900	Serbin
Rosina Polnick				
Agnes	4 Nov. 1913	Serbin		
Fr. August Herzog	12 Dec. 1845	Niethen	15 Mar. 1906	Fedor
Ernst Hilscher	21 Nov. 1855	Dauban	13 Dec. 1938	Winchester
Amalia Foerster	1864	Dauban	1922	
Andreas Hobratschk	13 Jan. 1824	Wurschen	26 Feb. 1893	Warda
Hanna Jacob	22 Oct. 1833	Teichnitz	2 Feb. 1892	Warda
*George Hocker	12 Apr. 1805	Förstgen	24 Dec. 1869	Serbin
Magdalena Schulze	1806		24 Nov. 1858	Serbin
Magdalena Kerk	1827	Dauban	10 Dec. 1863	Serbin
*Johann Hohle (Kruper)	25 Jan. 1825	Jahmen	12 Oct. 1889	Serbin
Rosina Jurak	1830	Reichwalde	22 June 1858	Serbin
Hanna Domaschk (Janak) n. Sarodnik	30 Apr. 1826	Dauban	12 May 1870	Serbin
Herta Krakowski	1837		4 Mar. 1899	Serbin
*Matthaus Hohle (Kruper)	11 April 1830	Jahmen	2 Aug. 1912	New Ulm
Maria Schram	1836	Kolpen	19 Oct. 1910	New Ulm
*Johann Hollas	18 Feb. 1821	Oelsa	23 Nov. 1900	Serbin
Hanna Schiwart, n. Schuster	16 Dec. 1823		20 Feb. 1909	Serbin

Name	Date and Place of Birth		Date and Place of Death	
John Hopenz	1820	Maltitz		
Christiane Roitsch	1833			
Oscar Horn	8 Dec. 1853	Mulkwitz	18 May 1935	Paige
Ida Schade	9 Aug. 1857			
Andreas Hottas	23 May 1805	Spree	1 July 1868	Serbin
Rosina Schulz		Reichwalde		
Maria Tilscher	June 1822	Reichwalde	10 Dec. 1890	Serbin
*George Iselt (Mrosk)	18 Sept. 1814	Dürrbach	16 Dec. 1874	Fedor
Rosina Bamsch	16 Aug. 1810	Dürrbach	18 Dec. 1863	Serbin
Magdalena Lehmann	27 Oct. 1865	Weissenberg		
*Rosina Schuster Iselt		Nappatsch	15 Oct. 1854	
Christian Jakob (Grossa)	8 Mar. 1849	Spreewitz	5 Feb. 1908	Copperas Cove
Maria Ssucky	16 Apr. 1857		31 Jan. 1921	Copperas Cove
Matthes Jakobik	5 May 1852	Trebendorf	1 Oct. 1930	Giddings
Magdalena Bohot	10 May 1852	Neustadt	12 Oct. 1933	Giddings
Johann Jannasch	27 Oct. 1829	Plotzen	16 Mar. 1881	Serbin
Anna Czech	18 Nov. 1829	Wawitz	12 Sept. 1881	
*Johann Jannasch	4 May 1809	Weissenberg	14 Aug. 1855	Houston
Magdalena	30 Jan. 1815		12 Aug. 1855	Houston
Christian Jatzlau	21 Oct. 1834	Zerre	3 Apr. 1880	Warda
Magdalena Socke	26 Mar. 1830	Oelsa	28 Sept. 1899	Warda

Gottlob Jentho	11 Apr. 1863	Schleifa	Aug. 1926	The Grove
Anna Maria Boriack	22 Dec. 1861	Neustadt	22 June 1914	Albany
Matthaus Jurischk	15 Sept. 1846	Spreewitz	5 Nov. 1888	Serbin
Maria Berghold	13 May 1849	Spreewitz	8 June 1926	Winchester
Peter Jurk	17 Sept. 1831	Dubrauke	8 June 1916	Warda
Johanna Zoch, n. Koal	9 Oct. 1842	Spreewitz	20 May 1929	Warda
Johann Chr. Kalmbach	10 Nov. 1833	Muskau	7 Apr. 1906	Walburg
Christoph Kambor	Jan. 1800	Wunscha	16 June 1855	Serbin
Maria Marko	1802	Viereichen	23 May 1882	Serbin
Andreas Kappler	6 Dec. 1832	Halbendorf	7 July 1902	Giddings
Agnes Groeschel	9 Apr. 1839	Särka	8 Oct. 1916	Giddings
*George Kaspar	2 June 1816	Kolpen	21 Jan. 1864	Serbin
Magdalena Schneider	6 Aug. 1823	Spreewitz	6 July 1895	
Carl Benjamin Weise				
Johann Kasparik	3 Oct. 1817	Neustadt	25 Nov. 1882	Warda
Hanna Jatzlau	Feb. 1813	Zerre	3 Feb. 1869	
*Christian Kasper	22 Jan. 1824	Neudorf	21 June 1855	
Dorothea	1823		28 May 1855	
Johann Kasper	1807	Kolpen	20 Oct. 1855	New Ulm
Hanna Schramm	2 Nov. 1819	Kolpen		
*Johann Pampel	Sept. 1807	Guttau	2 Jan. 1867	
Johann Kasper	1794	Jahmen	18 June 1856	Serbin
Maria Breda	1 Jan. 1796	Kaschel	9 Aug. 1880	

Name	Date and Place of Birth		Date and Place of Death	
Karl Ernst Keiling	21 Mar. 1827	Neider Seidau	1 Mar. 1903	Walburg
Therese Zieschang	30 Jan. 1835	Kreckwitz	9 May 1917	Walburg
Johann Kerk	6 Jan. 1798		20 Sept. 1879	
Agnes Schramm		Dauban		
Agnes Mros		Jetscheba		
Andreas Kieschnick [Elisabeth Korner]	13 Nov. 1828		23 Feb. 1900	Manheim
*Johann Kieschnick	Apr. 1795	Dauban	21 Nov. 1867	Serbin
Agnes Gersch	28 Apr. 1795		14 Oct. 1876	Serbin
*Johann Kiesling	14 Mar. 1787	Weigersdorf	17 Oct. 1854	
Hanna	1797		15 Oct. 1854	
Andreas Kiesling	31 Oct. 1827	Gross Radisch	14 Feb. 1910	Swiss Alp
Hanna Pietsch	21 June 1835	Gross Radisch	17 Oct. 1920	Swiss Alp
*Johann Kilian	22 Mar. 1811	Doehlen	12 Sept. 1884	Serbin
Maria Groeschel	1 July 1823	Särka	1 Jan. 1881	Serbin
Friedrich Kmoch	11 Aug. 1858	Spittel	23 Mar. 1922	Paige
Matthaius Kneschk	3 May 1834	Weisswasser	10 July 1909	Sagerton
Anna Wolsch				
*Johann Knippa	13 Sept. 1811	Buchwalde	27 July 1886	Swiss Alp
Christiana Schneider	17 Oct. 1831	Spreewitz	21 Dec. 1886	Swiss Alp

*Joh. Gottlieb Kohl	20 Oct. 1802	Muskau			
Johanne Ernstina	12 May 1827				
*Christoph Kokel	14 Jan. 1823	Reichwalde	14 Dec. 1868	Serbin	
Maria Schneider	1 Dec. 1820	Reichwalde	17 Mar. 1901	Walburg	
*Christian Kolba	22 May 1830	Neudorf	15 Oct. 1906	New Ulm, Minn.	
Maria Casparik	21 Oct. 1826		14 Feb. 1904	Reedsburg, Wis.	
*Matthaus Kolba		Neudorf	14 Oct. 1855	New Ulm, Minn.	
Heinrich Koslan	22 Mar. 1855	Weisswasser	17 Dec. 1930	Manheim	
Maria Ernstine Polnick	1860		10 June 1881	Manheim	
Maria Budschick	21 Apr. 1860	Weisswasser	3 Sept. 1931	Manheim	
George Krakosky	1831	Förstgen	8 Mar. 1903	Warda	
Amalie Freund	1834	Commerau	6 Aug. 1921	Warda	
Christoph Krause	23 Mar. 1817	Mucka	15 June 1869	Serbin	
Maria Michalk	21 Feb. 1828	Oelsa	26 July 1912		
Johann Krautschick	12 June 1825		26 Nov. 1904	Fedor	
Agnes Hattas	27 Sept. 1830	Spree	11 July 1911	Fedor	
*Johann Kubitz	12 Nov. 1810	Dubrauke	30 Aug. 1869	Serbin	
Maria Reben	1 May 1822	Dubrauke			
Maria Schklentscher		Weigersdorf			
Johann Kubitz	1806		27 July 1874	Serbin	
Johanna Bartsch	31 Mar. 1807				
Johann Kulke			18 Nov. 1922	Albany	
Agnes	13 Dec. 1831		11 Aug. 1889	Warda	

171

Name	Date and Place of Birth		Date and Place of Death	
Andreas Kunze	28 Jan. 1819	Neithen	7 Jan. 1879	Fedor
Hanna Dube	1828		19 Oct. 1870	Serbin
*Michael Kurio	20 Nov. 1820	Wurschen	8 Jan. 1902	Serbin
Magdalena Rudel	13 Apr. 1819	Rackel	9 Oct. 1854	
Johanna Christiane Dube	17 Sept. 1832	Rodewitz	12 June 1920	Warda
Andreas Lehmann	1 July 1807	Gr. Saubernitz	7 Nov. 1896	Warda
Anna Mehle	11 May 1811	Gr. Saubernitz	20 Jan. 1870	Serbin
*Johann Carl A. Lehmann	10 Aug. 1837	Weissenberg		
Johann Lehmann	1806	Weissenberg	16 Feb. 1862	Serbin
Johanna	1804			
*Johann Carl Lehmann	4 Mar. 1814	Dauban	15 Mar. 1888	Serbin
Magdalena Bosche	16 July 1820	Blösa	18 Jan. 1905	Serbin
Johann Leitko	13 Aug. 1854	Trebendorf	9 July 1916	Lincoln
Maria Nowusch	1866		4 July 1890	Lincoln
Johann Carl Leschber	27 Feb. 1823	Petershain	18 Dec. 1915	Walburg
Ernstine Johanne Paul	1 Dec. 1831	Petershain	15 Feb. 1916	Walburg
*George Lorentsk	3 Oct. 1816	Reichwalde	30 Sept. 1895	Serbin
Elisabeth Casper	19 Mar. 1815	Nochten	17 Nov. 1882	Serbin
*Andreas Lowke	1 Oct. 1814	Reichwalde	13 Apr. 1893	Serbin
Anna Schubert	21 July 1809	Klitten	21 Aug. 1869	Serbin
Hanna Jung, n. Schiwart	28 Apr. 1812		12 May 1901	Serbin

Andreas Lowke	14 Jan. 1831		24 Nov. 1914	Winchester
Henrietta	21 Mar. 1834		16 Jan. 1916	Winchester
*George Lowke	2 Apr. 1811	Klein Radisch	22 Apr. 1861	
Anna Kijank	9 Apr. 1810			
Johann Mitschke				
Johann Malke	1775	Weicha	29 Apr. 1856	Serbin
Hanna Gross	1795			
Matthes Maroske	1823		1903	Paige
Christiane Kruger	11 June 1841		8 Apr. 1923	Paige
*Hanna Matke	24 May 1816	Klitten	20 Oct. 1855	
Andreas Matthias (Mattiaschke)	29 Oct. 1831	Kippen	28 Jan. 1908	Frelsburg
[Rosina Mikeska]				
Mattiza				
Matthes Matthiez	11 Apr. 1821	Kaschel	4 Dec. 1880	
Dorothea Rehle	10 July 1822	Kaschel	4 May 1900	Serbin
Friedrich Matuschka	9 July 1838	Berlin	4 Mar. 1918	Lake Cr., MO
[Louise Horisch]	6 July 1838	Annaburg	27 June 1912	Lake Cr., MO
Johann Matz	3 Aug. 1837	Klitten	Mar. 1913	Warda
Anna Nowotnick			1905	
Peter Medack	13 Apr. 1833		1 Oct. 1904	Lincoln
Magdalena Drilling	16 July 1829		18 Nov. 1903	Lincoln

Name	Date and Place of Birth		Date and Place of Death	
*Andreas Melde	25 Dec. 1825	Doberschütz	30 Dec. 1903	Fedor
Magdalena Birnbaum n. Pillack	15 Aug. 1830	Rodewitz	16 July 1874	Fedor
Christiana Theresia Handrik	27 Dec. 1854	Rodewitz	12 July 1908	Fedor
*Johann Meltschak	20 July 1805	Königswartha		
Maria	16 May 1805			
Carl L. Mersiovsky	17 Jan. 1851	Oppach	14 Feb. 1907	Serbin
Maria Mirtsching	31 Mar. 1848	Hochkirch	14 Dec. 1880	Serbin
George Merting	1830			
Maria Schulze	10 Aug. 1836	Wunscha		
*Johann Mertink (Bartel)	9 Feb. 1824	Thomaswalde	3 Nov. 1878	Serbin
Hanna Hohle (Kruper)	Mar. 1826	Jahmen		
Rosina Becker,				
n. Drosche (Hofmann)	25 July 1826		14 May 1901	Serbin
Johann Carl Michalk	15 Aug. 1843	Sandförstgen	26 May 1901	Thorndale
Maria Birnbaum	8 Aug. 1850	Rodewitz	25 Feb. 1912	Thorndale
Carl Ernst Michalk	21 Aug. 1857	Sandförstgen		Victoria
Ernstine Zischang				
Andreas Michalk	23 Mar. 1840		23 Sept. 1903	Warda
Caroline Krakosky	6 Aug. 1846		24 Aug. 1897	
*Michael Mieksch		Loebau		

Johann Adam Miersch	12 Dec. 1830	Lehn	5 Oct. 1898	Walburg
Maria Bartke	28 June 1841	Baruth		
*Andreas Miertschin	22 Nov. 1809	Särke	28 Sept. 1854	
Anna Lehmann	1 Oct. 1809		29 Sept. 1854	
Johann Mikan	22 Dec. 1845	Weigersdorf	17 Apr. 1894	Walburg
Maria Magdalena Neitsch	5 June 1855	Galveston	9 Mar. 1924	Walburg
Johann Mitschke	25 Oct. 1841	Kaschel	12 Mar. 1912	Serbin
Hanna Matthiez	15 Aug. 1849		10 Mar. 1929	Serbin
Matthes Mitschke	11 Dec. 1817	Kaschel	24 May 1898	Serbin
Maria Kubitz	25 Aug. 1817	Kaschel	19 Dec. 1896	Serbin
*Ernst Adolph Moerbe	6 Aug. 1824	Klix		Serbin
Agnes Symny	1826	Klix	9 Jan. 1891	Serbin
Johann Symny				
*Ferdinand Jacob Moerbe	6 Dec. 1828	Neudörfel	13 Dec. 1896	Thorndale
Anna Holfeld	22 Dec. 1828	Neudörfel	29 Nov. 1854	
Johanna Rachel Dube	4 Aug. 1834	Rodewitz	15 Aug. 1917	Thorndale
Johann Moerbe	4 June 1830	Dauban	4 Feb. 1894	Warda
Maria Basche				
Maria Skade	27 Oct. 1843	Dauban	28 Mar. 1914	Warda
Matthaus Mrosko	13 Apr. 1814	Gröditz	Nov. 1902	Serbin
Hanna Schoellnick	1 Jan. 1818	Dürrbach		
Hanna	22 Mar. 1824		10 Dec. 1897	Serbin

Name	Date and Place of Birth		Date and Place of Death	
August Karl Mutschink	7 Sept. 1863	Rodewitz	6 Feb. 1939	Manheim
Emma Zschech	5 Apr. 1877	Serbin		
George Najorka	6 Aug. 1838	Muskau	26 Sept. 1876	Warda
Maria Kubitz	1841	Kaschel	28 Nov. 1907	Warda
Johann August Budschick				
Fr. Wm. Nakonz	19 Jan.	Spremberg	14 Feb. 1878	Warda
Maria Bohot	22 Jan. 1847	Spremberg	30 Sept. 1923	Serbin
*Johann Gottlieb Neitsch	19 Apr. 1829	Särka	22 Apr. 1902	Warda
Maria Symmank	30 July 1824	Weicha	9 Oct. 1905	Walburg
Johann Nerrettig	4 Nov. 1858		1 Aug. 1950	Copperas Cove
Anna Suck (Ssucy)	2 June 1863		6 Mar. 1942	Copperas Cove
*J. Carl Ed. Neumann	5 Apr. 1816	Weigersdorf	Sept. 1855	Houston
Maria Urban	24 Mar. 1818			
Johann Nickel	24 Jan. 1841		4 Apr. 1880	Serbin
Magdalena Domut	22 July 1841			
Johann Kubitz				
Andreas Niemtschk	1809	Malschwitz	26 July 1889	Lincoln
Andreas Niemtschk	7 Nov. 1850	Bautzen	11 Nov. 1920	Thorndale
Clara Richter	1857		24 Dec. 1910	Thorndale
Johann Niemtz (Njemz)	6 July 1873	Mühlrose	13 Jan. 1927	Dime Box
Theresia Maria Zoch				

Gottlieb Nitsche	3 June 1819	Burghammer	22 Mar. 1905	Serbin
Anna Pache (Petschick)			29 July 1886	Serbin
Andreas Noack	18 Sept. 1835	Maltitz	20 Nov. 1918	Lincoln
Anna Richter	15 Oct. 1840		13 Oct. 1930	Thorndale
*Christoph Noack	7 Sept. 1813	Sandförstgen	Oct. 1855	Houston
Johanna Christiane	1 June 1825			
Johann Noack	10 Aug. 1812		8 Nov. 1884	Warda
Maria	30 Nov. 1813		7 May 1887	Warda
Johann Noack	1 Mar. 1839	Molkwitz	22 Feb. 1913	Serbin
Maria Lowke	25 Oct. 1842			
Johann Noack	11 Jan. 1819	Rackel	3 June 1879	Manheim
Anna Wacker	30 Mar. 1824		9 Feb. 1895	Lincoln
*Johann Noack	Mar. 1823	Gröditz	15 Dec. 1907	Serbin
Magdalena	1812		22 Oct. 1854	
*Michael Noack	19 Feb. 1820	Wartha	27 May 1903	
Hanna Lehmann		Guttau		
Maria Handrick	5 Aug. 1839			
Maria Nowotnik	1828	Hoyerswerda	11 Oct. 1908	Lincoln
Johann Pallmer	4 Apr. 1831	Bederwitz	1 Sept. 1873	Serbin
[Helena Hermann]				
*Johann Pampel	Sept. 1807	Guttau	2 Jan. 1867	
Agnes Post				

Name	Date and Place of Birth		Date and Place of Death	
Agnes Belas [Hanna Kasper n. Schramm]		Klix	21 Nov. 1854	
*Michael Pampel Johanne Juliana	18 June 1819 30 Oct. 1827	Zittau		
*Peter Pampel Agnes Noack	18 Jan. 1808 1809	Wartha Wartha	Oct. 1855 18 Sept. 1854	Industry
*Carl August Patschke Hanna Matthieschk	19 Dec. 1818 22 Apr. 1826	Kolpen Lippen	24 June 1893 14 Dec. 1901	Fedor Fedor
Traugott Patschke Maria Krahl	13 May 1831 1832	Kolpen Schöpsdorf		
*Jacob Paulik Agnes Rosina Bartsch	1 Aug. 1800 28 Aug. 1786 24 Oct. 1822	Klitten	14 Apr. 1874 Mar. 1855 3 Feb. 1906	Serbin Fedor
Johann Paulik Maria Greulich	8 July 1850 8 Sept. 1857	Jahmen	3 June 1894	Serbin
Matthes Paulo Maria Broto (Sarodnik)	26 Dec. 1817 7 Mar. 1827	Schleife Spreewitz	27 Jan. 1903 7 Mar. 1911	Serbin Serbin
*Andreas Pehse Hanna Franke, n. Kunze Beata Simon	13 July 1819 3 Aug. 1814	Schadendorf Uhyst	10 Apr. 1900 29 Sept. 1882	Serbin Serbin
*Matthaus Peter Rosina Lushiz	29 Sept. 1789 June 1793	Reichwalde Reichwalde	5 Sept. 1873 16 May 1877	Serbin Serbin

Johann Petzold	24 June 1849	Rothenburg	7 Feb. 1902	Lexington
Maria Hultzsch	8 Aug. 1847	Rothenburg	8 Jan. 1904	Lexington
Gustave Pietsch	22 May 1867	Drehsa	22 June 1917	Giddings
Sidonie Hansel	24 July 1877	Drehsa	3 Feb. 1832	Giddings
*Andreas Pilak	17 Dec. 1797	Rodewitz	30 Sept. 1854	
Maria Urban	1800	Weigersdorf	1 Apr. 1873	Fedor
Johann Pobrau	24 Feb. 1852	Tzschellin	12 Dec. 1937	Walburg
Maria Domel	16 Mar. 1846			
August Polnick	12 Mar. 1823	Förstgen	25 July 1876	Fedor
Maria Wagner	3 Feb. 1823	Weigersdorf	8 May 1889	The Grove
George Polnick	2 Apr. 1825	Gr. Radisch	2 Oct. 1887	Fedor
Helene	1825			
Friedrich Poppelz	9 Dec. 1844	Weisswasser	20 Nov. 1935	Walburg
Anna Janusch			19 Nov. 1891	Walburg
Maria Handreck, n. Schlemmer	30 Jan. 1851	Rodewitz	July 1913	Walburg
*Matthes Prellop	7 Oct. 1822	Geisslitz	13 Aug. 1886	Serbin
Dorothea Schneider	1827	Spreewitz	16 Sept. 1884	Serbin
Johanna Hempel				
Johann August Proft	19 June 1844	Mutitz	22 Dec. 1896	Corning, MO
Andreas Proske	31 Mar. 1830	Förstgen	15 May 1911	Serbin
Johanna Kasper	5 June 1830	Petershain	20 Aug. 1898	Serbin

Name	Date and Place of Birth		Date and Place of Death	
Matthias Proske	19 Sept. 1832		7 Jan. 1886	Manheim
Magdalena Noack	16 Oct. 1834	Langölsa		
August Rackel	10 Oct. 1854		20 Mar. 1933	Loebau
Magdalena Noack	10 Sept. 1861	Klein Saubernitz	18 May 1936	Loebau
Johann Reinhardt	2 Jan. 1848		5 Dec. 1920	
Mary Lowke	4 Feb. 1847	Malschwitz	23 Jan. 1916	
Herman Roentsch	19 Apr. 1851	Kittlitz	22 Jan. 1889	Fedor
Andreas Richter	16 Dec. 1854	Weissenberg	22 Mar. 1931	Giddings
Magdalena Synatschk		Förstgen	6 Oct. 1885	
Maria Fritsche				
*Carl Ernst Richter	25 Oct. 1831	Viereichen		
Christian Richter	4 Oct. 1845	Spreewitz	7 Dec. 1911	Walburg
Magdalena Skoring	13 Jan. 1849	Zerre	20 Oct. 1914	Walburg
Johann Richter	10 Sept. 1837	Ruhetal	26 Sept. 1870	Serbin
Magdalena Hempel	20 Mar. 1837	Särke	7 July 1913	Fedor
August Zschech				
*Adam Ritter	13 June 1833	Rodewitz	25 Sept. 1907	Swiss Alp
[Maria Christiana Klein]				
Carl Roitsch		Maltitz	29 Oct. 1878	Swiss Alp
Maria Krause	9 June 1823		4 Apr. 1899	Swiss Alp

*Johann Gottlieb Scharath
Hanna Domann	28 Oct. 1805	Dauban	9 Apr. 1855	Industry
*Christoph Schatte
Rosina Domaschk	4 Apr. 1825
17 Aug. 1832	Klitten
Reichwalde	29 Apr. 1870
12 Sept. 1910	Serbin
Serbin
*Johann Schatte
Rosina	4 Apr. 1825	Klitten	30 Sept. 1854
26 Sept. 1854	Serbin
Serbin
*Matthaus Schatte (Mroske)
Rosina Wobaj	14 June 1802
21 Oct. 1801	Thomaswalde	22 Sept. 1854
18 Sept. 1854	Serbin
Serbin
Johann Schautschik
Maria Schubert	14 Dec. 1827
27 July 1839		12 Nov. 1897
17 May 1926	Serbin
Serbin
*Christoph Schelnick
Rosina Schwoibe	20 Sept. 1827
31 Jan. 1831	Dürrbach
Kaschel	19 Apr. 1902
11 Feb. 1904	Serbin
Serbin
Johann Schimank
Maria Kubitz	6 July 1845
2 Oct. 1848	Commerau	11 July 1931
20 Nov. 1919	Fedor
Fedor
*Christoph Schiwart
Hanna Schuster
Johann Hollas	29 Mar. 1825
18 Dec. 1823	Dürrbach	14 June 1859	New Ulm
George Schiwart
Johanna Domaschk
[Magdalena Warnasch]	1823
1827	Uhyst		
Johann Schiwart
Anna Wukasch	31 May 1821
12 Aug. 1822	Kaschel		

181

Name	Date and Place of Birth		Date and Place of Death	
Carl Heinrich Schkade	20 June 1850	Weigersdorf	14 Dec. 1917	Mannheim
Auguste Lehmann	23 July 1860			
*Andreas Schlemmer	20 Sept. 1820	Rodewitz	13 Sept. 1855	Houston
Theresia Polenz	1827	Drehsa	Sept. 1855	Houston
*Matthaus Schmidt	3 June 1802	Reichwalde	3 Aug. 1866	
Rosina Schneider	16 Apr. 1801	Reichwalde		
George Schmidt	23 Feb. 1843	Grosspostwitz	30 Sept. 1923	Serbin
Anna Krause	18 Aug. 1858		20 Mar. 1895	Serbin
Maria Beisert, n. Bohot	22 Jan. 1847	Neustadt	30 Sept. 1923	Serbin
Andreas Schneider	17 Mar. 1825	Tauer	14 Dec. 1897	Walburg
Maria [Wilhelmina Prachwitz]	12 Oct. 1835	Zimpel	25 Oct. 1873	Fedor
August Schneider	4 Jan. 1849		20 May 1902	Warda
Maria Noatnick	20 Oct. 1849		10 June 1895	Warda
Helena Domaschk				
Ernst Schneider	7 Dec. 1854	Preititz	8 Dec. 1912	Giddings
Maria Magdalena Kaestner	8 Jan. 1860	Gröditz	26 Aug. 1924	Giddings
*Johann Schneider	24 May 1829	Spreewitz	26 Jan. 1896	Warda
Magdalena Nowotnik	6 May 1834	Zerre		
*Michael Schneider	10 Apr. 1812	Nechern	7 Nov. 1867	Serbin
Maria Kerk	2 July 1824	Dauban		
Johanna Arldt				

Johann Schoellnik	13 Oct. 1793	Dürrbach	19 Oct. 1861	Serbin
Hanna Breda	Nov. 1793	Kaschel	4 Aug. 1865	
*Matthes Schoellnick	10 Dec. 1815	Dürrbach	30 Jan. 1883	Leeville
Anna Motz (Moze)	23 July 1809	Klitten	15 Aug. 1865	
Maria Zwahr, n. Dzjnkin	16 Oct. 1816	Klein-Saubernitz		
Michael Schoppa	18 Sept. 1833	Zerre	23 Feb. 1903	Warda
Maria Zoch	23 Jan. 1840	Sprey	15 Jan. 1881	Warda
Christiane Schur, n. Jassenk	4 Dec. 1831		27 Dec. 1893	Warda
Andreas Schubert	30 Oct. 1830	Tauer	15 Aug. 1897	
Maria Birke	23 Jan. 1828	Klein Saubernitz	24 Oct. 1915	
*George Schubert	15 June 1818	Tauer	8 Oct. 1870	Serbin
Rosina Born	Dec. 1816		13 Mar. 1903	Serbin
*Johann Schubert	25 July 1825	Kaschel		
Anna Mitschke	24 Oct. 1825	Kaschel		
Johann Schubert	12 Nov. 1806	Klitten		
Magdalena Petrik (Wuiz)	27 July 1825	Wunscha	31 Jan. 1879	Swiss Alp
Christian Schulz	4 Oct. 1862	Spreewitz	26 Feb. 1944	Warda
Magdalena Schoppa	1 Feb. 1866	Spreewitz	23 Jan. 1933	Warda
*Johann Schulze	30 Oct. 1801	Förstgen	26 Apr. 1884	Serbin
Maria	9 June 1799		22 Oct. 1858	
*Mattheus Schulze	17 Feb. 1807	Wunscha	10 Sept. 1854	
Hanna Juritz	1813	Wunscha	5 Oct. 1880	Serbin

Name	Date and Place of Birth		Date and Place of Death	
*Matthous Schulze	13 Mar. 1832	Särka	15 Nov. 1900	Serbin
Hanna Groeschel	24 Sept. 1836			
*Mattheus Schuster	17 May 1815	Förstgen	29 Jan. 1898	Serbin
Johanna Eleonore	17 July 1823		26 May 1907	Serbin
Matthias Schwausch	26 June 1832	Sabrodt	5 June 1886	Warda
Magdalena Schulze	31 July 1833	Weicha	30 Nov. 1920	Copperas Cove
Johann Kulke				
George Seiler	1857	Spreewitz		
Anna Jurisch	1857	Kaschel		
Friedrich Seydler	21 Feb. 1806	Bautzen	20 Nov. 1869	High Hill
Augusta Fiebiger	6 Aug. 1810	Bautzen	20 Aug. 1890	High Hill
*Carl August Simmank	29 May 1812	Carlsbrunn		
Ana Magdalena	19 Oct. 1812			
Traugott Skoreng	12 June 1843	Burghammer	9 Jan. 1868	
Maria Franz		Hoyerswerda		
*George Socke (Robel)	26 June 1812	Kaschel	10 Mar. 1862	Industry
Hanna Schiwart	28 Apr. 1812		12 May 1901	Serbin
[Philip Jung]				
*Andreas Lowke	1 Oct. 1814	Reichwalde		
*Johann Sommer	1 Aug. 1822	Qautitz	13 Apr. 1893	Serbin
[Gertraud]				

*George Sonsel			15 Mar. 1856	New Ulm
Hanna				
*Johann Spahn	1805	Lomischau		
	1828	Wartha		
Matthes Spreiz	20 July 1844	Mulkwitz	11 Sept. 1926	Winchester
Hanna Leitko	22 Apr. 1843			
Andreas Ssucky	24 Nov. 1825	Rachlau	7 Jan. 1875	Fedor
Anna Baer	22 July 1826	Kreckwitz	10 Apr. 1912	Copperas Cove
Carl August Stephan	1830	Gross-Saubernitz	10 July 1892	Warda
Hanna Roitsch	14 Feb. 1832	Maltitz	12 Oct. 1870	Serbin
Magdalena Bernstein, n. Jeremias	1832	Trauschwitz	30 May 1920	Albany
*Andreas Symmank	27 June 1808	Gröditz	9 Nov. 1882	Fedor
Maria Ritter	1817		6 June 1887	Fedor
*Andreas Symmank	28 Sept. 1821	Malschwitz	14 May 1893	Fedor
Christiane Fritsche	15 Sept. 1827	Malschwitz	1 Oct. 1876	
Anna Petschke (Betschik)	1841	Tzschellen	1904	Fedor
Johann Symmank	15 June 1835		4 Apr. 1903	Manheim
[Johanna Golner]				
George Symny	June 1804	Rackel	3 Mar. 1866	
Agnes Ponich	1803	Baschütz	27 May 1870	
Friedrich Synatsch	20 Apr. 1826		5 Aug. 1895	Serbin
Maria Schneider	13 Dec. 1837		23 Jan. 1912	Serbin
Johann Jacob Synatschk	15 Jan. 1822	Förstgen	19 May 1875	Serbin
Hanna Runar	12 Feb. 1828		11 Aug. 1873	Serbin

Name	Date and Place of Birth		Date and Place of Death	
*Carl Traugott Taeger	23 Sept. 1832	Weissenberg	19 Nov. 1904	Warda
*Johann Carl Teinert	13 Sept. 1816	Weigersdorf		
Maria Schneider			16 Nov. 1863	Serbin
Hanna Michalk	8 May 1825	Oelsa	20 May 1913	Terra Bella, Calif.
Hanna Symny	15 May 1835			
*Joh. Traugott Teschke (Tsechke)	26 Apr. 1813	Weicha	1 Oct. 1854	
Hanna	16 Sept. 1811			
*Gottfried Trinks		Sophienthal		
Elizabeth	1794		Oct. 1854	
Johann Tschatschula	1 Apr. 1810	Mulkwitz	29 Nov. 1880	Serbin
Maria Toper				
Matthes Tschatschula	23 Feb. 1811	Mulkwitz	22 Nov. 1879	Serbin
Anna Marusch				
*Johann Tschornak	1814	Dürrbach	5 Feb. 1863	Frelsburg
Hanna Herenz	1819	Oelsa		
*Andreas Urban	8 Mar. 1826	Kubschuetz	25 Feb. 1857	Serbin
Magdalena Bowyer	2 Mar. 1822			
John Heinrich Wenke				
*Johann Urban	17 May 1818	Rackel	25 Sept. 1903	Serbin
Anna Kschidl	June 22	Rackel	1 Jan. 1898	Serbin
*Michael Urban	18 June 1830	Weissenberg	25 Feb. 1898	Fedor
Johanna Chr. Schneider	29 Nov. 1822			
Carl August Dube				

Peter Urban	19 Oct. 1833	Weigersdorf	17 Dec. 1912	Fedor
Henriette Schiller	26 Sept. 1828	Weissenberg	13 Mar. 1912	Fedor
*Andreas Vogel	11 Feb. 1813	Förstgen	30 Mar. 1855	Houston
Agnes Hansk	23 Dec. 1809	Klitten		
*Christoph Vogel	1831	Dauban	2 Mar. 1903	Serbin
Agnes Jenke	1828	Rackel	24 Oct. 1857	Serbin
Magdalena Schulze	31 Mar. 1834	Förstgen	1914	
Carl Wagner	11 June 1828	Weigersdorf	26 June 1885	Fedor
[Pauline Strech]				
Carl Gottlieb Wagner	30 Oct. 1820	Cunewalde	4 June 1911	Serbin
Rachel Brabandt			1896	Serbin
*Mattheus Wagner	5 Feb. 1825	Halbendorf	10 Aug. 1872	Serbin
Maria Kjchidel	1825	Rackel	14 Aug. 1891	Serbin
Ernst Waiser	15 Feb. 1843	Serbin	21 Mar. 1918	Thorndale
Maria Moerbe	1 Oct. 1856		15 Jan. 1921	Thorndale
*Carl Benj. Weise	6 Feb. 1820	Olbersdorf	10 May 1908	Serbin
Maria Noack	1812	Wartha	30 Aug. 1862	Serbin
Magdalena Kaspar, n. Schneider	6 Aug. 1823	Spreewitz	6 July 1895	
Andreas Weiser	13 July 1833	Buchwalde	15 Oct. 1885	Manheim
Magdalena Mitschk	3 Oct. 1839		4 July 1919	Lincoln
August Weiser	2 July 1831	Rackel	8 May 1907	Fedor
Christiana Noack	2 June 1849		21 July 1927	Fedor

Name	Date and Place of Birth		Date and Place of Death	
*Carl Traugott Wenke	11 Apr. 1812	Wurschen	23 Oct. 1879	Serbin
Eleonore Schwarz	7 Dec. 1809	Kotitz	1877	Serbin
*Johann Wertschutz		Carlsbrunn		
August Winkler	29 Apr. 1805	Weigersdorf	31 July 1869	Serbin
Maria Hoebel	2 Feb. 1806	Lauske	18 May 1887	The Grove
Adolph Winzer				
Anna Jassynk		Terpe		Warda
Andreas Wirth	10 Oct. 1854	Wartha		
*Carl Wirthschutz	21 Nov. 1820	Carlsbrunn	13 Dec. 1883	Manheim
Johann Chris. Woythe	1 Feb. 1821	Zschernske		
Hanna Rensch	14 Jan. 1835	Wunscha		
*Christoph Wuensche	25 June 1812	Weissenberg	13 Feb. 1891	Serbin
Maria Wehle	2 Feb. 1804	Nostitz	25 June 1884	Fedor
Johann Wukasch	12 Oct. 1809	Buchwalde	3 Sept. 1870	Serbin
Agnes Wieder		Maukendorf	11 Feb. 1891	Serbin
Matthes Wukasch	29 May 1823	Buchwalde	15 Apr. 1906	Serbin
Anna Mrosack	6 Jan. 1818		1874	
Rosina Schatte, n. Domaschk	17 Aug. 1832	Reichwalde	12 Sept. 1910	Serbin
*Johann Zieschang	25 Nov. 1810	Förstgen	4 Mar. 1879	Fedor
Hanna	25 Nov. 1808			
Rosina Paulik, n. Bartsch				

Peter Zieschang (See Australia)			
Michael Zimmerman (Czjesslija)	1827	Kolhwesa	8 Mar. 1885 Serbin
Maria Theresia Wagner	12 July 1827	Steindörfel	5 Oct. 1872 Serbin
Traugott Zindler	1826	Burghammer	
Hanna Simmank	1824		
*Christian Zoch	13 Dec. 1825	Spreewitz	26 July 1899 Serbin
Maria Schneider	3 Nov. 1821	Spreewitz	
Johann Zoch	9 Sept. 1814	Neudorf	24 Sept. 1873 Serbin
Anna Schneider (Krautz)	29 Aug. 1818	Burghammer	
August Zschech	4 Aug. 1843	Baruth	26 Feb. 1894 Fedor
Magdalena Richter, n. Hempel	20 Mar. 1837	Särka	7 July 1913 Fedor
Johann Gottlieb Zschech	20 Apr. 1836	Wawitz	8 Jan. 1928 Fedor
Anna Lehmann [Karoline Bosse]	1835		18 June 1871 Serbin
Johann Gottlieb Zschiesche	1826	Kühnicht	4 Aug. 1867 Serbin
Maria Nowotnik	1822		22 Nov. 1867
Agnesa Wenk Zwahr	4 June 1827	Binnewitz	15 Jan. 1895 Austin
*Andreas Zwahr	5 Dec. 1813	Sandförstgen	29 Sept. 1855 Frelsburg
Maria Dzjnkin	16 Oct. 1816	Klein Saubernitz	
Matthes Schoellnick			
George Adolph Zwahr [Emma Rothenburg]	4 Feb. 1849	Binnewitz	24 July 1941 Brenham

Notes

Chapter 1—The European Background

1. S. Harrison Thomson, "The Sorbs (or Wends) of Lusatia," *A Handbook of Slavic Studies*, ed. Leonid I. Strakhovsky (Cambridge, Mass.: Harvard University Press, 1949), 177. In earlier history the boundaries carried political significance and the area was known as Mark Lausitz (Rudolph Lehmann, *Geschichte der Niederlausitz* [Berlin: Walter de Gruyter & Co., 1963], 1).

2. *Die Sorben: Wissenswertes aus Vergangenheit und Gegenwart der sorbischen nationalen Minderheit* (Bautzen: VEB Domowina-Verlag, 1970), 214.

3. Nat Mickan of Ebenezer, South Australia, told the story during an interview on July 24, 1969. Essentially the same pun and retort were recorded in Leopold Haupt and J. E. Schmaler, *Volkslieder der Sorben in der Ober- und Nieder-Lausitz*, Part II, Grimma, 1843 (Facsimile reprint, Berlin: Deutsche Akademie der Wissenschaften zu Berlin, 1953), 322.

4. The single most helpful book on the European Sorbs is Gerald Stone's *The Smallest Slavonic Nation: The Sorbs of Lusatia* (London: Athlone Press, 1972). Other studies include C. T. Smith, *An Historical Geography of Western Europe before 1800* (New York: Frederick A. Praeger, 1967), which considers the economic life of the Slavs; and two by Francis Dvornik—*The Slavs: Their Early History and Civilization* (Boston: American Academy of Arts and Sciences, 1956), and *The Slavs in European History and Civilization* (New Brunswick, N.J.: Rutgers University Press, 1962)—which are valuable for the religious and political issues. Hermann Schreiber, *Teuton and Slav: The Struggle for Central Europe*, trans. James Cleugh (New York: Alfred A. Knopf, 1961), examines eastern Europe during the early tribal conflicts. The tenth century is the focus of both Samuel H. Cross, *Slavic Civilization through the Ages* (Cambridge, Mass.: Harvard University Press, 1948), and Austin Lane Poole, "Germany: Henry I to Otto the Great," in *Germany and the Western Empire*, vol. III of *Cambridge Medieval History*, ed. J. B. Bury et al. (New York: Macmillan, 1936).

5. Stone, *Smallest Slavonic Nation*, 37–40; *Die Sorben*, 44–46, 58–72, 93. For a description of present conditions see Stone, 161–85, and *Die Sorben*.

6. Haupt and Schmaler, *Volkslieder der Sorben*, 214; George C. Engerrand, *The So-Called Wends of Germany and Their Colonies in Texas and Australia* (Austin: University of Texas, 1934), 89. Even Martin Luther in his free-flowing conversation at the table engaged in stereotyping and referred to the Wends as "thieves and a very bad sort of people" (Theodore G. Tappert, ed. & trans., *Luther's Works* [Philadelphia: Fortress Press, 1967], LIV, 208, 387).

7. There are discrepancies in the population counts and estimates. Counts by Sorbs are often high while those by Germans are generally low. The 1930 count was reported by Thomson, "Sorbs of Lusatia," 177.

Chapter 2—The Australian Wends

1. Theodore S. Hamerow, *Restoration, Revolution, Reaction: Economics and Politics in Germany, 1815–1871* (Princeton, N.J.: Princeton University Press, 1958), 46–47, 77, 171. Despite legislation ending feudalism, in actual practice procedures did not necessarily change. Women often continued to work at the manor, and when crops ripened men were required to work on the lord's harvest first.

2. Ibid., 222, 232; *Gubener Heimatlexikon* (Guben: Rat der Stadt Wilhelm-Pieck-Stadt Guben Deutscher Kulturbund, 1971); Siegfried Ramoth, manuscript history of Werben, copy in the author's possession.

3. Gerhard Krüger, "Auswanderer nach Übersee aus dem Landkreise Cottbus in 19. Jahrhundert," in *Familienkundliche Hefte für die Niederlausitz* (Cottbus: Verein für Heimatkunde zu Cottbus, 1937), 3–6. To keep from starving, peasants around Peitz ground up roots of weeds to add to their flour; government officials considered the practice nourishing.

4. Frido Mětšk, *Do cuzeje zemje* (Berlin: Volk und Wissen Ludowy Nakład, 1957), 10; letter from Carl Traugott Hoehne, *Tydźenske Nowiny*, Dec. 13, 1851, 399.

5. Gerald Stone, *The Smallest Slavonic Nation: The Sorbs of Lusatia* (London: Athlone Press, 1972), 22.

6. Krüger, "Auswanderer nach Übersee," 6; Mětšk, *Do cuzeje*, 21–44.

7. *Tydźenske Nowiny*, Jan. 3, 1853, 5.

8. Mack Walker, *Germany and the Emigration, 1816–1885* (Cambridge, Mass.: Harvard University Press, 1964), 55–56.

9. Hamerow, *Restoration*, 154.

10. Mětšk, *Do cuzeje*, 10; Alfred Brauer, *Under the Southern Cross: History of the Evangelical Lutheran Church of Australia* (Adelaide: Lutheran Publishing House, 1956), 15.

11. Walker, *Germany and Emigration*, 157; Ramoth, History of Werben MS. Some studies report that considerably more than a thousand Wends migrated to Australia. This larger number is probably based on the booklet *Do cuzeje zemje* by Frido Mětšk. Mětšk in turn relied on Krüger's article, "Auswanderer nach Übersee." Krüger, however, listed all applicants from Lower Lusatia

who asked for permission to migrate and included Germans as well as some individuals who changed their minds and did not migrate to Australia at all.

12. Krüger, "Auswanderer nach Übersee," 5–6; Rudolph Lehmann, *Geschichte der Niederlausitz* (Berlin: Walter de Gruyter & Co., 1963), 659. Because Upper and Lower Lusatia experienced different economic and political development, designations for agricultural ranks also differed. Other terms used: *Gärtner* is comparable to *Kössat;* *Hüfner* and *Kleinbauer* have up to 60 *Morgen* of land; *Grossbauer* owns as many as 300 *Morgen*.

13. Walker, *Germany and Emigration*, 95.

14. Hildegard Rosenthal, *Die Auswanderung aus Sachsen im 19. Jahrhundert, 1815–1871* (Stuttgart: Ausland u. Heimat, 1931), 26; letter from Johann Dallwitz, July 29, 1842. Ota Wićaz archive, Sorbian Ethnological Institute, Bautzen.

15. Excerpt from Kotitz Kirchengalerie, MS, now in Weissenberg parish church, quoted in a letter from S. H. Wiedmer to Bill Biar, copy in author's possession; appeal to the parish of Kotitz, Mar. 11, 1845, copy in author's possession.

16. Ota Wićaz, "Serbske wucahowanja do Australije," *Předźenak*, 1931, 68–69; notes on Pjenck, Wićaz archive, Bautzen; Mětšk, *Do cuzeje*, 11.

17. Frido Mětšk, *Die Stellung der Sorben in der territorialen Verwaltungsgliederung des deutschen Feudalismus: Ein Beitrag zur Rechts und Verfassungsgeschichte des deutschen Feudalismus im Sorbenland* (Bautzen: Deutsche Akademie der Wissenschaften zu Berlin, 1968), 85–86.

18. Wićaz, "Serbske wucahowanja do Australije," 68. Martin Stephan of Leipzig led a large migration of Lutherans discontented with the liberal trends of the Saxon church to the United States in 1839. A few of Stephan's followers came from Lusatia, including Johann Domschka from Lauske, who lost his life when the *Amalia* sank. Wićaz links the Wendish migration to Australia with Stephan's migration to America.

19. Walker, *Germany and Emigration*, 69.

20. Wićaz, "Serbske wucahowanja do Australije," 68; letter from Johann Bryl, *Serbske Nowiny*, Dec. 15, 1855, 389, 397–98. Teschner reported that as they traveled to Klemzig they met a shepherd who identified himself as a Sorb who had left Upper Lusatia in 1825 and had eventually migrated to Australia (Mětšk, *Do cuzeje*, 19–21).

21. *South Australian Register*, Aug. 3, 1850. The sub-agent for Godeffroy and Sons was Dieseldorf and Company, and fares were twelve pounds or one hundred *Taler*.

22. Reminiscences of Mrs. Christiane Petschel Hiller, typewritten copy in possession of Len Huf, Hamilton, Victoria. Godeffroy owned two ships named *Alfred*. The master on the *Alfred* that carried the 1848 migrants was H. E. Decker and this ship's draft was approximately 635–750 tons.

23. Letters from Johann Zwar, *Tydźenske Nowiny*, Sept. 13, 1851, 294–95, and Sept. 20, 1851, 300–301.

24. Hiller, Reminiscences. Martin Teschner, sailing on the *Victoria*, re-

ported arguments and fights on board between the people of various countries ("The Coming of the Wends" [by Rupert J. Burger], in E. W. Wiebusch, ed., *Yearbook of the Luteran Church of Australia 1976*, 49).

25. Letter from Zwar, *Tydźenske Nowiny*, Sept. 20, 1851, 300–301.
26. *South Australian Register*, Nov. 29 and Dec. 9, 1848.
27. Passenger lists of *Victoria* and *Alfred*, South Australian Archives, Adelaide; Ernst Kaulvers, *Seereise nach Süd-Australien am 15. August 1848 von Hamburg aus mit einigen Hunderten deutscher Landsleute unternommen nebst der im Jahr 1853 stattgefundenen Rückreise* (Bautzen: J. E. Schmaler, 1855); Hiller, Reminiscences.
28. Hiller, Reminiscences.
29. Krüger, "Auswanderer nach Übersee," 7.
30. Kaulvers, *Seerise nach Süd-Australien*, 5; letter from Johann Mirtschin, *Serbske Nowiny*, Feb. 10, 1855, 43.
31. Hiller, Reminiscences; *South Australian Register*, Dec. 6, 1848.
32. *South Australian Register*, Nov. 8 and Dec. 9, 1848.
33. Hiller, Reminiscences.
34. During World War I many Australian place names of German derivation were changed to English.
35. Hiller, Reminiscences.
36. Ray Deutsher, *Deutscher: A Family History, 1848–1986* (Toorak, Victoria: Privately printed, 1986), 36–37.
37. Ibid.
38. Letter from Andreas and Gottlob Preusker, *Tydźenske Nowiny*, Mar. 9, 1850, 77–78.
39. Letters in *Tydźenske Nowiny* from: Carl Traugott Hoehne, Dec. 27, 1851, 413–14, and Michael Zwar, Jan. 10, 1852, 13–15, and Jan. 31, 1852, 36–37; Mary Burrows, *Riverton: Heart of the Gilbert Valley* (Netley, S.A., 1965), 20.
40. Hoehne and Zwar letters.
41. Letter from Andreas Preusker, *Tydźenske Nowiny*, Mar. 9, 1850, 77–78; letter from Johann Mirtschin, *Serbske Nowiny*, Feb. 10, 1855, 67.
42. Letters in *Tydźenske Nowiny* from: Kappler, Dec. 6, 1851, 392, Zwar, and Hoehne.
43. Letter from Johann Ponich. *Tydźenske Nowiny*, Aug. 21, 1852, 268; letter from Carl Hempel, 1874, Wićaz archive, Bautzen; letter from Johann Bryl, *Serbske Nowiny*, Dec. 15, 1855, 397.
44. Ponich letter; letter from C. T. A. Lehmann, Apr. 19, 1866, Wićaz archive.
45. *Victoria* passenger list; Supreme Court of Victoria, Register of Letters Patent 1851–61: Certificate for Karl August Krueger, 1875, CRS A 727 225, Certificate for Johann Krueger, 1860, CRS A 727 185, Australian Archives.
46. Letter from Michael Zwar, *Tydźenske Nowiny*, Jan. 24, 1852, 27–29; Robert Wuchatsch, *Westgarthtown: The German Settlement at Thomastown* (Melbourne: Privately printed, 1985), 6.
47. Kappler letter; Brauer, *Under the Southern Cross*, 89–90.

48. Wićaz, "Serbske wucahowanja do Australije," 68; Brauer, *Under the Southern Cross*, 89–90. Kappler's records are now housed in the Lutheran Archives in Adelaide.

49. Letters in *Tydźenske Nowiny* from: Johann Zwar, Nov. 5, 1853, 346, and Andreas Albert, Dec. 10, 1853, 385.

50. Letter from Johann Bryl, *Serbske Nowiny*, Dec. 15, 1855, 398.

51. H. F. W. Proeve, "Ebenezer and Neukirch, 1852–1952," MS, Lutheran Archives, Adelaide.

52. A "hundred" is a survey unit of approximately one hundred square miles in a roughly rectangular shape. The Hundred of Gilbert was 112½ square miles in size.

53. Burrows, *Riverton*, 8, 20, 27; Mětšk, *Do cuzeje*, 46.

54. Letter from Rev. J. F. Noack to Rev. G. Birkman, copy in Lutheran Archives, Adelaide; "Coming of the Wends," 36; Mětšk, *Die Stellung der Sorben*, 46, 49. The hymn is a translation of a hymn written by Albert Knapp, "One thing more than all my heart is craving."

55. Letter from Semlin, Apr. 20, 1867, Peter's Hill File, Lutheran Archives, Adelaide; interview with Con Huppatz, Sept. 29, 1969, Riverton, South Australia.

56. Letter from E. von Plönnies, Aug. 13, 1863, Lutheran Archives, Adelaide.

57. Letter from Jarick and Hondow, Apr. 9, 1863, Lutheran Archives, Adelaide; Teichelman to Hensel, June 2, 1865, Peter's Hill File for Mar. 17, 1868, Lutheran Archives, Adelaide; *Der Lutherische Kirchenbote für Australien*, Dec. 22, 1875, 22.

58. D. W. Meinig, *On the Margins of the Good Earth: The South Australian Wheat Frontier, 1869–1884* (Chicago: Association of American Geographers, 1962), 11, 20, 21.

59. Michael Williams. "The Spread of Settlement in South Australia," in Fay Gale and Graham H. Lawton, eds., *Settlement and Encounter* (Melbourne: Oxford University Press, 1969), 4.

60. Peter Burroughs, *Britain and Australia, 1831–1855: A Study in Imperial Relations and Crown Lands Administration* (Oxford: Oxford University Press, 1967), 365.

61. Williams, "Spread of Settlement," 22, 24; Meinig, *On the Margins*, 26, 43; D. H. Pike, *Paradise of Dissent: South Australia 1829–1857* (Melbourne: Melbourne University Press, 1957), 304.

62. Jan L. Perkowski, "The Sorbian Language in Australia," *Lětopis* (1968), 201–19. According to Perkowski, while most of the Wends were Lutheran, some were Catholic and a few from the Silesian area of Lausitz also migrated in 1848. They first went to Kangaroo Island and then to Sevenhill. I have been unable to substantiate this material, however.

63. M. L. Kiddle, *Men of Yesterday: A Social History of the Western District of Victoria* (Melbourne: Melbourne University Press, 1961), 156, 415.

64. Ibid., 177.

65. Letters in *Serbske Nowiny:* Maria Kaiser, May 9, 1857, 146–48, Johann Mirtschin, Feb. 10, 1854, 59, and Agnes Stephan, Oct. 10, 1857, 323; Wuchatsch, *Westgarthtown,* 26.

66. Hiller, Reminiscences.

67. South Australia General Register Office (Registrar-General of Deeds Dept.), Memorials of Naturalization, with unenrolled or uncollected Certificates, Australian Archive: A 821.

68. Letter from Andreas Albert, *Tydźenske Nowiny,* Dec. 10, 1853, 385.

69. Hiller, Reminiscences. See also "St. Luke's Ev. Lutheran Church, Ballarat Rd., Hamilton, Victoria, 1861–1951," typed copy in possession of Oscar Schurmann, Hamilton, Victoria. In South Australia the squatters did not lock up the lands as they did in Victoria (Burroughs, *Britain and Australia,* 367).

70. *75th Anniversary of St. Michael's Ev. Lutheran Church, Tarrington, Victoria, 1853–1928* (N.p., n.d.; hereafter cited as *Tarrington Centenary*); *One Hundred Years of Blessing, 1853–1953: Centenary Publications of the Evangelical Lutheran Church in Victoria* (N.p., n.d.); Brauer, *Under the Southern Cross,* 283–84.

71. *Tarrington Centenary;* letter from Deutscher to Kräuer and Schuermann, May 5, 1853, Lutheran Archives, Adelaide.

72. Kiddle, *Men of Yesterday,* 416; letter from Mirtschin, *Serbske Nowiny,* Feb. 10, 1854, 51, 59.

73. Mirtschin letter, 59; Brauer, *Under the Southern Cross,* 285; Hiller, Reminiscences.

74. *Tarrington Centenary;* Schuermann to Meyer, Nov. 15, 1855, Lutheran Archives, Adelaide; Brauer, *Under the Southern Cross,* 285.

75. Schuermann to Meyer, Oct. 16 and Nov. 22, 1854, Lutheran Archives, Adelaide.

76. Schuermann to Meyer, Oct. 16, 1854, and Oct. 25, 1855, Lutheran Archives, Adelaide.

77. *Alfred* passenger list; Deutscher to Meyer, July 14, 1855, Lutheran Archives, Adelaide.

78. Brauer, *Under the Southern Cross,* 70, 103, 285; Schuermann to *Kirchenkollegium,* May 19, 1857, Lutheran Archives, Adelaide.

79. Schuermann to Meyer, Oct. 25 and Nov. 15, 1855, May 19, 1857, Lutheran Archives, Adelaide.

80. Deutscher to Meyer, July 11, 1856, and Schuermann to *Kirchenkollegium,* May 19, 1857, Lutheran Archives, Adelaide.

81. Schuermann to *Kirchenkollegium,* May 19, 1857; "St. Luke's, 1861–1951."

82. Letter from Hensel and Oster to Deutscher, Oct. 12, 1860, copy in possession of Len Huf, Hamilton; Deutscher to *Kirchenkollegium,* Oct. 22, 1860, and Schuermann to Kilian, July 19, 1863, Lutheran Archives, Adelaide. Hiller, Reminiscences, provides a much more sympathetic account of Deutscher.

83. Schuermann to Kilian, July 19, 1863; "St. Luke's, 1861–1951"; *Australischer Christenbote für die evangelische lutherische Kirche in Australien,* Aug., 1864, 31; Deutsher, *Deutscher;* Hiller Reminiscences.

84. "An Ein Hochwürd. Ober-Kirchen-Kollegium der Evangel. luther. Kirche zu Süd-Australien," Oct. 22, 1860, Lutheran Archives, Adelaide.

85. Data provided by the Department of Crown Lands and Survey, Victoria.

86. Urban left the Prussian state church in the 1830s and his action encouraged others to question the merger. Although he helped found the congregation that called Kilian and later sent immigrants to Texas, Urban himself migrated to Australia in 1851, three years before Kilian's migration. Two of Urban's daughters did migrate to Texas. In the 1860s he was not influenced by the emotionalism of Deutscher, but remained a faithful member of Schuermann's flock. During the last twenty years of his life he kept a coffin in his home, ready for death, which came when was eighty-nine (*Der Lutherische Kirchenbote für Australien*, Mar. 14, 1879, 55).

87. Kiddle, *Men of Yesterday*, 230; J. N. Powell, *The Public Lands of the Australian Felix: Settlement and Land Appraisal in Victoria, 1834–91, with Special Reference to the Western Plain* (Melbourne: Oxford University Press, 1970), xxvii, 74, 164; A. R. Callaghan and A. J. Millington, *The Wheat Industry in Australia* (Sydney: Angas and Robertson, 1956), 184.

88. Powell, *Public Lands*, xxvii, 164.

89. Letters in Lutheran Archives, Adelaide: Schuermann to Hensel, Apr. 12, 1871, and Jan. 23, 1872; Schuermann to Oster, July 10, 1873. See also V. G. Roennfeld, "The Early Years of the Lutheran Church in the Wimmera," in E. W. Wiebusch, ed., *Yearbook of the Lutheran Church in Australia: 1972* (Adelaide, 1972), 30–49; John F. Klowss, Natimuk, Victoria, to author, Nov. 15, 1969.

90. V. G. Roennfeld, *A Brief Historical Review of St. John's Evangelical Lutheran Memorial Church, Murtoa, Vic.* (Horsham, 1966), 38.

91. Powell, *Public Lands*, xxvi, 230.

92. Stephen H. Roberts, *History of Australian Land Settlement, 1788–1920* (Melbourne: Macmillan & Co., 1924), 223; Gordon L. Buxton, *The Riverina, 1861–1891: An Australian Regional Study* (Carlton, Victoria: Melbourne University Press, 1967), 62.

93. F. J. H. Blaess, "One Hundred Years, Jindera, New South Wales, 1868–1968," in E. W. Wiebusch, ed., *Yearbook of the Lutheran Church of Australia: 1969* (Adelaide, 1969), 21.

94. *Centenary of the Trek from Ebenezer, S. A. to Walla Walla, N. S. W., 1868–1968* (N.p., n.d.).

95. Blaess, "One Hundred Years," 26–27.

96. Ibid., 29–30; *Der Lutherische Kirchenbote*, vol. III, no. 3, Mar. 11, 1876, 24.

97. Blaess, "One Hundred Years," 35.

98. *South Australian Register*. Mar. 5, 1851, Aug. 28, 1855.

99. Letter from M[ichael] F[alland], Nov. 3, 1871, Wićaz archive, Bautzen; *Australischer Christenbote*, July, 1888, vol. 29, no. 7, 100–101.

100. For a hostile view of the German tradition in Australia and a description of how the tradition was carried on until World War II, see Charles A. Price, *German Settlers in South Australia* (Carlton, Victoria: Melbourne University Press, 1945).

Chapter 3—The Texas Wends

1. Ethel Hander Geue, *New Homes in a New Land: German Immigration to Texas, 1847–1861* (Waco, Tex.: Texian Press, 1970), 33; Letter from Seydlers and others, *Serbske Nowiny*, July 7, 1855, 212; Robert G. Seydler, "The Seydlers," MS copy in possession of the author.

2. *Seventh Census of the United States*, Manuscript Schedule of Population, Austin County, Fayette County; Deed of Trust Record, County Clerk's Office, Austin County; Seydler, "The Seydlers."

3. Letter from Johann Kasper, *Serbske Nowiny*, Mar. 18, 1854, 84, 92; *Der Lutheraner*, Mar. 13, 1855, 118; Anne Blasig, *The Wends of Texas* (San Antonio: Naylor, 1954), 12; George C. Engerrand, *The So-Called Wends of Germany and Their Colonies in Texas and Australia* (Austin: University of Texas, 1934), 42.

4. Johann Kasper letter, *Serbske Nowiny*, Mar. 18, 1854, 92. That date of publication was seven days before Kilian received the call from the migrating congregation (*Der Lutheraner*, Mar. 13, 1855, 118). The members of the 1853 group included Christoph Krause (Frelsburg), Johann Noack (Frelsburg), Johann Kasper (New Ulm), Mathias Matthiez (New Ulm), Mathias Mitschke (Industry), August Polnick (Rabbs Creek), and possibly Johann Domaschk-Janak. In contrast to the Seydler and Helas families, these Wends joined the Kilian congregation.

5. E.g., Blasig, *Wends of Texas*, 11.

6. Hajo Holborn, *A History of Modern Germany, 1648–1840* (New York: Alfred A. Knopf, 1964), 488–89; Alfred Brauer, *Under the Southern Cross: History of the Evangelical Lutheran Church of Australia* (Adelaide: Luthern Publishing House, 1956), 4. The name for the Prussian church was the Evangelical Church (Erwin L. Lueker, ed., *Lutheran Cyclopedia* [St. Louis: Concordia Publishing House, 1954], 860). Kilian explained his motives in the following statement: "What the decrees and bulls of the Roman Pope are, namely statutes of men intended to enslave souls, such are also the cabinet orders of the pope of Berlin, the king of Prussia, according to which the Evangelical Lutheran Church, since the year 1830, has been violated with regard to the society rights guaranteed by the Peace of Westphalia and robbed of its earthly goods. By these regal cabinet orders, by which, arbitrarily and violently, a new church or a church of confusion has been made, the faithful Lutherans in Prussia have been placed in such distress that they are seriously suffering, no matter whether they leave the Church of the king or remain in it. This is the reason for the strong desire to emigrate, which takes hold even

of pious souls" (Quoted in P. E. Kretzmann, "The Early History of the Wendic Lutheran Colony in the State of Texas," *Concordia Historical Institute Quarterly* [July, 1930], 47–48).

7. "History of the Weigersdorf Church," by Andreas Dutschmann, June 14, 1847, MS in Ota Wićaz archive, Sorbian Ethnological Institute, Bautzen. A bell tower was erected in 1877 (Korla Eckert, "125lětny wosadny jubilej ew.-luth. wosady swj. Trojicy we Wukrančicach," photocopy in possession of the author).

8. *Der Lutheraner,* Mar. 13, 1855, 117, 118. Kilian preached a sermon in 1846 before he went to Weigersdorf on "The Care Required of Lutheran Christians in the Present State of Confessional Confusion. A Serious Word Addressed to the Lutheran People." The sermon was reprinted and widely distributed. The rigid pledge Kilian supported would be replaced by a lax vow in 1872 (*Lutheran Cyclopedia,* 946; Walter O. Forster, *Zion on the Mississippi: The Settlement of the Saxon Lutherans in Missouri, 1839–1841* [St. Louis: Concordia Publishing House, 1953], 2). In an attempt to secularize religious activity one rationalist pastor preached a Christmas sermon on the stall-feeding of cattle (Andrew L. Drummond, *German Protestantism since Luther* [London: Epworth Press, 1951], 102).

9. *Der Lutheraner,* Mar. 13, 1855, 118, and May 22, 1855, 159. This same type of criticism was directed against Kavel's migration to Australia and the Stephan migration to Missouri (Carl S. Meyer, ed., *Moving Frontiers: Readings in the History of the Lutheran Church–Missouri Synod* [St. Louis: Concordia Publishing House, 1946], 86). Approximately one-sixth of Kilian's congregation migrated (*Kirchenblatt für die evangelisch-lutherischen Gemeinden in Preusse,* Nov. 1, 1854).

10. Appeal to parish of Kotitz, Mar. 11, 1845, copy in author's possession. Gerhad Laser, the Sorbian pastor and church historian, believes that social and economic injustices also motivated the migrants (letter from Laser to Bill Biar, Feb. 5, 1972, copy in author's possession). Mack Walker in his study of German migration wrote that the Old Lutherans "spoke of religion as the motive of their emigration, but conceded that it was less a matter of state coercion, which had been relaxed with the accession of Frederick William IV, than conflict within the church. The religious motive was mixed, not to say dubious: many people undoubtedly attached themselves to the Old Lutheran columns as a way out of difficult circumstances" (*Germany and the Emigration, 1816–1855* [Cambridge, Mass., 1964], 78, 79). Although most of the Wends were Lutheran, few of those who belonged to the Catholic church migrated (Brauer, *Under the Southern Cross*). It has been suggested to me by J. C. E. Riotte that this can support the religious explanation (in that there was no religious discontent among the Catholics) and also the economic (in that the Convent of Marijna Hwězda treated its serfs better than did the German nobles). Kilian's Australian correspondence was with Pastor A. L. C. Kavel.

11. Arnošt Wjezar, "Serbska kolonija w Texas a jeje wjednik Jan Kilian," *Łužica,* 1930, 90; Kretzmann, "Early History," 48.

12. *Der Lutheraner,* Nov. 15, 1884, 171, 172. Kilian did experience enough restraints to his ministry to influence his decision to accept the call. While he does not identify the source, the annoyance could well have been the state (*Der Lutheraner,* Mar. 13, 1855, 118).

13. Call from congregation to Kilian, Mar. 25, 1854, Serbin Papers, Concordia Historical Institute, St. Louis, Missouri (hereafter cited as Serbin Papers, C.H.I.).

14. Kilian to Andreas Dutschmann, *Serbske Nowiny,* Mar. 19, 1855, 189; *Der Lutheraner,* May 22, 1855, 159; *Kirchenblatt,* Nov. 1, 1854. Kilian's divergent route was probably the basis for a charge that he had deserted the flock. Kilian's passport, now in the Serbin Collection, was approved on September 14 and specified his route as Minden, Ostende, and Liverpool.

15. "On the Ship *Inconstant,*" Oct. 9, 1854; Kilian to John Moncure, Aug. 2, 1861, Notes for congregational meeting, Oct. 14, 1855, and Kilian to Carl Buchholz, Nov. 8, 1865, all in Serbin Papers, C.H.I.; Kilian to Clamor W. Schuermann, Oct. and Nov., 1860, *Australischer Christenbote für evangelische Lutherische Kirche in Australien,* 46–47, 50, 55; Kilian to Carl August Matek, June 17, 1868, Wićaz archive, Bautzen. C. F. W. Walther, president of the Missouri Synod, insisted on the supremacy of each congregation (Arthur C. Repp, "St. Paul's and St. Peter's Lutheran Churches, Serbin, Texas, 1855–1905, Part 2," *Concordia Historical Institute Quarterly* [Jan., 1943], 121).

16. Call from congregation to Kilian, Mar. 25, 1854, and Kilian's Notes for congregational meeting of Oct. 14, 1855, Serbin Papers, C.H.I.

17. Agricultural ranking is explained in chapter 2. The Upper Lusatians did not use the categories of *Büdner* and *Kossät,* while the Lower Lusatians did not use the term *Gärtner.* A *Gärtner* owned one-eighth of a farm while a *Häusler* owned only a house and a small garden.

18. Walker, *Germany and Emigration,* 90; *Aufname-Schein der Koeniglich Preussisch concessionirten Auswanderer Befoerderung von Valt. Lorenz Meyer in Hamburg,* Anne Blasig Papers, 1854–1930, University of Texas Archives, Austin; "Hamburg Porträt: Hamburg als Auswandererstadt," pamphlet published by the Museum für Hamburgische Geschichte, 1984.

19. *Der Lutheraner,* May 21, 1918, 181; Ernest Matuschka to author, Oct. 25 and Nov. 5, 1987. Pastor Matuschka retained some connections with the Noack and Zoch families.

20. Kilian to Dutschmann, *Serbske Nowiny,* Mar. 19, 1855, 180, 189, 197, 204, 205.

21. Blasig, *Wends of Texas,* 19; Johann Teinert, "Ein Brief," Anne Blasig Papers; Joseph Wilson, "Pastor John Kilian's Shipboard Diary," *Concordia Historical Institute Quarterly* (Winter, 1985), 150–55.

22. Kilian to Dutschmann, *Serbske Nowiny,* Mar. 19, 1855, 205. Kilian said 81 died, but he may have included those who died en route to Bastrop County (Joseph Wilson, trans. and ed., *Baptismal Records of St. Paul Lutheran Church, Serbin, Texas, 1854–1883* [Serbin, Tex., 1985]). Peter Symmank was the infant who survived.

23. H. C. Ziehe, *A Centennial History of the Lutheran Church in Texas, 1851–1951* (Seguin, Tex., 1954), 40–42; "One Hundred Twenty-fifth Anniversary, 1851–1976: Souvenir of the First Evangelical Church" [Houston, Texas]; Arthur C. Repp, "Beginnings of Lutheranism in Houston, Texas," *Concordia Historical Institute Quarterly* (July, 1953), 58. Two of the orphans were probably the children of Johann and Magdalena Jannausch, who both died in August, 1855.

24. Kilian to Dutschmann, *Serbske Nowiny*, Mar. 19, 1855, 205; George Merting and Carl Lehmann took care of Kilian's property (Minutes of congregational meeting, Oct. 14, 1855, Serbin Papers, C.H.I.)

25. *Serbske Nowiny*, July 7, 1855, 212, 213; and July 14, 1855, 220.

26. *Der Lutheraner*, Mar. 13, 1855; Minutes of the congregational meeting, Mar. 22, 1857, Serbin Papers, C.H.I.

27. Johann Teinert, "Ein Brief." The Wend predilections for wood was so great that people would build with stone only when wood was scarce and expensive (Leopold Haupt and J. E. Schmaler, *Volkslieder der Wenden in der Ober-und Nieder-Lausitz*, Part II, Grimma, 1843 (Facsimile reprint, Berlin, 1953], 211).

28. *Der Lutheraner*, May 13, 1855, 118; letter from Kilian to Dutschmann, *Serbske Nowiny*, Mar. 19, 1855, 205.

29. Transcribed Deed Records, Bastrop County, County Clerk's Office, Lee County, Texas. Somehow the tradition started that the Delaplain land sold for 50 cents an acre and that some land near Winchester was rejected because it commanded a dollar per acre (Blasig, *Wends of Texas*, 31). A full league and a labor total 4,605.53 acres.

30. Kretzmann, "Early History," 50, 51; Teinert, "Ein Brief"; Blasig, *Wends of Texas*, 42.

31. C. A. Weslager, *The Log Cabin in America from Pioneer Days to the Present* (New Brunswick, N.H.: Rutgers University Press, 1969), 72–74; Engerrand, *So-Called Wends*, 103, 106.

32. Note to congregational meeting, Oct. 14, 1855, Serbin Papers, C.H.I.

33. Notes of Pastor Kilian, 1856 and 1857, Serbin Papers, C.H.I. The original language is German.

34. Kilian to Dutschmann, *Serbske Nowiny*, Mar. 19, 1855, 205.

35. The basis for Tables 1–4 is the manuscript census schedule of the United States agricultural census for Bastrop (1860 and 1870), Fayette (1870 and 1880), and Lee (1880) counties. That portion of Bastrop County inhabited by the Wends was added to Lee County when it was created in 1874. All Wends whose names could be identified were used, but the spelling of the census enumerator makes selection difficult. Many residents were not enrolled because of the isolation of the frontier, and more Wends farmed in Texas than were included on the census records. All persons listed for Bastrop County in 1860 and 1870 were used, but for Lee County in 1880 only the persons on odd pages from 1 to 31 residing in Precinct #1 were counted. The statistics for the Germans came from Terry G. Jordan, *German Seed in Texas Soil* (Austin: University of Texas Press, 1966), where he randomly selected

persons from Austin and Waller counties. Statistics for the 1860 and 1880 censuses were based on information from 1859 and 1879, both drought years. The drought would have had a depressing effect on productivity and land values and would show the lands along rivers and creeks to advantage.

The number of farmers in each group for the three census years was as follows: 1860—26 Wends, 600 Texans, 210 Germans; 1870—67 Wends, 720 Texans, 307 Germans; 1880—188 Wends, 160 Texans, 213 Germans.

36. The Biar family of Texas sent cotton seed to the Biars of Australia, but the St. Kitt's rainfall was too low and the soil too hard (Magdalena Biar to Herman Biar, Dec. 5, 1904, letter in possession of Bill Biar).

37. Engerrand, *So-Called Wends*, 105, 106; Blasig, *Wends of Texas*, 49. Jordan argues that the Germans were satisfied with the smaller farms; possibly the Wends were satisfied with even less (Jordan, *German Seed*, 101).

38. The twenty-one Fayette County Wends reported the following averages in 1880: 184 bushels of corn, 12 bales of cotton, 2 oxen, 3 horses, 2 mules, 8 milk cows, 8 additional cattle, 9 swine, 35 improved acres, 194 unimproved acres, $304 worth of livestock, $750 total production, $1,733 cash value of the farm, $3.24 farm production per acre, and $7.49 cash value per acre.

39. Kilian to C. F. W. Walther, June 25, 1858, Serbin Papers, C.H.I.

40. In 1859 Kilian believed that the pietism of Johann Arndt, a Lutheran pastor in Germany was opposed to Lutheranism (Kilian to C. Schaller, Oct. 20, 1859, Serbin Papers, C.H.I.). In 1876, however, Kilian ordered two copies of Arndt's devotional books (Wićaz archive, Bautzen). In 1876 Kilian also vocally supported chiliasm (Repp, "St. Paul's and St. Peter's Lutheran Churches, Serbin, Texas, 1855–1905, Part 5," *Concordia Historical Institute Quarterly*, [Apr., 1944], 15).

41. Kilian to Schuermann, *Australischer Christenbote*, Oct., 1860, 47; Repp, "St. Paul's and St. Peter's Lutheran Churches, Serbin, Texas, 1855–1905, Part 1," *Concordia Historical Institute Quarterly*, (July, 1942), 45. For more on the association between Kilian and Schuermann see J. B. Koch, *When the Murray Meets the Mississippi: A Survey of Australian and American Lutheran Contacts 1838–1974* (Adelaide, S.A.: Lutheran Publishing House, 1975), 30–31; *Kirchenblatt*, Sept. 1, 1858.

42. Kilian to Schuermann, *Australischer Christenbote*, Oct., 1860, 47; Kilian to C. F. W. Walther, June 25, 1858, Serbin Papers, C.H.I.

43. Regional divisions of the Lutheran Church–Missouri Synod are called districts, while in other Lutheran bodies they are called synods. In the mid-nineteenth century the Texas Synod was autonomous but affiliated with the national General Synod. Kilian noticed the unionistic tendencies of the Texas Synod already in 1855, when he had to select a religious body that would identify him as a clergyman so that he could be licensed to perform civil acts. In 1855, he affiliated with the Missouri Synod rather than with the Lutheran body of Texas, and the congregation joined the Missouri Synod in 1865 (Kilian to C. F. W. Walther, Feb. 9, 1855, Serbin Papers, C.H.I.).

44. Numbers 16. The parallel is that of the laity opposing the priesthood.

45. Sources on this first schism are Repp, "St. Paul's and St. Peter's, Part 2," 11, and "Part 3," 18, 19; Kretzmann, "Earth History," 52; Kilian to Schuermann, *Australischer Christenbote*, Oct., 1860, 46, 47. In 1859 there were fifty families and some single men in Kilian's congregation and twenty other families scattered outside the Serbin area.

46. George R. Nielsen, "Folklore of the German-Wends in Texas," *Singers and Storytellers*, Publications of the Texas Folklore Society XXX, (1961), 256. On occasion the men hid in trees that were covered with dense grape vines (Mrs. James C. Killen, ed., *History of Lee County Texas* [Quanah, Tex., 1974], 215).

47. National Archives Index, Confederate Muster Rolls, Texas State Archives, Austin.

48. Kilian to John Moncure, Aug. 2, 1861; Kilian to Kirchenrath Wildenhahn, Bautzen, June 10, 1864, and Dec. 22, 1865, and Kilian to Carl Buchholz, Nov. 8, 1865, Serbin Papers, C.H.I.; Repp, "St. Paul's and St. Peter's, Part 2," 119; Killen, *History of Lee County*, 27, 28.

49. Mato Kosyk alluded to the preference for German among both the Serbin people and some distinguished Sorbs in Lusatia ("Serbja w Texasu," *Łužica*, 1884, 69).

50. Repp, "St. Paul's and St. Peter's, Part 2," 119, 122; Minutes of congregational meeting, Dec. 28, 1862, Serbin Papers, C.H.I.; Blasig, *Wends of Texas*, 61. The first class to be confirmed in German was on April 18, 1862.

51. Anne Blasig supports these views, citing an article about Jan Kilian in the 1927 issue of *Předźenak*. Jan Cyž, an authority on Sorbian history, identifies the article's author as Ota Wićaz and describes it as being utopian and written for the faithful (Jan Cyž to the author, Aug. 6, 1974).

52. *Der Lutheraner*, Feb. 15, 1871, 95.

53. Kilian letter, Dec. 22, 1865, Wićaz archive, Bautzen; Kilian to Albert Ebert, Mar. 11, 1868, and Lehnigk to Kilian, Sept. 18, 1867, Serbin Papers, C.H.I.; Repp, "St. Paul's and St. Peter's, Part 2," 123, and "Part 3," 21–23. In 1865 Kilian hoped to return to Europe, but something in the return correspondence dissuaded him. Then in 1867, he hoped for a position on the faculty of Concordia Seminary in St. Louis or for a Bohemian congregation there. Not only was he unhappy with the congregational affairs, but he was concerned with the lack of educational opportunity for his children.

54. Serbin Papers, C.H.I.: Letter to the congregational meeting, Aug. 8, 1896; announcements to the congregation, May 22, 1870, and Aug. 28, 1879; minutes of congregational meeting, June 12, 1870.

55. *Der Lutheraner*, Mar. 6, 1860, 119. Wendish confirmation classes ended in 1881 (Repp, "St. Paul's and St. Peter's, Part 2," 119).

56. Engerrand, *So-Called Wends*, 115; G. Birkmann, "Aus den ersten Jahren der Gemeinden in Fedor, Texas, 1870–1875," *Giddings Deutsches Volksblatt*, Oct. 5, 1939.

57. *Copies of Lists of Passengers Arriving at Miscellaneous Ports on the Atlantic and Gulf Coasts and at Ports on the Great Lakes*, Galveston, Texas, Roll 3, National Archives; list of new communicants, Feb. 23, 1873, Serbin Papers, C.H.I.

58. Melde settled in Fedor as early as 1856 (Engerrand, *So-Called Wends*, 119).

59. Proft's unassuming manner endeared him to Kilian, and they became fast friends (Arthur C. Repp, "Daughters of Serbin, 1870–1905: History of the Lutheran Churches at Fedor and Warda, Texas," *Concordia Historical Institute Quarterly* (July, 1948), 51. Proft used his early training in designing the windows for the churches at Serbin and Warda (Birkmann, "Aus den ersten Jahren").

60. H. W. Bewie, *Missouri in Texas: A History of the Lutheran Church–Missouri Synod in Texas, 1855–1941* (Austin: Steck Company, 1952), 15; "Geschichte der Dreieinigkeits Gemeinde zu Fedor, 1870–1940," mimeograph copy in Texas District Archives; Repp, "Daughters of Serbin," 55.

61. Kilian to J. G. Buenger, Oct. 21, 1872, and J. G. Buenger to Kilian, Mar. 2, 1871, Serbin Papers, C.H.I. The cemetery is across the road from the Dunk residence.

62. Arthur C. Repp, "History of Holy Cross, Warda, Texas, Daughters of Serbin, 1873–1905," *Concordia Historical Institute Quarterly* (Apr., 1953) 3, 4, 7. Steimke was so popular that in a letter to his son, Herman, Kilian reported that about one-seventh of his congregation desired to leave.

63. G. Birkmann, "Von der Wendenkolonie in Serbin," *Giddings Deutsches Volksblatt*, Sept. 22, 1932.

64. *Centennial Anniversary 1867–1967: Philadelphia Evangelical Lutheran Church, Swiss Alp, Texas*, by F. Erhard Eilers, pamphlet in possession of author.

65. Arthur C. Repp, *Concordia Historical Institute Quarterly* (Oct. 1942), 116.

66. The Wends in Texas who spoke no German were called "Stockenwenden"; G. Birkmann, "Von der Wendenkolonie."

67. Engerrand, *So-Called Wends*, 142.

68. Notes of Pastor Kilian, 1856 and 1857, Serbin Papers, C.H.I. Some Wends also spoke Spanish, according to Mato Kosyk.

69. Joseph Wilson, professor of German at Rice University, has written several articles on the use of German in central Texas. See "The Texas German of Lee and Fayette Counties," *Rice Institute Pamphlet* 47 (1960), 83–98.

CHAPTER 4—THE WENDS IN CANADA, NEBRASKA, AND SOUTH AFRICA

1. Brenda Lee-Whiting, *Harvest of Stones: The German Settlement in Renfrew County* (Toronto: University of Toronto Press, 1985), 18.

2. Ibid, 37, 295; *100th Anniversary of Lutheran Services in Pembroke and the 80th Anniversary of the Organization of Zion Congregation, 1863–1883–1963* (N.p., n.d.).

3. Records of Green Lake Lutheran Church, Green Lake, Ontario; J. Henry Getz, ed., *A Century in Canada, 1864–1964: The Canada Conference of the Evangelical United Brethren Church* (Kitchner, Ontario: Evangelical United Brethren Church, 1964).

4. Gerhard Krüger, "Auswanderer nach Übersee aus dem Landkreise Cottbus im 19. Jahrhundert," in *Familienkundliche Hefte für die Niederlausitz* (Cottbus: Verein für Heimatkunde zu Cottbus, 1937).

5. Lee-Whiting, *Harvest of Stones*, 43, 297; *100th Anniversary.*

6. Interview with Mrs. Mary Jonas and Mrs. Lillian Hempel, Aug. 9, 1974, Rankin, Ontario.

7. Joseph S. Roucek, ed., *Slavonic Encyclopedia* (New York: Philosophical Library, 1949), 1365. Mato Kosyk in 1884 said that he could find no Sorbian families in Chicago ("Serbja w Texasu," *Łužica*, 1884, 69ff.). The Wends of Bethlehem, Pennsylvania, are from Yugoslavia and not Lusatia (John Bodnar to the author, July 9, 1975). See also Preston A. Laury, *The History of the Allentown Conference of the Ministerium of Pennsylvania* (Kutztown, Pa.: Kutztown Publishing Company, 1926), 364.

8. St. John Lutheran Church, Sterling, Nebraska; Archives of the Lutheran Church in America, Nebraska Synod, Omaha, Nebraska.

9. Kosyk, "Serbja w Texasu"; *Story of the Midwest Synod, U.L.C.A., 1890–1950* (N.p., n.d.); Richard Dalitz and Gerald Stone, "Mato Kosyk in America," *Lětopis*, 1977, 42–79.

10. E. L. G. Schnell, *For Men Must Work* (Cape Town: Maskew Miller, 1954); Werner Schmidt-Pretoria, *Deutsche Wanderung nach Südafrika im 19. Jahrhundert* (Berlin: Dietrich Reimer Verlag, 1955).

11. Schmidt-Pretoria, *Deutsche Wanderung*, 357.

12. "The Coming of the Wends" [by Rupert J. Burger], in E. W. Wiebusch, ed., *Yearbook of the Lutheran Church of Australia: 1976*, 49; Denver A. Webb to author, Aug. 24, 1987. Artifacts and some records of the South African Wends are located in the Kaffrarian Museum, King William's Town.

Chapter 5—Wendish Folkways

1. Edmund Schneeweis, *Feste und Volksbräuche der Sorben* (Berlin: Deutsche Akademie der Wissenschaften zu Berlin, 1953), 3, 129; George C. Engerrand, *The So-Called Wends of Germany and Their Colonies in Texas and Australia* (Austin: University of Texas, 1934), 51. Schneeweis is the major source used throughout on Wendish customs prior to migration out of Lusatia.

2. Lillia Moerbe Caldwell, *Texas Wends: Their First Half Century* (Salado, Tex., 1961); interviews with Mrs. A. Eckermann, Aug. 19, 1969, Broadview, S. A., and William H. Nielsen, Oct. 20, 1974, Stephenville, Tex.

3. Caldwell, *Texas Wends*, 145; Anne Blasig, *The Wends of Texas* (San Antonio: Naylor, 1954), 60.

4. Blasig, *Wends of Texas*, 60; interview with Mrs. Mary Jonas and Mrs. Lillian Hempel, Aug. 9, 1974, Rankin, Ont.; Mato Kosyk, "Serbja w Texasu," *Łužica*, 1884, 69ff. Kosyk's information was based on the reports of August Urban, who had gone to Springfield, Ill., to study for the ministry, but remained in the city to become a merchant.

5. Schneeweis, *Feste und Volksbräuche*, 117; interview with Annie Tschatschula, July 11, 1987, Elgin, Tex.
6. Schneeweis, *Feste und Volksbräuche*, 20, 30.
7. Letter from Carl Hempel, 1874, Ota Wićaz archive, Sorbian Ethnological Institute, Bautzen; interview with Mrs. Alma Muegge, Oct. 2, 1969, Linden Park, S.A.
8. Blasig, *Wends of Texas*, 55; Caldwell, *Texas Wends*, 234, 237; Engerrand, *So-Called Wends*, 110; letter from Bill Biar to author, Aug. 5, 1983. The beer and barbecue weddings of the Texas Wends, although lasting only one night, are memorable events.
9. Engerrand, *So-Called Wends*, 27, 28.
10. Ibid., 110.
11. Arnošt Wjezar, "Serbska kolonija w Teksasu a jeje wjednik Jan Kilian," *Łužica*, 1930, 90ff.
12. Schneeweis, *Feste und Volksbräuche*, 169.
13. Interview with Mr. and Mrs. G. J. R. Gersch, Sept. 13, 1969, Horsham, Victoria.
14. Caldwell, *Texas Wends*, 211; interviews with Mrs. Pauline Dreckow, Oct. 30, 1969, Mt. Mary, S.A., with Anna Lieschke Wenke and Mrs. Musgrove, Dec. 4, 1969, Caronulla, N.S.W., and with Mrs. Mary Jonas and Mrs. Lillian Hempel.
15. Engerrand, *So-Called Wends*, 107; interviews with C. A. Biar, Nov. 8, 1969, Nuriootpa, S.A., with Mrs. Amalie Noack Doering and Mrs. Minnie Roehr, July 31, 1969, Ebenezer, S.A., with Mr. and Mrs. Gersch, and with Mrs. Musgrove.
16. George R. Nielsen, "Folklore of the German-Wends in Texas," *Singers and Storytellers*, Publications of the Texas Folklore Society 30 (1961), 249; interview with Arthur H. Zwar, Aug. 21, 1969, Payneham, S.A.
17. "The Coming of the Wends" [by Rupert J. Burger], in E. W. Wiebusch, ed., *Yearbook of the Lutheran Church of Australia: 1976* (Adelaide: Lutheran Publishing House, 1976), 55; Kosyk, "Serbja w Texasu," 49ff.
18. Interviews with Mrs. Doering, and with Mr. William H. Nielsen.
19. Interview with J. H. Biar, Sept. 9, 1969, Hamilton, Victoria.

Chapter 6—The Wends, Comparative Frontiers, and Turner

1. Frederick Jackson Turner, "The Significance of the Frontier in American History," *Annual Report of the American Historical Association* (1893), 199–227; Turner, *The Significance of Section in American History* (New York: H. Holt and Company, 1932), 18–19; George Rogers Taylor, *The Turner Thesis Concerning the Role of the Frontier in American History* (Boston: D. C. Heath and Company, 1972).
2. W. Turrentine Jackson "A Brief Message for the Young and/or Ambitious: Comparative Frontiers as a Field for Investigations." *Western Historical*

Quarterly (Jan., 1978), 8; Martin Ridge, "Frederick Jackson Turner, Ray Allen Billington, and American Frontier History," *Western Historical Quarterly* (Jan., 1988), 6–10.

3. Paul F. Sharp, "Three Frontiers: Some Comparative Studies of Canadian, American, and Australian Settlement," *Pacific Historical Review* (1955), 369–77.

4. Taylor, *Turner Thesis*, 2.

5. Ibid., 14. Turner opposed the germ theory of politics, which maintained that democracy originated among the tribes in Germany, then was transferred to England by invading tribes, and finally was brought to America by immigrants from England.

Index

adaptation, 27, 30, 32, 127–29. *See also* assimilation
Adelaide, Australia, 29, 31, 32
Albany, Tex., 110
Albert, Agneta, 45
Albert, Andreas, 30, 35, 45, 47, 48
Albert family, 55
Albion, Okla., 117
Albury, Australia, 58
Alfred, 24–27, 32, 51
Altus, Agneta, 17
Altus family, 23, 41
Andreas family, 110
Angus, George Fife, 17, 44
Appila, Australia, 43
Arldt family, 76
assimilation, xi, xii, 30, 60–63. *See also* adaptation
Austin, Tex., 110
Australia, 24, 31; agriculture in, 30; early migration to, 23, 24, 27; goldfields in, 44, 46, 49; house construction in, 28; land in, 41, 42, 48, 55–57, 60; squatters in, 48; voyage to, 25–27
Australia, settlement by regions: New South Wales, 57–60; South Australia, 28, 29, 32, 35–37, 41–43; Victoria, 43–57

Bamsch, George, 80, 83
Barossa Valley, Australia, 35
Bartsch, Adam, 25, 35, 58
Bartsch, Maria, 74
Bartsch family, 59
Baschzisch, Anna, 17
Bautzen, Upper Lusatia, 4, 6, 9, 23, 24, 34, 65, 70, 78; Treaty of, 7
Beechworth, Australia, 32
Behla family, 57
Beisert family, 108

Ben Nevis, 72, 75, 97
Bernstein family, 110
Bethany, Australia, 35, 37, 47
Bethany-Lobenthal Synod, 36, 64
Bethel, Australia, 35, 41, 59
Biar, Johann, 82
Biar family, 36, 43
Biele family, 23, 41
Bielefeld, 41
Birds' Wedding, 120
Birdwood, Australia, 43
Birnbaum, Joseph, 75
Birnbaum family, 106
Bishop, Tex., 107
Blandowski, Wilhelm, 44
Blumberg, 57
Boback, George, 32, 105
Boehme, ———, 116
Booleroo Center, Australia, 43
Borrack, Matthes, 37
Bramborski serski Casnik, 16
Bramke family, 55
Braun, Caspar, 75, 76
Brownlow, Australia, 43
Bryl, Peter, 24
Budarick family, 113
Buder family, 113
Budyšin. *See* Bautzen
Burger, Magdalena, 55
Burger, Peter, 45, 47
Burger family, 35, 45, 48, 55
Byaduk, Australia, 55

Calvinism, 23, 66. *See also* Prussian Union
Canada, 113, 114, 116
Carlsruhe, Australia, 39
cholera, 72, 75
Cisco, Tex., 110
comparative frontiers, xi, 125–31

INDEX

conflict, language, 98, 101
controversy. *See* religious controversies
Copperas Cove, Tex., 110
Cottbus, Australia, 4, 7, 9, 14, 17, 21, 34, 36
customs: Christmas, 120; Easter, 119, 120; feather stripping, 123; marriage, 120, 121; medicine and cures, 123; quilting, 123; spinning, 123

Dalitz family, 57
Dallwitz, Johann, 20
Dallwitz family, 35
Decker, H. E., 24, 25
Delaplain League, 78, 81, 91; division of, 80
Delius, Edward, 44
Deutscher, Agneta Albert, 45
Deutscher, Andreas, 25, 45, 53, 57, 60
Deutscher, Christiane, 53
Deutscher, Michael, 24, 25, 29, 47, 50–53
Deutscher family, 45, 48
diet and food, Wendish, 123, 128, 129
Dimboola, Australia, 56, 57
Dime Box, Tex., 107, 108
Doecke, Peter, 26
Doecke family, 35, 43
Domachenz family, 43
Doman family, 106
Domasch, Math., 80
Domasch-Jurz, Matth., 83
Domaschenz family, 57
Domaschk, Johann, 80, 83
Domaschk family, 106, 110
Domaschk-Janak, Johann, 65
Domaschk-Jurz, Johann, 82, 83
Domowina, 11
Drewitz, 15
Drung Drung, Australia, 55–57
Dry Creek, Australia, 44
Dube, August, 83
Dube, Johann, 80, 83
Dube, John, 78
Dube, Michael, 80
Dube family, 106, 108
Duck Creek, Australia, 60
Duldig, Johann, 36
Duschka, Christian, 17
Duschka family, 57
Duschke, Charles, 25
Dushke family, 57
Dutschmann family, 110

Eben Ezer congregation, Texas, 106, 107
Ebenezer, Australia, 34–36, 39, 54, 58, 59, 61

Ebenezer-Neukirch, 36
Ebenezer-Stockwell, 62
Eckert family, 43
economy: and migration, 14, 20, 21, 61
Egen, Rev. Theo. I., 59
Elsa, 75
emigrants: occupations of, 74; profile of, 17, 20, 23, 74; Prussian restrictions on, 20
Emu Downs, Australia, 43
Engelke, F. A., 80
Engerrand, George, 111
Eudunda, Australia, 39
Eyre Peninsula, Australia, 43

Falke family, 106, 110
Fedor, Tex., 105, 106
folkways, 119; Birds' Wedding, 120; costumes, 128; cures, 123, 124; feather stripping, 123; folk tales and magic, 124; weddings, 120, 121. *See also* customs
Freund family, 43
Fritsche, Peter, 80, 83
Fritzsche, G. D., 51
frontiers, comparative, xi, 125–31

Galveston, 66, 75
Gardi family, 55, 57
Gawler, Australia, 43
Geitz family, 43, 57, 59
German Democratic Republic, 11
Germans: conflict with Wends, 5–7
Gerndt, Ludwig Hermann, 114
Gerogery, Australia, 59
Gersch family, 36, 57
Giddings Deutsches Volksblatt, 111, 112
Gniel family, 57
Godeffroy, J. C., 24, 117, 118
Goessling, J. F., 59
Grabia family, 43
Graf, Carl, 80
Graf family, 110
Graff, Johann, 32, 44
Green Lake, Australia, 55, 57
Green Lake, Ontario, 116
Greschke, I. M., 57
Greschke, S. C., 57
Greschke family, 59
Greulich, Johann, 75, 76
Groch family, 59
Groeschel, August, 80, 83
Groeschel, Maria, 71
Groeschel family, 75, 76, 82
Grove, The, 110
Gruetzner, Mrs. Johann, 105

208

Index

Gruetzner family, 32
Gude, Johann, 35, 47
Gude family, 41, 55
Gulbin family, 57
Gulf of St. Vincent, Australia, 43

Hakert, ———, 17
Hamburg, 65
Hamilton, Australia, 48, 49, 54, 56, 58
Handreck family, 55
Handrick, Johann, 80
Handrick family, 106
Harms, Ludwig, 53
Harms family, 59
Harnath family, 57
Hattas, Johann, 83
Hawker, Australia, 43
Helas, George, 65, 76
Helas family, 66, 78
Helena, 21, 24, 26, 31, 35
Hempel, Carl, 31, 44, 121
Hennersdorf, Peter, 58
Hennersdorf family, 59
Hensel, Carl A., 53, 56, 59
Henty, Thomas, 29, 46
Henty family, 48, 60
Herbrig family, 110
Herlitz, Herman, 59
High Hill, Tex., 64
Hiller, C. G., 53, 59
Hiller family, 56
Hilscher family, 110
Hochkirch, Tex., 110
Hochkirch, Victoria, 50
Hocker, George, 80, 83
Hoehne, Carl Traugott, 16, 31
Hoffnungsthal, Australia, 28, 29, 32, 41
Hohle, Johann (John), 73, 80, 83
homesickness, 31
Hondow, Martin, 30, 37
Hope Valley, Australia, 34, 36, 41, 61
Hopetown, Australia, 57
Horsham, Australia, 55, 57
Houston, Tex., 75, 76, 110
Huf, Johann, 45
Huf family, 47
Hundrack, Johann, 45
Hundrack family, 35, 47–49
Huppatz cemetery, Australia, 38

Inconstant, 72, 75
Iselt, George, 80, 83
Iselt family, 108

Jackson, W. Turrentine, 126
Jakob family, 106, 110

Jannasch, John, 80
Jannausch, Johann, 76
Jarick, Christian, 17, 38
Jarick family, 59
Jatzlau family, 108
Jeitz family, 55
Jenc, August, 21
Jentho family, 110
Jeparit, Australia, 57
Jindera, Australia, 58, 59
Jonas family, 116
Jurak, Magdalena, 80
Jurischk family, 110

Kaiser, Maria, 44
Kangaroo Island, Australia, 43
Kappler, Andreas, 21, 23, 25, 26, 34, 80
Kappler family, 34
Kapunda, Australia, 30, 37, 41
Kasper, Johann, 65, 96
Kasper family, 110
Kasperick family, 110
Katyil, Australia, 57
Kaulvers, Ernst, 25
Kavel, A. L. C., 17, 51
Kelo, ———, 116
Kiata, Australia, 57
Kielow families, 43, 113
Kieschnick, Andreas, 80
Kieschnick family, 106
Kiesling family, 110
Kilian, Gerhard, 71, 108, 109
Kilian, Jan (Johann), 9, 20, 21, 23, 34, 36, 52, 65–72, 76, 77, 78, 81–84, 92–94, 96, 97–103, 105, 108, 117, 122, 130; career of, 70; complaints against, 76, 77, 92–94, 101; and discontent, 72, 81; and leadership, 69–71, 73, 77
Kilian, Maria Theresia, 76
Kilian, Michael, 70
Kilian, Peter, 70
Kilian, Peter T., 103
Kilo family, 55, 59
Kleinig family, 35
Klemke, Johann G., 58, 59
Klemzig, Australia, 27
Klowss family, 57, 59
Knippa, Johann, 75
Knippa family, 110
Koal family, 113
Kokel, Christoph, 73, 80, 82, 83
Kolba family, 110
Kollosche family, 43
Konzag, Friedrich, 17
Kornheim, Australia, 57

INDEX

Kosch family, 55
Kossatz family, 43, 113
Kosyk, Mato, 6, 21, 117, 120, 124
Kotzur family, 55, 59, 60
Krakosky family, 110
Krause, Christoph, 65
Krause, Maria Michalk, 65
Krautschick family, 106
Krüger, Gerhard, 17, 20, 114, 116, 118
Krueger, Johann, 32
Krueger, Karl August, 32
Krummnow, ———, 51, 52, 54
Kubitz, Johann, 80
Kubitz, Mary, 80
Kubitz family, 76
Kulke family, 110
Kunze family, 106, 110
Kurijo, Michael, 82, 83

land legislation. *See* Australia, land in
language controversy, 96–103, 109
Lehmann, August, 106
Lehmann, Carl, 73, 78, 80, 82, 83
Lehmann, Martin, 38
Lehmann family, 57, 106
Lehnigk, Gottfried, 100, 101
Lehrack family, 55, 57
Leitko family, 107
Leubner, Ernst, 101, 102
Lewitzka family, 57
Lieb, J. George, 93
Liebeck, ———, 116
Lieschke, Andreas, 58–60
Light, Col. William, 41
Light Pass, Australia, 29, 57
Lincoln, Tex., 107
Lischke family, 35
Locksley, Ontario, 116
Loebau, Tex., 107
Loessel, Carl H. C., 53
Lorentschk (Lorentsk), George, 80, 83
Lowke, Andreas, 80, 82, 83
Lowke, Christoph, 96
Lowke family, 35, 110
Lusatia, 3–9; Lower, 13, 113, 117; Upper, 3, 4, 20, 121
Lutheran church, 8, 21, 23, 31, 34, 36, 39, 54, 58–60, 62, 63, 67–70, 72–74, 76, 80, 93, 100, 111, 114, 117; Old, 21, 23, 34, 50
Luzici, 6
Lyndoch Valley, Australia, 35

Malke, Johann, 80
Mallee, Australia, 57
Malvinia Vidal, 36
Manheim, Tex., 104, 106, 107
Markus, ———, 116
Maroske family, 57
Marschall, Christian, 17, 20
Mathiez, Andreas, 80
Matschka, Matthes, 17
Matthiez, Johann, 83
Matthiez, M., 80
Matthiez family, 108
Mattiez, Mathias, 65
Matuschka, Freidrich, 74
Matuschka family, 55, 57, 59
Medack family, 107
Melbourne, Australia, 29, 31, 32, 44; early immigration to, 43; Wends in, 44
Melcher, 116
Melde, Andreas, 105, 106
Methodism, 92, 93, 114
Merting (Mertink), George, 80, 82, 83
Merting (Mertink), Johann, 74, 80, 83
Meyer, Heinrich A. E., 35, 37, 47, 50–52
Meyer, J., 25
Meyer, Valentin Lorenz, 74
Meyer family, 38, 77
Miatke, George, 25
Miatke family, 113
Michalk, Charles, 96
Michalk family, 106
Mickan, Andreas, 58
Mickan, Johann, 80
Mickan family, 35, 58, 59
Miertschin family, 75
migration: to Australia, 23, 25–27; beginnings of, 16; and cholera, 72, 75; conditions of, on ship, 26; economic factors in, 14, 20, 21, 69; factors favoring, 13–15; food shortages and, 14, 17, 191 n. 3; and German ties, 15, 24; homesickness and, 31; language and, 62, 63; letters supporting, 15–17; newspapers and, 15, 16; population pressure and, 14, 15; post–Civil War, 104; rate of, 17, 23; route of, 24, 71, 74, 75; serfdom and, 14, 20; social and religious motives for, 20, 21; to Texas, 73, 76; transportation facilitating, 15, 24; from Upper Lusatia, 20
Milceni, 6
Mirtschin, Johann, 26, 44, 45
Mirtschin, 35, 45, 47, 48, 54
Missouri Synod, 69, 94, 109, 111, 112, 117, 201 n. 43
Mitchell, Thomas, 48
Mitschke, Mathias, 65
Mitschke, Matthes, 96
Mitschke family, 110

Index

Modra, Matthes, 17
Modra family, 43, 57
Moerbe, Ernst, 83
Moerbe, Ernst Adolph, 73, 75, 82
Moerbe, Jacob, 83, 96
Moerbe family, 106, 107
Morvian Brethren, 35, 51
Mt. Clay, Australia, 47
Mt. Gambier, Australia, 34, 46
Mt. Rouse, Australia, 50–52, 55
Mt. Torrens, Australia, 57
Mroske, Math., 80
Mudra family, 55, 57
Murtoa, Australia, 55–57

Nagora family, 113
Natimuk, Australia, 55–57
Neale's Flat, Australia, 43
Nebraska: Wends in, 116, 117
Neitsch family, 110
Nerettig family, 110
Neukirch, Australia, 35, 36, 57
Neumann, Carl, 76
Neumann, Johann, 80
New Ulm, Tex., 65, 66, 76
Nhill, Australia, 57
Ni Ni, Australia, 57
Niemtschk family, 107
Niquet, Rev. J. P., 58
Noack, Johann, 37, 65, 80, 92, 96
Noack family, 43, 57, 106, 110, 113, 116
Noack, Tex. 110
Nossack family, 57
Nowka, Mato, 16
Nuriootpa, Australia, 35

Old Lutheran church, 21, 23, 34, 50
Oster, Phillip J., 53

Pallmer, John, 102
Pallmer family, 103, 105
Palmer Rapids, Ontario, 116
Panko, Matthias, 117
Pampell, Peter, 80
Pannach family, 35
Patschke family, 106
Paulick, Jacob, 80
Peitz parish, 17
Penshurst, Australia, 48, 50, 55
Peter Godeffroy, 118
Peter's Hill, Australia, 30, 32, 34, 36, 37, 39, 41, 43, 54, 61, 119, 121, 122; controversy at, 38
Petschel, C. G., 45
Petschel, Christiane, 24–28, 45, 53
Petschel, Wilhelm (William), 28, 45, 51, 53

Petschel family, 27–29, 46–48, 53, 57
Pietism, 21, 34, 35, 52, 91, 92
Pilak, Johann, 83
Pilak, Magdalena, 75
Pillack, Johann, 80
Pillack family, 106
Pjenck, Andreas, 21
Pleasant Hills, Australia, 60
Poesch, Martin, 20
Point Pass, Australia, 43
Polnich, Andreas, 35
Polnick (Polnik), August, 65, 76, 82, 83, 106
Ponich, Johann (John), 31, 32, 44
Port Arthur, Tex., 110
Port Lincoln, Australia, 47
Port Phillip, Australia, 44
Portland, Victoria, 29, 35, 45–47
Předźenak, 110
Prellop, George, 96
Preusker, Andreas, 25, 29
Preusker, Peter, 25
Preusker, Traugott, 25, 29
Pribislav, 21, 32, 44
Prochno, Jacob, 32
Proft, J. A., 105, 106, 107
Proposch, George, 25
Proposch family, 57
Proske family, 106, 107
Prussian Union, 23, 66, 197 n. 6
Pumpa family, 55, 57, 59, 60

Quorn, Australia, 43

Rabbs Creek, Tex., 76
Rainbow, Australia, 57
religion: among emigrants, 36–39, 45, 49
religious controversies, 38, 39, 50–54, 66, 91–94. *See also* language controversy
Rentsch, Anna, 45
Rentsch, J., 45
Rentsch, Johann, 45, 55
Rentsch family, 35, 41, 47, 55
Richter, Johann, 76
Ridge, Martin, 126
Ritter family, 110
Riverina, Australia, 55, 57–60
Robe, Australia, 43
Rosel family, 32
Rosenthal, Australia, 28, 29, 32, 35, 44–47
Rudi, C. C., 93
Ruschen family, 60
Rychtar, Jan, 24

INDEX

St. Kitts, Australia, 36, 41, 43
St. Peter's, Serbin, 103
Salmann, 57
Salzke, Christian, 58
Salzke, Johann, 58
Salzke family, 55, 59
San Francisco, 32
Schatte, Christoph, 80, 82, 83
Schatte, Hanna, 75
Schatte, Matthias, 75
Scheetz family, 57, 59
Schellnick (Schelnick), Christoph, 80, 83
Schellnick (Schelnick), George, 80, 83
Schellnick (Schelnick), Matthaus, 83
Schilling, Matheas, 80
Schimmens, ———, 116
Schiwart family, 110
Schkade family, 106, 107
Schlemmer family, 41
Schmidt, Andrew, 109
Schmidt, Herman, 104
Schmidt, Mathias, 80
Schmidt, Matthaus, 82
Schmienz family, 113
Schneider, ———, 47, 51
Schneider, Andreas, 35
Schneider, Johann, 51
Schneider, Kasper, 51
Schneider, Rev. E., 92
Schneider family, 110
Schoelnick (Schellnick), Matthias, 75
Schoknecht, Rev. C., 56
Schondorf, Christoph S. D., 35, 36, 41
Schoppa family, 110
Schubert, Hanna, 74
Schuermann, Clamour W., 47–50, 54–56, 59, 92; and Deutscher, 50, 54
Schulze, Matthaus (Mattheus), 75, 82
Schulze family, 110
Schuppan family, 43
Schuster, Matth., 80, 83
Schwabe, William, 124
Semlin, Friedrich, 38
Serbin, 23, 93, 94
Serbo-Lusatians, 4
Serbske Nowiny, 65, 110
serfdom, 14, 20
settlement. *See* Australia; Texas
Seydler, Friedrich Gustave, 64, 76, 78
Seydler family, 64, 65
Sharp, Paul, 126
Simank, Charles, 80
Simank family, 109
Smoler, Jan, 16
Sorbian language, 5
Sorbian nationalism, 5, 9

Sorbs, xiii, xiv, 4, 5. *See also* Wends
South Africa, 117
South Australian Register, 62
Spree River, 4
Spreewald, 4
Springton, Australia, 43
Starick family, 57
Steinwärder, 36
Stephan, Agnes Kaiser, 44
Stephan, Johann, 32
Stephan families, 48, 110
Sterling, Neb., 116, 117
Stiemke, A. L. Y., 109
Sucky, John, 80
Swiss Alp, Tex., 110
Swjela, Kito, 38
Symank family, 106, 107

Tabor, Australia, 55
Tanunda, Australia, 27
Tanunda-Light Pass Synod, 36
Tarrington, Australia, 23, 50, 54, 55, 61
Teichelmann, C. G., 38, 47
Teinert, Carl (Karl), 73, 76, 101, 103, 108, 109
Teinert family, 106
Temora, Australia, 60
Teschner, Martin, 16, 25, 36, 37
Teschner families, 43, 113
Texas: Delaplain League in, 78, 80; early migration to, 64, 65, 75–77; farming in, 84–91; housing construction in, 81–83; post–Civil War migration to, 104; Wendish expansion in, 105–10
Thomastown, Australia, 32, 44. *See also* Dry Creek
Thorndale, Tex., 107
Towk family, 55, 57
Turner, Frederick Jackson, 125, 126, 130, 131
Twartz family, 43
Tydźenske Nowiny, 16, 31

Urban, Andreas, 47, 48, 54, 67, 76
Urban, Johann, 73, 75, 80, 83, 92, 93
Urban families, 35, 59, 106, 107

Vectis, Australia, 57
Vernon, Tex., 110
Vogel, Andreas, 76
Von Plönnies, E., 38

Wagner, Mathias (Mattheus), 80, 83
Wagner, Robert, 65, 76, 78
Walburg, Tex., 110
Walla Walla, Australia, 58, 59

Index

Walther, C. F. W., 70
Warda, Tex., 104, 108, 110
Warraquil, Australia, 62
Weise family, 110
Weiser family, 107, 110
Wends, xiii, xiv, 4, 13–17, 98; agricultural production of, 84, 85, 90; agricultural wealth of, 88, 89; aid to immigrants by, 35, 44; animal husbandry of, 85–87; assimilation of, xi, xii, 94, 104, 105, 110, 111, 114, 115, 118; in Australia, 32, 34, 35, 36, 50; in Canada, 113–16; Catholics among, 194 n. 62, 198 n. 10; Christianization of, 6, 8; in Civil War, 94; culture of, 6, 105; democracy and, 72, 130, 131; and Germans, 4, 7, 11, 60, 191 n. 6; early history of, 5–7; in gold fields, 32, 35, 44, 49; homesickness among, 31; identification of, xii, xiii, 114; integration of, into Australian society, 60–63; intermarriage among, 61; land-holding by, 88; language of, 5, 11, 96, 97; motives for migration of, 65–69, 198 n. 10; nationalism among, 5, 9; naturalization of, 45; in Nebraska, 116, 117; population of, 11, 12; religion among, 6, 8, 9, 130; size of migration by, xii, 191 n. 11; in South Africa, 117, 118; in Texas, 64, 65, 66, 91, 104, 105–10; wealth of, 90, 91; and World War I, 62, 63. *See also* Sorbs
Wenke, Carl, 80
Wenke, Carl Traugott, 83
Wenke, Michael, 58
Wenke family, 35, 58, 59
Westgarth, William, 43
Wiese, Rev. H., 59
Wilson, Tex., 110
Wimmera, Australia, 54, 55, 57
Winchester, Tex., 110
Winian, Australia, 57, 62
Winkler family, 106
Wodonga, Australia, 59
Woito family, 113
Wuchatsch family, 32
Wuensche, Christoph, 83
Wuensche family, 106, 107, 110
Wukasch (Wukash), Matthias (Mathes), 80, 83
Wusk, Gottlieb, 117
Wusk, Matthaus, 117

Yorke Peninsula, Australia, 43

Zapf, Eduard, 109
Zieschang, Peter, 53
Zieschang family, 41, 110
Zieschank (Zischang), Johann (John), 80, 82, 83
Zimmer, Michael, 44
Zimmer family, 32
Zoch family, 110
Zschech, Johann, 36
Zschech family, 36, 55, 57, 106, 108
Zwahr, Anna, 80
Zwar, Johann, 21, 23, 24, 25, 34, 35, 58, 124
Zwar, Michael, 30–32

www.ingramcontent.com/pod-product-compliance
Lightning Source LLC
Chambersburg PA
CBHW030317080526
44584CB00012B/592